TRANSFORMING CULTURE

Transforming Culture

Creating and Sustaining Effective Organizations

Elizabeth K. Briody, Robert T. Trotter II, and Tracy L. Meerwarth

palgrave
macmillan

TRANSFORMING CULTURE

Copyright © Elizabeth K. Briody, Robert T. Trotter II, and Tracy
L. Meerwarth, 2010.

First published in hardcover in 2010 by PALGRAVE MACMILLAN®
in the United States—a division of St. Martin's Press LLC, 175 Fifth
Avenue, New York, NY 10010.

Where this book is distributed in the UK, Europe and the rest of
the world, this is by Palgrave Macmillan, a division of Macmillan
Publishers Limited, registered in England, company number 785998,
of Houndmills, Basingstoke, Hampshire RG21 6XS.

Palgrave Macmillan is the global academic imprint of the above
companies and has companies and representatives throughout the
world.

Palgrave® and Macmillan® are registered trademarks in the United
States, the United Kingdom, Europe and other countries.

ISBN: 978-1-137-40819-8

The Library of Congress has cataloged the hardcover edition as
follows:

Briody, Elizabeth Kathleen.
   Transforming culture: creating and sustaining a better manufacturing
organization / Elizabeth K. Briody, Robert T. Trotter, Tracy L.
Meerwarth.
      p. cm.
   ISBN: 978-0-230-62346-0
   Includes bibliographical references and index.
   1. Corporate culture—United States. 2.   Organizational change—
United States. 3.   Industrial sociology—United States.   I. Trotter,
Robert T. II. Meerwarth, Tracy L. III. Title.
   HD58.7.B745 2010
   658.4'063—dc22   2009039551

A catalogue record of the book is available from the British Library.

Design by Scribe Inc.

First PALGRAVE MACMILLAN paperback edition: February 2014

10 9 8 7 6 5 4 3 2 1

Transferred to Digital Printing in 2013

Elizabeth dedicates this book to Marc Robinson
for his wisdom, support, and love.

Bob dedicates this book to Sally Trotter for all of her encouragement
and support over the years, to his kids (Hara, Talbot, David, and Rayne)
for the stimulus and excitement they have given in their lives, and to
his colleagues and friends for interesting times and valuable
opportunities in the overall scheme of things.

Tracy dedicates this book to the men and women at the
stamping plant that allowed her to learn from their stories.

CONTENTS

Figures

FOREWORD

When *Transforming Culture* was published in 2010, it was based on years of data collection and analysis associated with General Motors (GM) assembly and stamping plants. The original subtitle—*Creating and Sustaining a Better Manufacturing Organization*—reflected the context of this case study. Yet, even as my coauthors and I wrote about the cultural models, transformation process, and tools, we recognized that this work could be applied in many different organizations. Indeed, the book should appeal to organizations that are planning for or in the throes of change and to students in anthropology and other university programs interested in organizational culture and cultural change. Accordingly, we have changed the subtitle so that it now reads *Creating and Sustaining Effective Organizations.*

My consulting work at Cultural Keys LLC has brought me in contact with a variety of organizations—both for-profit and nonprofit—in several industries, including health care, long-term care, consumer products, and hospitality. Organizations planning cultural transformation can benefit from our research and applications regardless of industry. For example, with the help of the Cultural Change Team at a large, regional hospital, the Bridge Model of Cultural Transformation was adapted for the hospital's new "patient-centric" vision. The bridge model was a powerful visual metaphor, charting the direction of change from task-based patient care to responsive and empathetic patient care. In addition, we applied the bridge model to illustrate the kinds of organizational-culture changes needed to accompany this orientation toward patient centeredness.

Similarly, we have used *Transforming Culture*'s steps in the process of cultural transformation to help hospital leaders and employees understand the roadmap for change. We identified the "obstacles" to change and "enablers" of change from our ethnographic fieldwork.

Hospital personnel now rely on a systematic analysis of their culture as they continue to plan for and implement change initiatives. We also designed several applications or tools that could address cultural weaknesses within such a health care setting, one of which provided a structure and a format for creating small, problem-solving teams customized for a siloed organizational culture. In sum, the models, processes, and tools related to cultural transformation not only reinforce those aspects of hospital culture that are working well, but they are also contributing to a reconceptualization of what the hospital's future ideal culture should be given the extensive changes occurring in U.S. health care policy and practices.

Aside from the book's usefulness to business and organizational leaders planning for change, we believe the book has broad appeal as a classroom text. Anthropology students, whether at the undergraduate or graduate level, will see that the book focuses on the cultural aspects of automotive work. The book portrays a cultural history of automotive manufacturing in a dynamic and evolving global context. Its ethnographic detail brings to life GM plant culture from the mid-1980s to the late 2000s. As Ann Jordan points out in her review of our work, "The analysis of GM's successes and failures and the description of practices on the shop floor are reasons enough to read this book and also to consider it for class adoption."[1] However, the book also documents an applied research project from theory (cultural models) to application (cultural transformation process and tools). It lays out the domains of cultural adaptiveness and cultural responsiveness as critical to cultural problem solving and transformation. It also describes how we worked in partnership with GM and union leadership to develop, validate, and test ten tools to strengthen the importance of collaboration (the future ideal) on the plant floor. Because there is so little anthropological work on organizational culture change, this book helps to fill that gap. Recognition of this contribution came in November 2012 when our book won the Robert B. Textor and Family Prize for Excellence in Anticipatory Anthropology from the American Anthropological Association. As stated in the award letter, "Their [the authors'] use of anthropology in the private sector anticipates and provides a signpost for others who will engage in an area of increasing importance for both anthropological scholarship and practice."

Yet this book was not written solely for anthropologists or those training in anthropology. Other university students are likely to find the book useful as a text as well. Business, engineering, industrial relations, informatics, cultural studies, and history students will be able to draw on the book's longitudinal case study at an important global organization as well as the book's practical tools for organizational improvement. Comparisons between American mass production and Japanese flexible and lean production help sort out differences in the structure of work (e.g., work practices, processes, status and role, technology) and the dynamics of work (e.g., work relationships, patterns of work force perceptions and behavior). American manufacturing has been struggling to remain competitive. GM, for example, has been shrinking for thirty years, with thousands of people affected by its layoffs and plant closures. We think this book provides insight into what American organizations can do to improve their competitiveness in the global economy. These readers may be interested to learn that our analyses do not conform to a bifurcated view of manufacturing culture in which members are reducible to either management or labor. They may also find that anthropologists tend to be inclusive—speaking with everyone and anyone. While GM management and union leadership played critical roles in the project, they represented only a portion of our entire sample. Finally, these students may discover that an anthropological perspective is useful in describing and explaining cultural themes and patterns and in using that knowledge base to help the culture transform. Indeed, a work culture based on collaboration, as we suggested for GM, is a too-often overlooked strategy for securing a competitive advantage in the global economy.

Elizabeth K. Briody, PhD
Cultural Keys LLC
2013

Preface

The auto industry of the last thirty years has not been for the faint of heart. The U.S. domestic industry, in particular, has been in continuous transformation for most of that time period. The modern auto business is one of the few truly global industries. Today, there are more similarities than differences in the product designs, materials used, and processes of manufacture among the global competitors. Yet, significant differences are found in the various results of each. Success is difficult and eludes many.

I began working in the car business as a young engineer over three decades ago. As I prepare to retire from a senior leadership position at General Motors (GM), I look back on a career that never lacked for challenges and opportunities. I come from a family of autoworkers. My father was an hourly employee who provided for his family by working in the factory every day for over forty years. My first engineering assignments started on those same factory floors. My extensive plant experience has given me a unique perspective from which to consider the waves of change that buffet the domestic automakers. I have seen incredible acts of initiative and selfless contributions from hundreds of employees like my father. The value of their conscientious acts could be counted into the many millions of dollars. Yet I have seen firsthand the errors and acts of waste of demotivated workers as well. Both groups entered the work force to do their very best. At one time, they all shared the same excitement and sense of wonder at how cars and trucks are produced. Yet, somewhere along the way, that excitement was lost for some and replaced with boredom, apathy, and—at times—resentment. Like my colleagues, I have read much on manufacturing and workers. Some of what I have read has been insightful. Much of it is of little use to the supervisor or manager on the front lines of the factory floor attempting to deal with these circumstances.

The Lansing Delta Township facility is GM's newest American assembly plant at the time of this writing. The location, building, facilities, and tools represent the latest manufacturing technology from around the world. Yet the work force is men and women from a combination of several older and closed facilities in central Michigan. It is a work force from one of the most strongly unionized areas of the country. During a routine review of the project, a simple question was asked: What's the plan for the people? We had spent hours reviewing details related to the physical attributes of the plant but much less time on the preparations related to the readiness of the work force. All present at the review recognized that the men and women who would someday staff the facility were the real key to success of this billion-dollar investment. Future meetings would review reporting relationships and team sizes, as well as other metrics, but how would we prepare the people to work together? How would we create a culture of world-class safety, quality, and productivity?

The answer would come from the unlikely source of cultural anthropology in the person of a dedicated scientist from GM Research. In addition to the best practices found in management texts, the study brought to our effort a process that created learning events from the very problems and issues that we hoped to avoid. These events, often unseen, can sow the seeds of future distrust and disruption and—ultimately—demotivate portions of the work force. This effort has generated a set of lessons and tools that continue to grow and bear fruit. When I began my career as a manufacturing engineer, I had a keen interest in understanding how to reliably reproduce a particular result or product. I am grateful to Dr. Elizabeth Briody not only for her contribution to the successful launch of a world-class manufacturing team but also for her documentation of these efforts in such a way that others can reproduce these results to the benefit of the teams of which they are a part.

Troy A. Clarke
President of GM North America
September 13, 2009

Acknowledgments

Many people played a role in the publication of this book. We are extremely grateful to GM for its financial and technical support of this research program for six years. We also thank the people of GM. Over 400 employees shared their time, their stories, and their experiences with us so that we could understand their views of manufacturing culture—past and present—and their expressed hopes for the future. This book is their book as much as it is ours. It is their story of life on the plant floor and of cultural transformation that we did our best to capture. For confidentiality reasons, we do not reveal their names.

The idea for the project, originating with Steve Holland at GM Research and Development (R&D), was quickly supported by other managers at R&D including Alan Taub, Jan Aase, and Tom Seder. Support grew within GM's manufacturing organization, with Troy Clarke serving as the original project sponsor, executive advisor, and, ultimately, manuscript reviewer. His global perspective and his manufacturing background positioned him to add considerable value to the final product. Randy Thayer, who became plant manager of GM's newest U.S. assembly plant, Lansing Delta Township, was an ongoing source of support for our work. His interest in innovation and plant culture predated the plant's construction, continued through the plant's successful start-up, and was maintained long after our research group reported its results and delivered the tools. He and his Joint Leadership Team worked tirelessly with us to refine our ideas and develop and validate customized applications to help build and maintain a collaborative plant culture. Local union leaders Art Luna and Steve Bramos were an integral part of Randy Thayer's team, as were plant Quality Network leaders; in particular, Don A. Smith and Mark Strolle were always available to answer our questions and offer insights into emerging cultural patterns. GM's Global Manufacturing System employees, working directly with the manufacturing plants, acted as advocates for the project. We especially appreciated the interest and perspectives offered by Gerry Knesek, John Ciupak, and Chris Turner.

Several senior manufacturing executives provided assistance and guidance in disseminating project results in GM's U.S. facilities and in sponsoring the pilot testing of the tools we developed. They included Larry Zahner, Joe Ponce, Bill Boggs, Arvin Jones, Jim DeLuca, Joe Spielman, and Gary Cowger. The project was supported by Greg Fedak, Mike Hall, and John Bussineau of the International Union, United Automobile, Aerospace and Agricultural Implement Workers of America (UAW)-GM Quality Network. Several GM employees, including Karen Sutton, Matt Albee, Sharon Zielinski, Mark Beltramo, Tom Schenk, and Jeff O'Neal helped in the identification or compilation of documentary data and/or library support services. We were very grateful for their assistance.

A number of researchers worked with us during the research, validation, analysis, and applications-development phases of the project. Gülcin Sengir, a computer scientist by training, adapted quickly to the world of anthropological fieldwork. Her perspective and modeling efforts led to the creation of the Ideal Cultural Model, which became a core element of the study. Linda Catlin, an experienced consulting anthropologist (Claymore Associates, Inc.), also participated fully in the fieldwork. Her skill in facilitating discussions with manufacturing leaders, while offering insights from a variety of field projects in which she had been involved, always proved highly relevant and useful. Emily Altimare contributed her expertise in anthropology during the pilot-testing phase of the study and in the testing phase of the *ExplorePlantCulture* computer game. She also built on our research to design her own dissertation fieldwork at the Lansing Delta Township plant. Lee Ridenour adapted some of our tools for additional testing as part of his honor's thesis. Wolf Gumerman, Honors Director for Northern Arizona University and a fellow anthropologist, documented and chronicled parts of the Ideal Plant Culture project for dissemination to the American Anthropological Association. He also contributed to our understanding of the culture through his photographs and videos and his excellent questions about working within GM culture.

The artwork for the book's cover was done by Perry Kuey. He also used his artistic style to design all of the graphic illustrations. The photograph on the cover was taken by Linda Johnson. George Dan Pirvu, the patient and creative developer of the *ExplorePlantCulture* computer game, created the computer graphics screenshot.

On a personal note, Elizabeth Briody would like to thank some special people who have been great sources of support for her. Her husband, Marc Robinson, played an important role in the book. He offered many technical contributions, including a broad economic and strategy perspective that helped situate the findings within a broader context. He provided insights on the perspective over time of both GM management and the UAW. He offered editorial advice and encouragement and adapted his schedule, as much as possible, to the book's pace. Their children, Andrew, Kathleen, and Anton Robinson, understood the importance of the project and helped out in many ways. Urszula Wawer easily and cheerfully took on many of the Robinson household and childcare responsibilities during the writing phase of the book. Two other individuals deserve special recognition for what they personally taught Elizabeth about the importance of collaboration. Both Ina Rosenthal-Urey, professor emeritus of anthropology at Wheaton College, Norton, Massachusetts, and Bob Frosch, retired vice president of the GM Research Labs, modeled a collaborative research style that became the basis of the way in which the Ideal Plant Culture research group worked with each other and with those who participated in the study.

About the Authors

Elizabeth K. Briody, PhD, is a cultural anthropologist who has been engaged in cultural change efforts for over twenty-five years. She founded Cultural Keys LLC, a consulting firm that helps organizations transform their culture, reach their potential, and attract and retain new customers. She has worked in a variety of industries including manufacturing, health care, long-term care, and consumer products. She is coauthor of *The Cultural Dimension of Global Business*, 7th ed. with Gary P. Ferraro (Pearson, 2013) and coeditor of *Partnering for Organizational Performance* with Robert T. Trotter II (Rowman & Littlefield, 2008). She is a member of the executive board of the American Anthropological Association, past president of the National Association for the Practice of Anthropology, and adjunct professor at several universities.

Robert T. Trotter II, PhD, is an Arizona Regents' Professor and current chair of the Anthropology Department at Northern Arizona University. His research interests include cross-cultural–health care issues, organizational models for change, social networks and social structures, innovation and cultural models, exploring advanced ethnographic methods, and applied anthropology. He is the coeditor of *Partnering for Organizational Performance* with Elizabeth K. Briody and coauthor of *Ethics for Anthropological Research and Practice* with Linda M. Whiteford (Waveland, 2008). He has conducted applied anthropological research for GM, the World Health Organization, the Centers for Disease Control and Prevention, the National Institutes of Health, and the Surgeon General's Office of HIV/AIDs Policy.

Tracy L. Meerwarth, MA, is a Corporate Officer at Consolidated Bearings Co., Cedar Knolls, New Jersey. She worked at GM R&D from 2001 through 2008, prior to which she received her MA in applied anthropology from Northern Arizona University with an emphasis on organizational studies. She applied her interests in cultural modeling, and cognitive and symbolic anthropology to various projects at GM, including collaboration and workspace studies. She and her coinventors hold a U.S. and international patent entitled, "System and Model for Performance Value Based Collaborative Relationships" (U.S. Patent No. 7,280,977, October 9, 2007). She is coeditor of *Mobile Work, Mobile Lives: Cultural Accounts of Lived Experiences* with Julia C. Gluesing and Brigitte Jordan (Blackwell, 2008).

CHAPTER 1

INTRODUCTION TO THE AMERICAN
MANUFACTURING CULTURE STORY

The modern automotive assembly plant is a wonder; in fact, tours—
virtual or real—of assembly plants are popular features of Disney's
Epcot Theme Park and The Henry Ford Museum. Thousands of parts
from a vast array of suppliers arrive daily, often in the precise quantity
and sequence that will be needed during that day or even that hour.
Workers at hundreds of stations wield sophisticated, specialized tools
to put those parts into systems and subsystems and integrate them
with vehicle underbodies and sheet metal. The metal parts are welded
by advanced robots and painted in high-technology booths using
cutting-edge chemicals and processes. The final products that emerge
are often beautiful and symbolic dream machines, as memorialized in
countless songs, but are also increasingly electronic marvels with chips
controlling everything from engine performance, to braking, to satel-
lite communications. Despite being produced with a dizzying variety
of body styles, models, options, and colors on a single assembly line,
vehicle quality is at levels far above a generation ago.

It is easy to be blinded by the technology of product and process
and miss the people who do the work—whether they are production workers, managers, skilled tradesmen, manufacturing engineers,
or support staff—or to view them as little different from the welding
robots. Yet forgetting the people would be a profound error. The
production system is dependent on people. They solve the problems.
They come up with the innovations. And, they have the capacity to
adapt to changing conditions—whether a temporary breakdown on
the line, the launch of a new product, or a streamlined change in the
production process.

Both the recent turmoil and the longer history of the automotive
industry make it clear that change is relentless—coming from tougher
vehicle requirements and fluctuations in tastes of customers and

policymakers, from fierce competitors both old and new, from ideas and inventions, and from dramatic swings in the economic environment. Competition, globalization, ingenuity, and work practices all play a role in the automotive evolution. Innovations appear, traditions are reshaped, mistakes are made, and winners and losers can switch places in the process. The stakes get higher and higher as more players arrive in the global marketplace to offer their products, services, and knowledge. With more consumer choice, organizations must cope by exploring new options for getting to market faster with higher quality and lower cost. The ability of people to adjust and respond to change effectively is critical to success in automotive manufacturing, and, indeed, to success in most work settings. Yet change is often perceived as difficult. At a minimum, obstacles to change must be overcome, including resistance to new ideas and initiatives, and the whole change process must fit into a number of important cultural environments (e.g., organizational, national).

Culture plays a critical role in this cyclical process of innovation and adaptation, though its explanatory impact is not often explored or understood. Our definition of culture, "assumptions, expectations, beliefs, social structures, and values guiding behavior,"[1] targets the organization and specifically the manufacturing function. We view the elements of culture as fluid and interdependent; a change in one part of the culture (e.g., how employees are treated) can have broad ramifications in other parts of the culture (e.g., how problem solving does or does not occur). Culture affects how a plant or workplace functions, how managers and line workers relate to each other, and how change is perceived. Culture also influences the type of response that people make and which approaches to change will be effective and durable. Indeed, ignoring culture is a major reason why most change efforts fail.[2]

This pattern of adaptation and response is part of the cultural change or transformation process, a core concept around which this book is written. Examining cultural transformation within the automotive industry provides a view of the past and present, as well as potential insights into a future trajectory of work and culture. There is no "one best way" for any culture to function or to change. Indeed, there are often multiple "best ways" and "worst ways" that play out. In this book we offer a process for finding out what individuals in the culture (and not just a subset of the culture, such as the senior leadership) think is the "best way forward."

We describe and explain the cultural transformation process using our multiyear, multisite ethnographic study[3] of General Motors (GM) manufacturing operations in the United States. We link the historical record with anthropological field data to portray the evolving process of cultural change and to point a way forward. It turns out that a consensus view from inside the culture suggests a "one best collaborative way" for the future of the firm. Across the board, we found an emphasis on the importance of a cohesive, unified, and collaborative approach to work as a strategy for improving organizational effectiveness. GM's cultural-transformation story, including its successes and failures, offers lessons for other organizations and industries as they try to adapt in a rapidly changing world.

THE DECLINE OF AN AMERICAN ICON

GM was once the archetype of the American organization and is now under attack as a failure of American competitiveness. For most of its hundred-year history, GM has been viewed as the embodiment of American culture. Hard work, technological innovation, and successful products were all part of the American dream. GM was, at one time, the master of mass production methods, generating high-volume products characterized by their styling and power. Yet, GM was slow to make the transition to lean production in which flexible production methods and multiskilled worker teams produce high-quality results;[4] it was also slow to change its overall cultural orientation in the face of new vehicle models in both the United States and abroad.

GM, and the American automotive industry generally, found itself losing ground to competitors as Toyota, Honda, Nissan, and then Hyundai, took advantage of both their cultural milieu and structural advantages, such as protected home markets, to compete, increasingly successfully, in the global market. These Asian firms first spearheaded quality improvements and then became masters at reducing waste and cost, reducing lead time to market, and learning effectively from their mistakes. Though Detroit's vehicles have improved dramatically in recent years, often exceeding the ratings of competitors, their customer base in the United States continued to slip because of cost disadvantages and the lagging customer perception of their product quality. As the twentieth century came to a close, GM was beset with other problems. It found itself overstaffed, lacking a strategic plan, and making decisions consistent with its parochial Midwestern mindset rather than a global orientation (e.g., lacking "sophistication in its understanding of foreign competition"[5]).

In addition to product development and marketplace difficulties, GM and the other Detroit automotive companies also faced challenges in implementing changes in manufacturing practices. Hourly workers at almost all of GM's U.S. facilities are represented by the UAW.[6] The UAW is a powerful union with a long history of contentious relations with U.S. auto manufacturers, including GM. Historically, the UAW has been concerned with preserving the jobs, plant floor work rules, and lifestyles of members and has been resistant to key management efforts to make changes. The power of the UAW ensures that most changes on the plant floor require its tacit or explicit cooperation. Gradually over the last twenty-five years, the confrontational stance was muted somewhat, though the devastating 1998 strike at GM signaled that the conflict persisted. As the UAW became increasingly convinced that Detroit's survival was at stake (ca. 2005), it agreed to a series of concessions that reduced the competitive gap in wages, benefits, and work rules with foreign manufacturers, particularly those on U.S. soil. After a historic labor agreement with the UAW in 2007, GM management was convinced that the company was poised for success.

And then GM's world began unraveling at breakneck speed. Experiencing bankruptcy, leadership changes, massive restructuring and downsizing, GM had to grapple with, redefine, and then manage its core operations despite the changeable and unpredictable conditions in the world around it. Some of the traditional strengths of GM and American culture (e.g., the individual nature of work and creativity, the emphasis on meritocracy and career advancement) are no longer sufficient for ensuring survival. To thrive in the twenty-first century requires breaking down the barriers associated with GM's autonomous and decentralized (i.e., silo-based) cultural tradition, improving the ability of the collective to learn and adapt, and shoring up the sense of community within the GM work force.

The erosion of GM's market share, the decline in value of GM's brands, and the high cost of labor at GM and at its key supplier, Delphi, created a life-threatening crisis. These problems were compounded in the late 2000s after a spike in fuel prices, a collapse in demand for profitable GM trucks, and a global credit crisis that froze credit and destroyed consumer confidence—all in rapid succession. GM was forced to seek U.S. government assistance to continue operating and was vilified in the process by Congress, the media, and much of the American public. All parts of the political spectrum found fault with past GM decisions—whether related to labor, fuel economy, or product—and exhibited significant resistance to public support of private companies. GM was ultimately supported by both the Bush and Obama administrations because of its importance and because of the vulnerability of the economy. However, the Presidential Task Force on Automotive Restructuring viewed the company's plans as insufficient, forced out CEO Rick Wagoner, and helped push the company through bankruptcy.

Prompted largely by external (and to some extent internal) critiques, and shaken by the demands of the Task Force, GM leaders launched an intense effort to change the dysfunctional culture of the "old GM." As the company emerged from bankruptcy in July 2009, new CEO Fritz Henderson described a "new culture" for the restructured company focused on customer and products, speed (especially with respect to decision making), risk taking, and accountability. One of the strategies for influencing the change process, and one that GM employed, is storytelling—on broadcasts, in meetings, and in other places where employees gather. "Cultural-change agents" exemplifying the new culture tell stories that express their hopes for the future, including stories that "correct" some failure from the past. This approach to cultural change promotes both the messages and the individuals themselves who model the behavior of the new culture. Cultural change may have been accelerated when Henderson was replaced by an outsider, Ed Whitaker, in December 2009. The jury is still out on how effective GM's cultural change efforts will be and whether they will yield long-term success.

GENESIS OF THE PROJECT

Though the research on which this book is based was complete before GM appealed for government assistance, the need for the book became even clearer as GM continued to make the headlines day after day. This book focuses on the process of cultural change that is going to be necessary to reshape U.S. manufacturing and other American workplaces if the United States is to be successful in the current drive for innovation and global competitiveness. The basic research was triggered by an initial series of questions about American culture and the American workplace that were raised during a discussion involving our anthropological research group and a senior GM executive, Troy Clarke, who, at the time, was GM's executive in charge of manufacturing and labor relations. He had previous international experience with GM manufacturing in Mexico, Asia, and other international locations. His ideas are reflected in these questions, which linked differences in manufacturing plant culture with the national cultures in which those plants were located:

- How can we transfer the highly successful organizational and work culture we experience in Mexico to the United States?
- How can we help American workers achieve a more ideal work culture that is beneficial to the company and to their lives and not in conflict with either or both?
- How can we achieve the kinds of strong relationships among employees and management that we observe in other cultures?
- What kinds of changes are needed to make American workers and management successful within a global context?
- What should be the new American ideal work culture?
- How will that new ideal work?

We address these questions throughout the book using culture-change and evolutionary theories. There are a number of classic theories of cultural evolution and the process of cultural change in the social science literature. These theories are based on anthropology's focus on the interactive combination of human biological evolution,[7] the evolutionary development of prehistoric human societies,[8] and the study of contemporary cultural change.[9] Application of those concepts has produced a long and fertile "point-counterpoint" exploration of cultural change that is now being applied to organizations and organizational-culture change.[10]

Our empirical research is grounded in ethnographic data (e.g., stories, statements, observations, interviews, pilot tests) that we intensively collected at GM at two points in time—the mid-1980s and the mid-2000s—and collected continuously at a less-intensive level from the mid-1980s to the present. As our analysis reveals, we identify a key weakness in GM culture for which we offer a set of validated tools to help transform that limitation into a strength. The weakness we refer to is in the area of relationships—specifically, cooperative workplace interactions and collaborative problem solving.

GM, like many other U.S. organizational cultures, focuses so much on work tasks and work process that they overlook the potential value of collaborative relationships as a way to improve workplace effectiveness. This pattern is particularly evident for people living in low-context cultures (e.g., American national culture, Scandinavian, and German-language–based cultures). In the workplace, low-context culture tends to favor the development of many transitory rather than close relationships among fellow workers.[11] Higher-intensity, more complex relationships tend to be reserved for home and friends. The two can overlap, but often do not. A low-context culture workplace tends to favor direct forms of communication in which the message is highly structured and detailed, with less emphasis on non-verbal cues or cultural assumptions. Things are "spelled out in detail," and there is heavy reliance on the written word. By contrast, people in high-context cultures (e.g., Japanese national culture, Chinese national culture) emphasize the importance of interpersonal relationships in everything they do, including work. They are oriented to the welfare of the group rather than to individual goals. They also tend to be heavily reliant on nonverbal communication and general social rules and value indirect verbal interaction. Based on our data, we suggest that an important reason that the firms from high-context cultures, such as Toyota, have been successful in outperforming and outproducing GM is because of their stronger orientation toward relationships and the ways in which those relationships affect other cultural elements (e.g., learning, diffusion of new ideas). This cultural insight led us to investigate relationships in the workplace and eventually recommend that GM needed to focus a portion of its energy and attention to improve its relationship processes. We believe that other U.S. organizations can benefit from this insight as well.

Defining what collaboration is, and is not, is useful in understanding our perspective. According to Webster's Dictionary, the word "collaboration," with its roots in the Latin words *com* (with) and *laborare* (to labor), means "to work together." For our purposes, collaboration involves working in concert with others in pursuit of particular goals. The emphasis on the working relationship, the work tasks, and the work goals are interwoven into our concept. Collaboration may take a variety of forms in a work environment (e.g., problem-solving discussions, assistance in completing a task). Our usage incorporates the connotation of cooperation and respect. The way in which we use the term neither implies friendship, on the one hand (though work-based relationships are often strengthened through cooperative activities), nor favoritism or cronyism, on the other. It does not necessarily mean consensus or agreement on work objectives, methods, or tasks. In fact, tensions may be generated that require organizational time and attention. Collaboration simply involves the willingness and the ability to engage with others in collective or cooperative work-related efforts.

THE CULTURAL TRANSFORMATION PROCESS

Our focus in this book is squarely on the transformation of American workplace culture[12] (which includes the concept of collaboration) and the process of cultural change in both a specific organizational culture as well as the broader social context. Because cultural inertia and cultural change are inextricably tied with people—their roles, beliefs and values, and the changes in their relationships over time—we highlight both the details of our study and the implications it provides for a broader cultural context. We use various sources of data to examine what the manufacturing culture was, what it is, and what it could (or should) become. We document employee perspectives of the culture-change process, including their past, current, and ideal worldviews (i.e., conceptualizations or mental models) associated with plant culture. We discuss ways in which the work force can become engaged in the culture-change process and help sustain the desired changes. And we discuss the process of producing culture-specific tools that are directed at planned cultural change. We believe that these ideas and the tools stemming from them can be adapted for use in a variety of American organizational settings and not just in manufacturing environments.

Cultural transformation is a process of cultural change that produces a cohesive pattern of change in an organizational culture. The change can be actual or ideal, intended or serendipitous, and should become integrated into the firm's organizational structure, beliefs and expectations, and behavior rather than being a "cosmetic" or transitory change. We use the phrase "cultural transformation" within the context of an organizational culture to refer to the change process rather than to identify some result of that transformation.

During cultural transformation, an end point or goal should be identifiable. Identifiable goals, or end points, can include ideal or intended end points. Alternately, if the change is unplanned, the identifiable end point may be the starting point for a retrospective view of the transformation process. The process of cultural transformation can entail a series of stages (or subprocesses) that include the following:

1. Identification or recognition of the need to initiate a change
2. Identification of the direction the change should take or identification of an end point to achieve at the end of the change process
3. Identification of the focus of the change, including conditions and processes that need to change
4. Implementation of the change process (which would involve identifying obstacles that have the potential to derail the attainment of the ideal and activating the enablers or positive elements of the culture that can support the change to the ideal)

5. Establishment and maintenance of a feedback loop that would measure changes in behaviors, beliefs, and conditions in relation to the ideal
6. Decision to celebrate the achievement of the ideal or restart the transformation process due to an inability to reach that ideal

We use two primary domains or cultural concepts that help explain the overall process of cultural transformation and make that process accessible to those who want or need to transform GM or other manufacturing cultures. These domains are cultural adaptiveness and cultural responsiveness. *Cultural adaptiveness* occurs when members of the culture are aware of the world around them and are prepared to modify their culture as necessary, when warranted. In many ways, it is the ideological element of transformation—the willingness to recognize the need to change and the will to change. They know the overall cultural context of their society and are able to integrate (or transform) changes in the larger cultural environment into a more adaptive organizational culture. The general literature on cultural change demonstrates that some cultures are more amenable to adaptation than others. All cultures change, and all cultures resist change, but cultures do vary in terms of their willingness to support or resist change as a general theme or process. Higher cultural adaptability requires a view of the world that accepts the need for transforming the present into a different future, rather than maintaining the past into an indefinite present. Manufacturing culture adaptiveness occurs when a company "gets it," that is, the company understands that when the culture surrounding the firm changes in unanticipated directions or at an unexpected pace (e.g., a drastic rise in oil prices, a political change in response to global warming, an economic crisis), the company must adapt its worldview to address these new issues. Simply fighting for the status quo or inappropriately attempting to slow the pace of change internally when that pace is driven by external forces are behaviors that run counter to a culturally adaptive firm.

Cultural responsiveness is the ability of an organization to maintain an appropriate pace of transformation, an appropriate response process (either evolutionary or revolutionary), and appropriate targeting of organizational transformation in relation to its surrounding environment. It entails a negotiated (or interactive) change in worldview[13] that occurs when the manufacturing culture has to be actively negotiated between members of the organizational culture and either outsiders (e.g., customers) or insiders (e.g., other employees) to respond appropriately to a new worldview or a changed environment. Culturally appropriate responsiveness results in changed relationships, roles, processes, rules, or similar conditions and occurs at the point in time when those interactions are important to solidify the new culture and move beyond the old. It is a combination of appropriate action and timeliness.

When we combine the two concepts of cultural adaptiveness and cultural responsiveness, some of the successes and the failures of GM, or any organization, can be placed in a framework that shows what works and how it works in relation to the overall cultural environment surrounding it. GM has been highly adaptive and minimally adaptive at different points in time, as well as highly responsive and inappropriately responsive at other times. The same is the case for all organizations. The overall long-term success of an organization depends on a continuing overall positive match between adaptiveness and responsiveness in spite of short-term failures.

Understanding the transformative elements inherent in the two domains of cultural adaptiveness and cultural responsiveness leads directly to *cultural problem solving*. This process utilizes our knowledge about cultural transformation and turns it into a set of actions (see Figure 1.1). The proactive use of these actions has the potential to change the culture in the desired direction by reinforcing the positive aspects of organizational culture and diminishing the negative aspects. The basic steps in cultural problem solving involve (1) identifying the cultural conditions that are in play, (2) identifying the response to the problem that best resolves the problem in a positive direction, and (3) implementing the solution.

The process of cultural problem solving requires an understanding of the appropriateness of proposed or attempted solutions, the timeliness of those solutions, an understanding of the cultural obstacles that work against cultural transformation, and the enablers that mitigate the impact of the obstacles—all of which are described later in this book. All of these elements combine to form an overall model of cultural transformation.

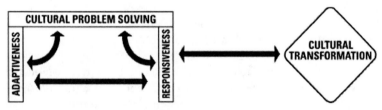

Figure 1.1 Elements of cultural transformation

THE IDEAL PLANT CULTURE PROJECT

Earlier cultural transformations in U.S. automotive manufacturing (e.g., Fordism, lean engineering) serve as an important historical backdrop for our study. We used a carefully designed ethnographic approach, combined with anthropological theory, to gather statements and stories associated with life on the plant floor—how it was in the past, how it is currently, and how it could be in the future. We wanted to understand manufacturing culture holistically from a variety of perspectives. Consequently, we sought the views of a cross-section of employees[14] who were able to articulate their views of an ideal plant culture and how that ideal contrasted with either current or past circumstances. Their "ideal" conceptualization focuses on what happens internally within the work environment. It is here where we focus our analysis and from here where we gain our insights. We try to understand their culture from their point of view.

Throughout this book we use a "cultural-models"[15] approach to understand and explain manufacturing culture.[16] The approach involves asking members of a culture to describe a key element of their culture and then to construct a consensus description (or model) of the culture that is simultaneously validated by members of the culture and by the empirical data collected by the researchers.[17] Our cultural-models approach allows us to construct a basic model of the "insider's view" of an ideal plant culture and present an empirically constructed view (i.e., our explanations) of that model.[18]

The development of a model of the ideal plant culture, discussed later, reflects the cultural-models approach and is an example of cultural transformation. It reconfigures relationships and activities to address necessary changes in internal conditions (e.g., employee participation in problem solving activities). Our results demonstrate the propensity for change away from an individualistic orientation to work toward one that engages organizational members in a collaborative fashion. Indeed, we found a strong desire during the four-year field and validation phases of our project for a cultural ideal based on unity, cooperation, and collaboration. This finding reinforces American eagerness to counter individualism with community,[19] in spite of the longstanding national-culture emphasis on individualism and self-reliance.[20] Given the strong consensus surrounding the importance and value of collaboration to manufacturing culture today and the likelihood that its potential has not been fully activated in low-context cultures, exploring options for incorporating collaboration as an integral part of workplace cultures is a key way to enhance organizational performance.

For cultural transformation to be effective, a different orientation or mindset is necessary. A top-down approach to cultural change is partial, at best, if it does not have the ability to expand to incorporate the perspectives of the whole. Certainly in GM, and probably in many other organizational settings, there is little recognition that culture belongs to and is shared by everyone. Indeed, there is a strong belief that culture is the purview of the executive suite to plan, to create, to control, and to change at will. There is little understanding that soliciting viewpoints and sharing perspectives about the direction of cultural change and the process of achieving it can actually increase the long-term probability of success. Cultural change can be more powerfully embedded and sustained if all parts of the cultural system are working in concert and toward a potential future that reflects, broadly, the views of the whole.

There is another important dimension of the transformation process that requires immediate and sustained attention. Expressing the objectives of change through stories (as exemplified by the "new GM" postbankruptcy) is but an initial step in any cultural transformation. Change is not possible unless there is a specific implementation process to realize those objectives. The cultural transformation model we use to identify positive (or adaptive) change and to identify appropriate responsiveness within GM can serve as a model for other organizations who seek change in ways consistent with their future plans and their surrounding cultural environments.

As the implementation process gets underway, it will face resistance. Consequently, it will be critical to identify and cope with the barriers that emerge to prevent the cultural transformation from occurring. Organizations will need to be proactive, rather than reactive, in this regard. Moreover, the follow-up actions to assess the direction and extent of the change will be necessary to keep the transformation process on course. This book offers a model for the cultural transformation process that can be applied across organizations and industries and illustrates how organizational-culture change can be successful in spite of, or perhaps because of, the challenges faced on the plant floor and in the global market place.

One other dimension of cultural transformation involves the identification and ongoing use of mechanisms to support the cultural ideals. We led an effort to design a set of collaboration tools that would strengthen and help sustain GM's collaborative ideal. Because these applications (or cultural problem-solving actions) are the product of the cultural transformation process described above, they are structured to include the key stages of that process (e.g., recognition of the need to change, identification of obstacles likely to prevent change). At the same time, the tools are flexible enough to incorporate new ideas and initiatives—such as the "new" cultural priorities the leadership team has identified. We believe that these tools offer a template for change for the world beyond GM manufacturing. They can be adapted for use in other organizations in the exploration of their future cultural directions and help those organizations chart the paths that make sense to them.

The rest of the book tells the story of how American workplace culture needs and provides answers to the basic questions that we have posed and how the answers we received should be seen within both old and newly forming U.S. work cultures. Now more than ever, given the persistent economic challenges to U.S. manufacturing enterprises, this book is relevant and useful for organizations in the process of change. One of the core strengths of the book is that it is an ethnographic case of a company that represents American culture and American cultural transformations at a critical time in history. In the broadest context, the book attempts to address the American view of an "ideal" work culture, and the issues of cultural change and innovation in the workplace, and what the people in the trenches see as the critically needed changes in the nature of relationships within existing U.S. organizational cultures.

While numerous books have been written about improving organizational competitiveness, most discount the role played by organizational and national culture. Their emphasis on prescription and application of best practices without taking the cultural context into account can derail or slow the change process. This book suggests an alternative approach that directs the focus back on the culture—that interlocking set of elements including the expectations, preferences, and behaviors of organizational members—as a way to secure a competitive advantage and does so by relying on the knowledge, experiences, and talents of all organizational members. It offers a culturally appropriate process for moving U.S.-based organizations in new, uncharted directions that are still compatible with American national-culture principles and ideals.

CHAPTER 2

SIGNIFICANT CULTURAL TRANSFORMATIONS IN THE AUTOMOTIVE INDUSTRY

The manufacturing history of Europe, the United States, and the world is an intertwined flow of cultural transformations. Understanding the broad sweep of those transformations is an excellent way to explore current patterns because any cultural transformation has three elements that define it, explain it, and predict where it will end up. These elements are a history, a present configuration, and future potential. A famous aphorism states, "Those who cannot remember the past are condemned to repeat it." In both the social sciences and in most human relationships, the things a person has done in the past are often the best predictors of future behavior. Unfortunately, being the best predictor is not necessarily synonymous with being a reliable predictor, only the most reliable predictor we have. People, cultures, and environments can change in unanticipated directions that make the future less certain.

The historical context of automotive manufacturing provides an important, necessary, and relevant background for the Ideal Plant Culture study and the transformations that are embedded in or necessary to understanding the lessons and tools derived from the study. The historical framing in this chapter focuses on the cultural patterns of manufacturing that arose over the past century to shape the course of the automotive industry. It illustrates the ways in which the dominant manufacturers established their competitive edge and influenced the marketplace. It allows us to draw attention to the ways in which "underdog" firms sought to become competitive by inventing, borrowing, and adapting approaches and techniques that they hoped would put them on the path to prosperity. This kind of history offers both a view of the past mediated by an understanding of the cultural context in which successes and failures occurred and the cultural interpretation of the transformation process and its outcomes from the standpoint of the firms involved and their competitors.

CULTURAL AND ENVIRONMENTAL CONDITIONS INFLUENCING CULTURAL TRANSFORMATION

The external environment has a significant impact on the viability of change as well as the impact of the speed of change.[1] Numerous cultural and environmental conditions have shaped how production work has been conceived and implemented and how it has evolved in the automotive industry. By *production-work paradigms*, we mean the centralizing elements (e.g., organization of work, ideologies, relationships, work practices) characterizing a particular approach to manufacturing work. We call attention to three sets of conditions affecting any given production-work paradigm: national-culture effects, external-environment effects, and organizational-culture effects.[2] The work-related ideologies that culturally frame these conditions reinforce, raise questions about, or, ultimately, lead to the refutation of that paradigm while simultaneously preparing the groundwork for its successor. Sometimes the change is a classic dialectic (thesis–antithesis–synthesis), and sometimes it arises from an innovative leap that seems not to follow a pathway of incremental change.

National-culture ideals, assumptions, and patterns of behavior affect the way in which production-work paradigms are conceptualized, executed, and evaluated. Individualism, a central theme in American culture, involves the pursuit of one's self-interest (e.g., knowledge, career considerations, hobbies) with values, rights, and duties grounded in the individual. Americans pride themselves on being self-reliant, or "their own person," such that they typically are concerned about the success of their own welfare rather than that of some larger group or organization.[3] Group activities are certainly present in American culture (e.g., team sports, charitable committees, organizational task forces). However, commitment to a group effort tends to be "only for a specified and frequently short period of time" so that goals can be accomplished and a particular problem can be solved.[4] Individualism and its allied concept of autonomy are woven into the fabric of American organizations. For example, work tasks are typically assigned to individuals and then individuals are evaluated on their performance. Individual units within an organization may be distinctive and differentiated from other units by a set of traditions and shared identity. Moreover, American organizations typically value independence and self-reliance.[5] Mass production, as practiced in the United States, has been influenced heavily by individualism.

A contrasting national-culture example is Japanese culture, where the emphasis is on the group. Ties to the group are strong to the point that "members feel a collective sense of responsibility for each other's actions."[6] Unlike the United States, Japan is on the groupism end of the spectrum, though individuals and individual activities are valued (e.g., Yoko Ono, Nobel Prize winners, Sumo wrestlers). This groupism, with its strong, relational foundation, affects the ways in which work in Japanese organizations is coordinated and carried out. Members of work teams typically engage in problem-solving exercises as one way to improve their performance. Consensus is a highly valued ideal; it can build and reinforce group bonds so that the group's focus is on a set of shared goals. Group boundaries can expand to accommodate business and trade—as in the case of the Japanese Keiretsu, a set of companies with interwoven business relationships.[7] The production-work paradigm associated with many Asian manufacturers, particularly with Toyota Motor Company, Ltd., is replete with relationship-based elements such as teamwork.

Production-work paradigms take into account external environment effects, including such forces as economics, politics, and technology. For example, the domain of public policy has had an important impact on production-work paradigms. U.S. government regulation, led by consumer advocates during the 1970s, resulted in an array of safety-related actions by manufacturers, including the production of safer vehicles.[8] Such regulation had an effect on manufacturing generally, though it had a particularly notable impact on GM's version of mass production. New technology is another domain linked with external environment effects. During the twentieth century, many mass-production manufacturers shifted to automation to reduce labor costs and lessen labor-management difficulties. Success was not always assured due to factors such as manufacturing inflexibility (e.g., downtime due to problems in the automated system) and employee fear about losing their jobs.[9] These examples indicate that production-work paradigms are affected and sometimes severely constrained by elements in the external environment.

Organizational culture also plays a role in the creation and trajectory of production-work paradigms. For example, Toyota lacked the resources in its early days to purchase special-purpose machine tools as Ford had done. Instead, Toyota acquired machines that were "adjustable" to design changes, laying them out according to the sequence of work activities to create a smooth production flow.[10] Similarly,

Toyota's tooling strategy was an important element in the creation of its production process. These factors helped to shape the development of Toyota's production process, which later was characterized by its flexibility. Within the mass-production paradigm, Ford's organizational culture was greatly influenced by its founder, Henry Ford, who opted to centralize and compartmentalize its operations, reserving much of the decision making for himself.[11] GM's variant of mass production exhibited a greater degree of decentralization during the same time period,[12] though it, too, became more centralized over time.[13]

Two Influential Production-Work Paradigms in the Automotive Industry

Two production-work paradigms have had a sustained impact on the automotive industry: mass production, and flexible and lean production. Each consists of an integrated set of attributes that constitute a recognizable innovation in manufacturing and a significant departure from the past. We discuss these two paradigms using Weber's concept of "ideal types"—"the construction of certain elements of reality into a logically precise conception."[14] To these ideal types, we apply the comparative method,[15] acknowledging that these production-work paradigms followed a particular evolutionary progression. Comparison allows us to examine the elements that are shared between the ideal types and view the differences in their historical context. We also can identify the elements that are retained, discarded, or modified as the evolutionary trajectory proceeds.

We divide the discussion of each paradigm into two parts: the structure of work and the dynamics of work. By structure, we mean the elements that shape the organization and coordination of work: work practices, processes, tasks, technology, resources, status and roles, human resource practices (e.g., compensation, hiring practices), and the physical plant environment. We define the dynamics of work as the relationships associated with the work environment, patterns of work force perceptions and behavior, and the quality of interactions. The structural side of the work environment is interwoven with the relationship-dynamics side; both are mutually reinforcing.

Mass Production

The production-work paradigm that has come to be known as mass production had its origins in selected types of large-scale European manufacturing (e.g., small arms, textile mills) and was distinguished from craft systems;[16] a more recent configuration of mass production from the twentieth century was pioneered by Henry Ford and then diffused all over the world. The term "mass" in mass production can be understood in two ways: as an adjective it implies the quantity produced, while as a noun it signals those who may purchase the product—the mass consumers.[17] Mass production has been defined as the "manufacture of standardized products in high volumes using special-purpose machinery and predominately unskilled labour."[18] Other features include interchangeable parts, "highly mechanized production, moving line assembly, high wages, and low prices on products."[19] Factory organization is increasingly centralized, paralleling the subdivision of work tasks into fewer and fewer elements.[20]

Mass production represented a major cultural transformation from craft production—that is, a small-scale production process involving skilled workers who created products with or without specialized tools or customer involvement. Craft production engaged the social as well as the material aspects of the culture,[21] with workers participating in all phases of the work, from the design, to the procurement of materials, to their manufacture, and, sometimes, to their sale. The acquisition of craft knowledge was dependent on relationships—whether involving a parent-child or master-apprentice pair.[22]

In nineteenth-century America, a production process on a larger scale than craft specialization emerged as the immediate precursor to mass production. Labeled the "American system of manufactures," it referred to the methods of key manufacturers such as Isaac Singer (sewing machines), Samuel Colt (firearms), and Cyrus McCormick (the McCormick reaper), among others.[23] These manufacturers produced their goods in an organized, coordinated fashion using a combination of skilled workers and extensive mechanization. This "American system" spread to the nascent automotive industry through two, frequently related mechanisms: (1) specific techniques such as the manufacture of interchangeable parts (i.e., standardized and uniform) and (2) competent and inventive individuals with experience in more than one industry (e.g., Henry M. Leland, founder of Cadillac, moved from firearms to machine tools and sewing machines to automobiles). Two of these industries in particular, bicycle makers and carriage and wagon manufacturers, were among those that "turned their efforts to automobile production."[24] The diffusion of manufacturing ideas between New England and the Midwest ultimately resulted in the establishment of the center of automotive mass production in Michigan.

Structure of Work: Compartmentalized, Mechanized, and Centralized
The "*act* of mass-producing the Model T"[25] entailed several interlocking concepts all working in unison: an efficient plant layout, a continuous flow of materials, a subdivision of work tasks, continuous labor efforts, specialized machinery, consistent work standards, and a centralized direction. With its emphasis on efficiency and productivity, configuration of key elements, and scale of operations, mass production represented a significant cultural transformation in work goals, work processes, and work output. Production became increasingly formalized and compartmentalized with differentiation in roles and work practices not found in craft production. The initial stationary assembly phase, in which both the assemblers and the vehicle were static, progressed to a phase in which workers moved among the vehicles (placed on stands) to complete their tasks.[26] Laborers distributed parts at each station, timing their deliveries to occur just before they were assembled. Teams or "gangs" moved from station to station completing the assembly tasks they had been assigned, fixing the same components on each station.[27] Subassemblers stood at workbenches adjacent to which were bins holding the various parts.[28]

By 1913, the assembly line was in full operation at Ford Motor Company, with the work moving to workers who were stationary. With each successive phase in the organization of work at Ford, the work became easier to supervise, since it was further divided into increasingly discrete tasks.[29] Indeed, production work became so fragmented that the tasks of any given worker represented a smaller and smaller part of the whole production effort: "The workers had been instructed by the foreman to place one particular part in the assembly or perhaps start a few nuts or even just tighten them and then push the flywheel down the row to the next worker. Having pushed it down eighteen or perhaps thirty-six inches, the workers repeated the same process, over and over, nine hours, over and over."[30]

Unlike most craft production where workers develop a product from start to finish,[31] assembly workers were only responsible for completing specific tasks. In fact, some have argued that worker deskilling under capitalism has been a strategy to reduce production costs and increase productivity.[32] In the context of the Fordist mass-production paradigm, work became configured in ways consistent with individualism in American culture—especially in the assignment of particular work tasks to individuals.

Plant machinery played an increasingly crucial role in the development of mass production. Ford became convinced of the interchangeability of parts, made possible by precision machining within the American system, and hired highly skilled mechanics to ensure that the parts produced were standardized.[33] One of these mechanics hired to "superintend" Ford's Bellevue plant later reminisced that Ford realized that "to create great quantity of production, your interchangeability must be fine and unique in order to accomplish the rapid assembly of units. There can't be much hand work or fitting if you are going to accomplish great things."[34] Henry Ford wrote, "Every part must be produced to fit at once into the design for which it is made. In mass production, there are no fitters."[35] Mass production was a new form of work that ultimately proved to be less time consuming and labor intensive given the volume produced in comparison with craft specialization.[36] Mastering the interchangeability of parts led to reductions in labor costs. No longer was it necessary to have as many skilled workers as in the past. Ford was now positioned to hire a work force composed largely of unskilled laborers.

Mechanization first contributed significantly to the effective and efficient production of parts and later to the assembly process. It was to become an important defining element of mass-production cultures; a strong belief in the value and utility of mechanization persisted even after later attempts to design a fully automated plant failed.[37] Many of the machines performed multiple operations as a way to standardize production,[38] with machine layout an important feature. Machine tools were arranged according to the sequence of operations on the parts (rather than by types of machines)—another element borrowed from the American system. This sequencing created a flow to the machining process and foreshadowed the conveyors, gravity slides, and, ultimately, the assembly line. It also has been characterized as "continuous step by step improvements in workflow,"[39] resulting in significant savings in labor costs. Once Ford settled on producing the Model T, he invested in special-purpose, rather than general-purpose, machine tools. The benefit at the time was cost reduction through economies of scale and the expansion of the market for standardized goods.[40]

Centralization represented another component of the structure of work under mass production. As an enterprise grows, centralization becomes an option for planning and coordinating work, with management taking over control of how the work is organized;[41] in craft production, the master maintains control over specialized skills and knowledge (e.g., craft "secrets")[42] as well as how and when the work gets done. Ford wanted centralized control with those he trusted in charge. He was likened to a sea captain whose "foresight and insight" were alone able to "guide the ship."[43] He surrounded himself with a cadre of technical specialists who conducted extensive experimentation. His "hard-driving production engineers" operated in a "project-centered, flat and informal organization."[44] In his autobiography, Ford described his expectations for connecting his enterprise into a cohesive whole: "It is not necessary for any one department to know what any other department is doing . . . It is the business of those who plan the entire work to see that all of the departments are working properly toward the same end."[45]

Centralization occurred in phases. With the launch of the Model T in 1908, matters pertaining to machines and machine purchases were handled by a central department rather than by individual foremen.[46] As "machine work became more specialized and work studies more prevalent, the direction and evaluation of work became more centralized."[47] Ford conducted analyses of work routines and flows, though he claimed he did not rely on a Taylorist approach.[48] With the introduction of the assembly line in Ford operations, the new employment office took over some of the foremen's responsibilities, including the transfer or firing of workers.[49] Accounting and inspection departments also were created.[50] The creation of these new functions ushered in a new group of professional managers who "became responsible for the tasks of factory coordination and control, tasks which had formerly been the preserve of skilled workers."[51]

Ford also found that he had to deal with the structural problem known as the "constancy of labor effort."[52] Unlike craftwork, Ford needed access to increasingly greater numbers of workers as business expanded. Production work was hard, backbreaking work. Providing a financial incentive was a key way to address both problems. Though Ford initially offered workers a bonus beginning in 1908, he ultimately settled on the unprecedented wage rate of five dollars per day in 1914—assuming the workers met service and behavior conditions.[53] This wage "effectively doubled the earnings of Ford workers and provided a tremendous incentive for workers to stay 'on the line.'"[54] And, once the Machinery Molders Union was defeated in 1907, Ford faced no serious union challenges for about thirty years.

Workplace Dynamics: Directive, Impersonal, and Elitist
Just as the structural elements of mass production evolved, so too did the dynamic or relationship aspects of the culture change. The relationship between Ford and his employees was characterized as paternalistic in the early years of the 1900s when the work force was relatively small. He "frequently moved about the factory, jesting, telling stories in off moments, and playing practical pranks on the hands,

but scrutinizing every operation. 'Everybody used to call him Hank or Henry . . . and he used to know everybody by name.'"[55] By 1906, the work force had grown, making it more difficult to maintain these personal ties. Moreover, there was evidence of poor supervision and quality, leading Ford to increase the authority of his foremen over the workers and later to establish centralized control through bureaucratic departments.[56] The social and cultural distance between Ford and his employees widened; he became more directive and was even said to be "deeply autocratic."[57] Under mass production, power was linked with increasingly higher levels of supervisory authority. Ford himself was situated in the most powerful role at the pinnacle of the organizational hierarchy where he orchestrated the production process. As the Ford organization expanded, relations became more impersonal. These new patterns contrasted with the personalized relations associated with craft production in which the master craftsman or employer engaged in the work alongside the apprentice or employee.[58]

Ford believed that the performance of repetitive tasks was not problematic for the "majority of minds." He believed, "above all, he [the average worker] wants a job in which he does not have to think."[59] This pattern contrasted with craft specialization where cognitive (e.g., planning, design) and other skills mattered to the successful execution of the final product. Ford accepted as a given "inequalities of ability."[60] Consistent with these beliefs, he expected and sought "malleable workers"[61] who would be compliant and hard working. It was as if the workers were simply extensions of the machines rather than resourceful and innovative contributors in their own right. Ford was the sole, and final, decision maker vis-à-vis his senior managers. While he solicited input from them, and certainly encouraged innovative thinking and experimentation, he expected to make the calls. For example, once the Model A was launched in 1927, he required all engineering changes to be funneled through one particular design engineer, who would then seek his approval on each change.[62]

Relationships on the plant floor were mixed. Some supervisor-subordinate relationships were highly valued. Around the time of the Model A changeover, Ford fired many of the supervisory personnel on the plant floor and hired a new manager in charge of assembly. Lower-ranking supervisors were apparently "demoralized" to see "their longtime supervisors summarily dismissed."[63] Fear and a certain inevitability characterized the iron hand of Henry Ford. One foreman later reminisced, "I knew what was going to happen. They were all going to be fired, not only me but all the fellows from Highland Park."[64] The quality of relationships in the craftwork paradigm could also vary. However, when a master takes on an apprentice, the relationship is face to face, personal, and typically solidified by "filial status" or "kin fosterage" in which "introduced sons live as dependent members of the household."[65] Bonds of kinship, such as parent to child, also matter when both are engaged in craft production[66] as do "comradeship and community."[67]

Patterns of hierarchical authority characterized many of the foreman-worker relationships. There were labor problems—often involving the worker and his foreman—in which the foremen were seen as "prejudiced" or "arbitrary."[68] Some foremen were heavy handed with their workers, as evident in the high levels of worker dissatisfaction from a 1913 Ford survey.[69] In 1913, there were high annual levels of worker turnover at Ford—reaching 370 percent (while the average turnover rate in Detroit was 100 percent), as well as absenteeism—equaling 10 percent of Ford's work force.[70] The decision to create the employment office had mixed effects on worker morale overall. For some, it represented a positive, progressive change. For others, particularly nonnative English speakers, it was mostly problematic. When foremen were in charge of hiring, they often hired those of their own ethnic group, thereby creating groups of culturally and linguistically similar workers on the plant floor. But Ford's strategy and intent was one of assimilation in which he sought to eliminate ethnic differences so that he could "fit them [workers] for their increasingly standardized role."[71] That aim was well served by the employment office. It also may have reduced preferential hiring of friends and family members and led to some guidelines for hiring—and firing.

Given his desire to centralize operations, Ford saw no compelling reason for his employees to engage with one another: "It is not necessary to have meetings to establish good feelings between individuals or departments. It is not necessary for people to love each other in order to work together. Too much fellowship may indeed be a very bad thing, for it may lead to one man trying to cover up the faults of another."[72] Ford wanted his employees to stay on task. Personal relationships, particularly when they led to favoritism, had the potential to interfere with work goals and work output. Ford settled on an impersonal approach to production work, believing it would enhance productivity. By contrast, craft production's master-apprentice relationship entailed continuous interaction through observation and practice so that the apprentice would learn the trade;[73] moreover, the degree of technical skills required for the particular craft played a role in dictating the duration of the relationship, with some crafts such as ironmaking necessitating long apprenticeships.[74]

Ford viewed the dealer-customer relationship differently than relationships among his employees. He issued a policy concerning the customer relationship: "A dealer or a salesman ought to have the name of every possible automobile buyer in his territory, including all those who have never given the matter a thought. He should then personally solicit by visitation if possible—by correspondence at the least—every man on that list and then making necessary memoranda, know the automobile situation as related to every resident so solicited. If your territory is too large to permit this, you have too much territory."[75] Thus, while the development of relationships with potential vehicle buyers was essential to Ford's operation, collaboration on the plant floor was not. One writer described the role of factory employees as "human appendages" in the "mechanized, conveyor-laced, assembly-line-dominated factory."[76]

Creativity, experimentation, openness to technical changes, and continual technical improvements represented critical dimensions of Ford's overarching work philosophy. He placed a high value on "pressing forward" in the exploration of new frontiers and the discovery of workable, effective solutions.[77] He indicated, "If we have a tradition it is this: Everything can always be done better than it is being done," and "If there is any fixed theory—any fixed rule—it is that no job is being done well enough."[78] Yet, the Fordist philosophy reflected an elitism in which only the most competent technical specialists played a role in Ford's inner circle, adapting techniques from other industries, experimenting with alternative options, and developing innovative strategies that solidified the change to mass production. This elitist approach contrasted both with the importance of innovation to individual craftsmen[79] and with successive work paradigms that permitted or encouraged innovation within the work force on a broader scale.

Visual images of this production-work paradigm are now part of the historical record. Diego Rivera's frescoes at the Detroit Institute of Arts were completed in 1933 after eight months of work. Both the north and south walls of the garden court depict scenes from the automotive industry, including the production of the engine and transmission of the 1932 Ford V8 engine at the River Rouge complex. The multiracial and multiethnic work force is shown engaged in strenuous, physical work against a backdrop dominated by factory machinery.[80] Mass production exhibited sociocultural, linguistic, ethnic, and regional differences that set it apart from craft production, where there tended to be greater population homogeneity and an alignment of particular forms of craftwork with particular family units. Film also contributed to the characterization of mass production. The

1936 comedy *Modern Times* features Charlie Chaplin as the Little Tramp, a factory worker who suffers a mental breakdown due to the demands of the repetitive tasks. The film captures the tensions among assembly line workers and between workers and management as the line pace increases. In the contrasting case of craft production, the master was able to maintain some degree of control over the amount and pace of the work. Art forms such as the frescoes and film provide insight into dimensions of the mass-production paradigm whose "real, inner truth" is found in the work culture "of the factory, not its product."[81]

Ford's mass-production paradigm was perceived around the world as the highly successful manufacturing ideal. It was innovative, productive, and profitable. It employed a large work force at wages superior to the competition. It also manufactured products that were highly desirable and for many, affordable. Yet the plant-floor culture fell far short of ideal as this 1914 letter from a housewife to Henry Ford attests, "The chain system you have is a *slave driver! My God!*, Mr. Ford. My husband has come home & thrown himself down & won't eat his supper—so done out! Can't it be remedied? . . . That $5 a day is a blessing—a bigger one than you know but *oh* they earn it."[82] The backbreaking, monotonous work, the relentless pace of the line, the tensions surrounding making the daily quota, and the accidents and injuries tied to the production process all left their mark on employees and on manufacturing culture. The gulf between management and labor widened. It reached an all-time low when the media captured Ford Motor Company security guards, described as "goons," beating up UAW organizers at the "Battle of the Overpass" at the River Rouge Plant in 1937. This incident increased support for the labor movement and damaged Ford's reputation. The emergence of the UAW was a response to the treatment of manufacturing workers, though the UAW found it had little influence over plant operations.

Flexible and Lean Production

As mass production grew in popularity, its methods and techniques spread all over the world. Many firms found that they were unable to adopt all of its fundamentals completely because of differences in local conditions (e.g., economic, political, ideological).[83] Instead, they adapted those elements that made sense, given their particular context, and borrowed and developed other elements to create alternative work paradigms.

Convergence around a set of key elements emerged as a recognizable alternative to mass production. Associated particularly with Japanese manufacturers, this new paradigm of "flexible specialization" represented a "strategy of permanent innovation: accommodation to ceaseless change, rather than an effort to control it . . . [that] is based on flexible—multiuse—equipment; skilled workers; and the creation, through politics, of an industrial community that restricts the form of competition to those favoring innovation."[84]

The long-term success of flexible specialization depends on "an irreducible minimum of trust and co-operation among economic actors, not only between employers and workers, but also between firms and their subcontractors or subsidiaries."[85] Other writers prefer the label "new manufacturing organization,"[86] "flexible manufacturing,"[87] or "lean production."[88] The term "lean" connotes "less of everything compared with mass production" (e.g., tool investment, manufacturing space, engineering hours, human resources) and a focus on achieving goals such as "continually declining costs, zero defects, zero inventories, and endless product variety."[89] Still others make explicit reference to the overwhelming impact that the Toyota Motor Company has had on manufacturing and simply refer to this confluence of characteristics as the "Toyota Production System" (TPS) or the "Toyota Way."[90]

Those writing about flexible specialization have called attention to two prominent dimensions of the reaction to the mass-production paradigm—flexibility and leanness. Other features of flexible specialization include the central role of connections—particularly the supervisor-subordinate pair and the work team—in learning and in the application of that learning, the structured ways to foster ongoing improvements in work process to enhance efficiency and productivity, and the dissemination of new or adapted techniques, approaches, and practices within the entire supply chain (i.e., suppliers, employees, dealers, customers). All of these features exhibit points of contrast with mass production—both as separate elements and as an integrated configuration. Applying an all-encompassing descriptor to this production-work paradigm is challenging. We have opted to label this paradigm "flexible and lean production" to capture its most well-publicized elements. There are many examples of this work paradigm,[91] though the one revered as the ideal is TPS. Consequently, we describe TPS's historical roots, its fundamental elements, and the ways in which it differs from mass production.

Structure of Work: Economizing, Standardized, and Selective
In its earliest form, flexible and lean began with attention to quality in the textile industry. Sakichi Toyoda, whose family name in its slightly altered form, "Toyota,"[92] is now among the most recognizable names in the world, was a weaver who invented an automatic loom in 1926. This loom was capable of detecting a broken thread; it would stop automatically (referred to as autonomation) so that a repair could be made. While mechanization had enabled the transformation from weaving as a form of craft production, autonomation ensured quality that was not previously possible. This particular feature would eventually challenge mass production, which did not have fail-safe mechanisms to ensure consistency in product quality. The possibility of preventing the manufacture of a poor quality piece in loom technology[93] foreshadowed the future of his family's legacy in motor vehicle manufacturing. By the early 1960s, devices had been installed throughout Toyota to stop the line if there were equipment malfunctions or quality problems.[94] Perhaps the most well-known equivalent today of the loom's ability to interrupt the weaving process is the *andon* [95] cord, used by an assembly operator to stop the line and signal that help is needed. The problem can be addressed immediately at the point in the process where the problem has occurred. "Built-in" quality, in which a solution is found "in station" at its source, is now a core feature of TPS.

With the money from the sale of the patent rights on the automatic loom, the automotive business was launched. Many experts were recruited from both academia and industry in such areas as machine tools, steel manufacturing, vehicle design, and factory layout. During the 1930s, investments were made in simple and flexible equipment that "would enable many of the concepts essential to TPS."[96] "Universal machine tools or easily adaptable specialized machinery" were purchased[97] rather than the special-purpose machines installed by Ford and other firms reliant on mass production. Toyota's machinery purchases represented a cultural response in keeping with its own environmental context, where resources were more limited compared with Ford's and where customer demand was more differentiated and changeable. These universal tools positioned Toyota for relative ease in product-design changes,[98] a diverse set of market offerings, and the anticipated low-volume production runs.[99]

Toyota worked to create a "smooth flow of production." The factory organization was influenced by the German *Producktionstakt* method[100] in which the body of the aircraft was moved step-by-step through the production process. *Takt* time, or available production time divided by the rate of customer demand, represented a later evolution of this method and was viewed as a way to increase output. This method, borrowed from abroad, had an important impact on streamlining Toyota's production process. Facing capital constraints, Toyota also emphasized product development through "indirect technology transfer" or "reverse engineering" in which foreign vehicles were purchased, studied, tested, and then reproduced.[101] Thus, early in its organizational history, Toyota began adopting and adapting production features, as well as product-development techniques, that could be gleaned from its automotive competitors and from other industries.

Before 1948, Toyota tried to produce as much product as possible in line with the mass-production orientation. Toyota had a centralized organization, as did Ford. But Toyota's production-management initiatives shifted with an emphasis on economizing; workers should produce only what was needed for the next process. Materials and components were no longer pushed through the process, as was common in mass production, but were pulled by final assembly. Using this "just-in-time" (JIT) method, "workers moved backwards to previous stations to take only what they needed, 'just in time' for their operation."[102] A rising Toyota leader reported, "In 1949 and 1950, when I was in charge of the machining shop, I tried to create 'flow of production' as the first step for introducing a 'Just-in-Time' system. In order to create the flow . . . a single worker handled several machines."[103] For the production flow to work well, machines had to be reliable and have relatively short set-up times. Toyota's economizing strategy, well suited to produce and deliver only what the market was willing to purchase, was not a feature of the Ford paradigm.

JIT represented an opportunity to economize in other ways, including reducing various forms of *muda*, or waste (e.g., the elimination of inventories, reduction in factory space for storing inventories) and focusing on value-added work. The constraints facing the Toyota organization led to a particular set of cultural responses, including financial restraint and fast and efficient parts flow through the plants. Reducing *muda*, also known as the "economizing strategy,"[104] played a critical role in Toyota's cultural transformation away from the accumulation and storage of parts irrespective of demand as practiced by firms engaged in the mass-production paradigm. With parts produced in small lots, defects were immediately visible, making it possible to prevent quality problems. It was aided by the *kanban* system in which paper or metal signs accompanied parts in transit and signaled when parts needed to be replenished. *Kanban* evolved further when Toyota learned about the pull system embedded in American supermarket operations: customers create demand by purchasing food, forcing the supermarket to replenish its stock, which requires supermarket suppliers to produce new product. Principles like the "*kanban* supermarket" helped to illustrate the ways in which factory production was part of a larger context involving suppliers, dealers, and customers and allowed Toyota to respond to its domestic market, which demanded a large variety of vehicles but in small volumes.[105]

Another fundamental aspect of the flexible and lean work paradigm was the concept of standardized work. It was developed in response to production inefficiencies: "The shop floor in those days was controlled by foremen-craftsmen . . . [who] were always making excuses for production delay [*sic*]."[106] Standard operating procedures were created and posted above the workstations. Time studies were used to evaluate the efficiency of each working group.[107] Ford also used time studies but was focused more on product standardization than process standardization. Toyota applied these procedures to reduce waste and variation in its operations. In addition, Toyota standardization had the virtue of alerting employees to the current best practice. Indeed, Japanese firms "tend to think of standardization as spreading best practice."[108] Standardization also represents a platform for change "with one standard leading to another as continuing improvement efforts are made." Standardization has been illustrated as a series of steps;[109] the emphasis is on ongoing efforts to maintain while upgrading standards, reflecting the importance of *kaizen*, or continuous improvement efforts.

Toyota has a long tradition of selective borrowing of ideas, techniques, and processes associated with other firms. On one trip to study American manufacturing methods in 1950, Toyota learned about Ford Motor Company's suggestion plan in which "any workman [could] communicate any idea that comes to him and get action on it."[110] The suggestion plan, which was consistent with Toyota's step-by-step process improvements, became a core element of *kaizen*; all employees were heavily involved in improvement efforts, though there was pressure from managers to participate.[111] *Kaizen* was also directly linked with the emphasis on quality (e.g., in process, materials, design) brought by the U.S. military to Japan following World War II. The military recruited William Edwards Deming, who advocated the "14 Points for Management"[112] and the plan-do-check-action cycle of continual improvement;[113] both have had a long-lasting impact on Toyota and other manufacturers. The adoption of Ford's suggestion plan and Deming's methods strengthened the cultural tradition within Toyota of learning about, borrowing, and adapting techniques from outside Toyota. This ability to adjust to and learn from changing industrial circumstances represented a high level of cultural adaptiveness that would bode well for Toyota's future as a global enterprise. Other elements of *kaizen* include team problem solving, quality control circles, job rotation, off-site training, and other group activities to improve firm performance;[114] interestingly, it was the Japanese themselves, and not Deming, "who made a quantum leap to involve workers directly" in these work activities.[115] Such activities, with their expectation that all employees are expected to contribute to the firm, contrast with mass-production practices. In flexible and lean systems, the possibilities for change are endless but are dependent upon the efforts of the entire work force.

There also were structures put in place to maximize the potential for Toyota success. Even before the firm was incorporated in 1937, Toyota established a staff office to "solve problems in manufacturing or product designs, manage relations with dealers, gather technical information or feedback from customers, settle claims, and advise parts suppliers."[116] By contrast, Ford's interactions with dealers were designed primarily to elicit information on the customer base so as to increase sales. Toyota's post–World War II human resource system, consisting of such features as lifetime employment, remuneration based on seniority, and semiannual bonuses, not only helped bind employees to the firm but also decreased the likelihood of confrontation with management.[117] Typically in Japanese firms, recent graduates were recruited annually and then promoted according to a seniority-based wage system. Until the mid-1970s, it was common for an employee to remain with a firm for life.[118] Promotion was not a function of achievement but rather of company loyalty because "the key to everything in Japan is *ningen kankei*, human relations."[119] Loyalty was the key reason for extending lifetime employment to Toyota workers who supported the company during two months of intermittent strikes in 1950.[120]

Historically, Toyota has operated as a centrally regulated enterprise throughout the supply chain. For example, Toyota differentiated itself from its domestic and foreign competition in its relationship and interaction with its dealers. It provided financial, sales-training, and other forms of assistance and promised to treat dealers as "equal partners."[121] With its suppliers, Toyota engaged in the "black box parts" practice, first with Nippondenso after it separated from Toyota in 1949, and later with other core suppliers. This type of joint product helped to spread Toyota's engineering workload and served as a "key engine for diffusion" of knowledge and expertise between Toyota and its suppliers.[122] Moreover, Toyota has demonstrated repeatedly a desire for "mutual prosperity" for its suppliers.[123] At the same time, new technology and proprietary knowledge could be retained as a competitive edge "within the upper tiers of the value chain,"[124] and risk could be disseminated.[125] The significant cultural transformation of the automotive industry spearheaded by Toyota was inclusive, incorporating all parties in the work of and benefits associated with the enterprise.

Workplace Dynamics: Participative, Group Centered, and Risk Averse
The centrality of relationships is embedded in Toyota's organizational culture. Relationships are paramount in creating a cooperative and coordinated approach to work.[126] The regularity and frequency of interactions within and across work groups, departments, and organizations are an essential part of this flexible and lean paradigm. The dynamics of these relationships are complex and are typically structured to achieve company goals. Employees are expected to participate fully in all aspects of their work and in any company activities.

Toyota's location in Koromo (now called Toyota City) fostered interdependencies between the firm and the local rural population. Toyota hired "the same unskilled, malleable farm boys, with strong backs and communal loyalties," that led to the Toyoda family's successful weaving enterprise.[127] The rural location, the dearth of other employment options, and the fact that it was a family business combined to create "a special sense of loyalty and community not present to the same extent at more urban companies such as Nissan."[128] The high-context nature of Japanese culture—that is, its "extensive information networks among family, friends, colleagues, and clients"[129] and sensitivity to human relationships—undoubtedly worked to reinforce community and company norms.

The employment relationship found at Toyota differed from that found at Ford. The lure of high wages (not relationships) was a necessary condition in sealing the employment contract at Ford and in creating some degree of loyalty to the firm. As Ford discovered, however, loyalty was short lived as supervisory relationships and working conditions worsened and as alternate job opportunities became available elsewhere. A similarity between the two firms seems to have been in the type of worker hired. Two different writers, documenting the Toyota and Ford enterprises respectively, used the term "malleable" to describe a desirable worker characteristic.[130] One implication of this similarity is that workers would be more likely to do what they had been asked to do (with minimal or no commentary or quarrel), thereby aligning themselves with the organization's stated goals.

Katsuaki Watanabe, president of Toyota (2005–2009), described the culture of the "Toyota Way" as having the two pillars of continuous improvement and respect for people. These two themes are inextricably bound together, with each dependent on the other:

> Respect is necessary to work with people. By "people" we mean employees, supply partners, and customers. "Customer first" is one of the company's core tenets. We don't mean just the end customer; on the assembly line the person at the next workstation is also your customer. That leads to teamwork. If you adopt that principle, you'll also keep analyzing what you do in order to see if you're doing things perfectly, so you're not troubling your customer. That nurtures your ability to identify problems, and if you closely observe things, it will lead to kaizen: continuous improvement. The root of the Toyota Way is to be dissatisfied with the status quo.[131]

Participating in diverse ways in the culture of the workplace positions Toyota to improve its overall performance.

This "dynamic learning capability," said to be "at the heart of the success of TPS,"[132] was apparent early on in Toyota's history. *Genchi genbutsu*, or "go and see for yourself," was evident when Toyota sent its technical and managerial leaders to places such as the United States, Germany, and Great Britain to observe and analyze manufacturing methods. Upon their return to Japan, they discarded some processes, technologies, and work practices (e.g., stockpiled inventories) and adapted others (e.g., *kanban* supermarket) for Toyota's particular circumstances. The practice of "reverse engineering" American vehicles and engines enabled Toyota to investigate products firsthand by "tearing them down." The written word played a significant role in Toyota's ability to "catch up" with the West. There are various references in the literature to Japanese engineers studying American technical reports and other documents,[133] as well as Japanese publications as those became available such as the *Quality Control for the Foreman*, which was published by the Japanese Union of Scientists and Engineers.[134]

Learning and sharing insights at Toyota is often described as a collective and cooperative process. Set-based concurrent engineering requires that product development employees develop in-depth technical expertise, be familiar with data on related development issues, and share and manage the design inputs to optimize overall system performance.[135] Quality control (QC) circles support problem solving and the elimination of defects: "When people can get together to engage in convivial conversations, good results can multiply. Allowing the workers to have a convivial place to meet and discuss problems is one of the aims of QC circle activities. The Japanese people do not wish to be alone. They want a sense of belonging and to be in a group. QC circle activities take advantage of this Japanese predisposition."[136]

Yet within the group, one relationship matters above all else—that between the supervisor and the individual being supervised. This relationship is central to group functioning. Constructive motivational strategies, such as those in which the supervisor engages one-on-one with subordinates to foster learning[137] or conducts the "5-why" analysis that targets the root cause of a problem without an intent to blame,[138] also reinforce the importance of learning and continuous improvement. Moreover, the role of the supervisor differs from the top-down approach of the mass-production paradigm. Supervisors are "boundary managers and providers of resources," enabling the operators to do their jobs effectively and serve both their internal and external customers.[139]

The prominence of the paired supervisor-subordinate relationship as a conduit for learning and skill development at Toyota has more parallels with craft production than mass production; the master craftsman assigns and monitors tasks, offers support, and helps in the transmission of explicit and implicit rules.[140] While there is surely variation in the strength of the supervisor-subordinate relationship in Toyota, it is an alternative to the looser (and often less personal) connection between supervisors and their subordinates in the mass production system. The supervisor-subordinate pair is also a basic unit of work activity that is aligned with Toyota's well-known team problem-solving efforts. Learning techniques and experiences set Toyota apart from Ford's mass-production model in which knowledge resided largely in the senior leaders: whereas Toyota regularly solicited input from its work force, Ford did not routinely engage its work force in providing feedback, relying instead on its inner circle of trusted and respected professionals.

Today in particular, Toyota is held in high esteem by diverse publics from customers to the automotive media. Certainly, Toyota has set high global standards for vehicle quality, productivity, functionality, reliability, and the like. However, the TPS production-work paradigm has had to cope with thorny "people issues" that emerge in manufacturing culture. The writings of two former Toyota employees offer a perspective on Toyota's culture that seems inconsistent with the "idealized," public image associated with much of the business and organizational literature.[141] These writings from the "inside" reveal an organizational culture incongruent with its public image.

Kamata, a Japanese journalist, spent six months working on the line at Toyota between 1972 and 1973, while Mehri, an American engineer, spent three years between 1996 and 1999 working at Nizumi, "an upper level Toyota group company," as a computer simulation engineer.[142] What is remarkable about these two experiences, which occurred about twenty-five years apart—is the similarity in organizational-culture themes related to the nature of work and managerial control. Efficiency and risk aversion surface as key themes dominating Toyota plant culture, both taking their toll on the work force in the form of health and safety issues. Ford was similarly motivated to improve its efficiency, though its management strategies, by the late 1930s, were tempered by negotiated settlements with the UAW; the latter advocated for worker rights and specialized work rules.

The emphasis on Toyota efficiency is described cogently in the Japanese journalist's diary from his fifth day of work at the plant: "Once, when I saw Chaplin's *Modern Times*, I remember really laughing at his accelerated motions as he tried to keep up with the line. But I won't laugh any more—I'm doing the same thing now . . . The line is a machine, and for eight hours the humans working at it are required to operate with machinelike accuracy. The line demands speed—relentless, mechanical, and unchangeable."[143] After a few weeks of work on the line he commented, "I still fall behind at work. As soon as I push the alarm button, my team chief runs up to me and asks in a disgusted tone, 'Haven't you learned yet? Watch closely—I'll show you one more time.' Then he goes through the operation slowly and condescendingly. At a crucial point, he looks at me and says, 'See? Do it like this. Haven't you learned yet?'"[144]

The journalist linked the many occupational injuries and accidents occurring in the plant with the fast line speed that ensured plant output. He indicated that overtime was required if the production quota for the shift had not been met and reported one attempt by frustrated workers to complain at a meeting: "Sugimoto, who's about twenty-two, says, 'We can't stand up straight after ten hours on our legs. It's natural there are accidents when we try to do that work when we're exhausted.' We all silently agree with him, but most of us are too tired to say anything and just sit there on the bench. Finally someone hoots at the team chief, 'Write down what he said just now, will you?' But generally there's an air of resignation. Workers feel that nothing they say will reach the top [managers]."[145]

The American engineer, in his interviews with production workers, also discovered the overriding emphasis on plant efficiency. One individual indicated that the line speeds were so fast that "workers do not even have a second to wipe the sweat off their faces,"[146] while another reported that he had to work "60 full seconds for every minute on the line, with not a moment to rest. At that speed, accidents are unavoidable."[147] The engineer also pointed out that injuries were hidden to improve the safety record, with workers let go if they were hurt. There was little teamwork or collaboration, despite the general belief that the assembly line was *abunai*, or dangerous:[148] "If something happened on the line, if someone needed assistance from another group member—nobody helped," stated one production worker.[149] Thus in the early 1970s, Toyota employees were assigned a particular set of tasks that they performed throughout the shift (as was the pattern in mass-production plants) in their quest for plant efficiency.

Many of the cultural patterns described in the engineering function paralleled those that the engineer identified on the plant floor. He worked alone on his engineering projects, finding that the culture did not "allow the free flow of ideas, open discussion and debate, true team collaboration"; instead, the work culture forced compliance with the Toyota Way "blindly under the strict direction of . . . superiors."[150] The restrictions placed on creativity were partly due to the limited collaboration within and across groups. But another factor was at play as well. There were no opportunities to "think outside of the box"[151] and develop innovative designs. "Only concrete information that could be validated through experiments or through previous designs was considered acceptable for discussion."[152] The potential for an engineering "breakthrough" was unlikely given Toyota's discomfort with product design risk. Moreover, the strategy of incremental improvement would be less likely to upset Toyota's authority structure.[153]

The evidence from the Ford and Toyota "ideal types" suggests that the quality of interaction within those organizational cultures had a considerable range. The Fordist model of mass production emphasized task over relationships; relationships seemed to be largely inconsequential to getting the work done. Indeed, Ford himself discouraged interactions except as they pertained to directing the work process. The flexible and lean model created structures to foster interaction for a particular work purpose (e.g., "Quality Circles"), thereby creating opportunities to involve employees in the generation of ideas to strengthen the Toyota enterprise. But, at least some evidence from Toyota insiders indicates that Toyota did not benefit as fully as it might have from employee input given its particular cultural response to competition. The cultural dynamics of the Toyota manufacturing and engineering environments reveal a significant degree of employee stress. It was not evident that plant-personnel relationships were routinely, or even occasionally, activated to mitigate or arrest plant floor tensions, and there was no outside party like the UAW to intervene and mediate. Indeed, the quality of working relationships seemed to suffer as production pressures mounted. Thus, while the structured team concept at Toyota has proven its value in achieving continuous improvement, it does not appear to be effective in restoring relationship health.

Summary

Cultural and environmental conditions played a significant role in the development and evolution of the two dominant production-work paradigms in automotive manufacturing during the twentieth century. Both Ford and Toyota built on the practices and experiences of earlier industries, including firearms, bicycles, and carriages and wagons for Ford, and weaving and machining for Toyota. Both used their own national-culture characteristics to advantage with Ford emphasizing hard work for material gain, and Toyota emphasizing community loyalty and relationships. In working within their historical and cultural circumstances, their own organizational cultures and production processes emerged, characterized by an array of divergent features. Other firms followed in their paths, adapting elements of their production-work paradigms in ways that worked for them. GM was one such firm.

THE EVOLVING PRODUCTION CULTURE AT GM

GM's production-work paradigm was first a variant of Ford's mass production, and much later in its history, a modification of TPS. The best way to think of GM's evolution in terms of its production operations is as an evolving hybrid; GM's early production-work elements were largely aligned with mass production, while its most recent production-work configuration is more akin to TPS. As such, GM does not represent a distinct, independent type of production work. In this section, we examine GM's production culture through the historical record to situate it in a broader context. In later chapters of this book, we explore GM's production culture through the ethnographic record, linking back to the historical detail as appropriate and to the two influential paradigms that shaped its trajectory.

GM is in its second century of operations. Established on September 7, 1908 by William C. Durant in Flint, Michigan, GM was composed of many different car companies including Buick, Oldsmobile, Cadillac, Oakland (later known as Pontiac), and Chevrolet. Over the decades, GM came to be associated with both domestic and global brands. At its peak in 1962, GM held 50.7 percent of the U.S. vehicle market.[154] A history of its past trends and transformations furnish a valuable framework for understanding the challenges it faces in the near and longer-term future.

Diversified Mass Production under Alfred P. Sloan

GM's implementation of mass production veered sharply from Ford's in that it offered a range of models—each made on a dedicated assembly line. Led by Alfred P. Sloan, president of GM beginning in 1923, GM began introducing annual styling changes to cultivate sales. GM's cultural responsiveness led to setting "price class positions" for its brands,[155] which were reflected in the phrase "a car for every purse and purpose."[156] While one's first car might be a Chevrolet, the lowest-priced GM brand, one could always aspire to a Buick or Cadillac, the most expensive of the five U.S. brands. The implementation of this plan reflected a high degree of cultural adaptiveness to a purchasing public eager for updated designs. As a result of Sloan's consumer-oriented strategies, GM's U.S. market share rose from 16 percent in 1924 to 43 percent by 1927. Ford briefly took the market share lead again with the introduction of the Model A, but GM's winning product strategy enabled it to dominate all U.S. manufacturers by the early 1930s.[157] "'Sloanism' had triumphed over 'Fordism'"— that is, marketing triumphed over vehicle production.[158] Ford has not retaken the lead on market share, but the gap between Ford and GM has fluctuated.

Structure of Work: Differentiated and Decentralized
Structurally, GM was more complex than Ford due to the size and diversity of its operations, since it was formed from a merger of several independent companies. Ford had centralized power and control in a single individual—its founder—while GM's geographically scattered and differentiated divisions required an alternative form of coordination. Sloan appreciated and supported GM's decentralized structure in which each division "was a self-contained group of functions [engineering, production, sales, and the like]."[159] At the same time, he recognized the importance of the "common good,"

the "relation of the part to the whole," and divisional profits as a key factor in corporate responsibility.[160] Therefore, he settled on a "latticework of committees [that] melded GM's decision makers—with their varying functional views and time perspectives—into a responsive, unified managerial team."[161] These committees linked together the senior leaders in a corporate-wide hierarchy, though their allegiance was largely to their divisional home. Decentralization, with integration through committee structures, was a cultural and historical response to the past, given that GM's early divisions had once been independent companies.

Workplace Dynamics: Meritocratic and Autonomous

Sloan had a significant impact on GM's cultural dynamics, particularly in the 1920s and 1930s. He appreciated receiving input from his managers and prided himself on soliciting their views before making policy decisions.[162] One writer has argued, "Sloan didn't want yes-men; he wanted informed back talk, and he wanted the 'right' decision, even if he didn't agree with it. Once a decision had been made, Sloan was prepared to subordinate his status as chief executive to the weight of informed consensus."[163] Debate was cultivated resulting in a relatively "balanced, decentralized meritocracy,"[164] at least among the senior leaders. Sloan also valued customer input, visiting dealerships to understand customer preferences;[165] in that regard, his approach paralleled Toyota's, which also understood the importance of matching customer requirements with final product. Sloan recognized that customer satisfaction was critical for GM success. His desire to be customer oriented and responsive set him apart from Ford, famous for this statement about the Model T:[166] "Any customer can have a car painted any colour that he wants so long as it is black."[167]

Sloan's reinforcement of the decentralized organizational structure—through both his committees and his solicitation of input—was aligned with his expectations for independence and self-reliance within GM culture. Individualism and autonomy have continued to play a prominent role in company operations today—sometimes to the detriment of the organizational whole.[168] Colloquial terms used to describe GM's autonomy include "silos" (an agricultural metaphor referring to GM's largely self-contained functions and organizations), "fiefdoms," and "turf," to name a few. A key expression linked with GM's autonomy is the "not-invented-here" notion; that is, if an idea originates outside of a particular GM function or organization, its merit and potential impact are limited. Support for the idea would be weak because the "receiving" function or organization would not be able to take credit for it. GM's autonomy played a key role in preserving and optimizing the individual units, often sacrificing the "greater good" of the company as a whole.

Labor relations under Sloan were increasingly confrontational. Production workers faced harsh working conditions (e.g., assembly line speed-ups, insufficient breaks, tough factory managers, fear of dismissal).[169] As union organizing commenced, GM, like Ford, hired "spies and detectives to head off an uprising," which resulted in higher levels of distrust between management and labor.[170] Walter Reuther, organizing for the UAW, succeeded in getting GM to recognize the union after a six-week-long sit-down strike from 1936 to 1937. Though Reuther's career was dedicated largely to the ideals of democracy and equality, he was not successful in altering conditions on the shop floor. Consequently, he opted to bargain with GM management for "classification and seniority walls around the work considered most pleasant and dignified"[171] and for wages and benefits that improved union workers "purchasing power."[172] GM has been referred to as "Generous Motors" among employees, their family members, and others. It was the paycheck and benefits (e.g., health, vacation, savings) that surfaced as the ideal, providing a salve for those difficult and dysfunctional aspects of manufacturing culture.

Post–World War II Dominance and Rising Parochialism

A pent-up demand for automobiles arose in the aftermath of World War II, since GM and other domestic automakers ceased production of civilian vehicles during the war, converting their factories to make military vehicles and equipment. The postwar period was characterized by high levels of employment and prosperity, with American economic superiority evident in many industries, including the automotive industry. The conversion of manufacturing plants back to cars and trucks, powertrains, and components was successful and was an indicator of what GM could and did accomplish under a remarkable set of circumstances. America's dominance was linked with car size: "The Chevrolet had stretched more than one-and-a-half feet from 1953 to 1958"[173] under the styling leadership of Harvey Earl. "Large" cars were not only valued but also more profitable.

In a decided change from the past, GM's business was largely "manufacturing driven"[174] with effort and energy put into styling and new technology; little, if any attention, was given to customer input. Vehicle models were developed largely on the basis of an inward-looking corporate orientation that took little account of changing environmental circumstances or customer expectations. GM's parochialism was becoming more pronounced, more local, and more focused on retaining a neatly defined boundary between insiders and outsiders.[175] Increasingly, key product decisions were being made by finance, often over the objections of other corporate functions.[176] This pattern also has been described as a narrow or parochial worldview.[177] The power of GM's financial function, with its emphasis on minimizing cost leading to scrimping on product quality, became more apparent within GM's organizational culture. The cross-functional integration offered through Sloan's committee structure had deteriorated. Instead, the groundwork for a future where decision making relied excessively on cost considerations over much internal (e.g., engineering) and external (e.g., customer) input was being laid. GM's cultural responsiveness was becoming increasingly parochial, limiting, and unable to embrace a changing industry and market.

Beginning in the 1960s, GM's dominance of the U.S. market was challenged by imported vehicles, particularly from Germany and Japan. Tastes were changing; the smaller-sized imports were creating a niche. This emerging pattern "defied all the executives had been schooled to believe: Americans wanted luxury, comfort, roominess—in short, the status that could come only from owning a large car."[178] Customers associated with the "bread-and-butter market segments"[179] were switching to alternatives offered by foreign manufacturers. There was increasing misalignment between GM and its customer base.

Societal standards also were changing vis-à-vis safety, emissions, and fuel economy. As the U.S. automotive market leader, GM had the greatest visibility and was a key target for the ills of the industry. The safety issues associated with Chevrolet Corvair, as argued in a provocative book,[180] led to a tightening of regulations on the automotive industry. GM's vigorous opposition to government intervention further damaged its corporate image. Its success also was compromised by internal divisional competition, corporate promises of vehicle competitiveness, penny pinching, and dependency on automation during the launch and aftermath of the 1970 Chevrolet Vega.[181] At this point in its history, GM was a corporation embroiled in conflicts—within and across its own internal units that had moved away from Sloan's legacy of consensus, with the U.S. government that sought to curb its power, and with a consumer public it did not understand. As GM's economic dominance was receding, its relationship with the UAW faltered as well. The 1970 strike lasted for sixty-seven days and led to a loss of $1 billion in profits and a loss of 1.5 million production vehicles.[182] The GM-UAW relationship has continued to face challenging periods (particularly in years when the national contract is being renegotiated) interspersed with periods of calm and mutual accommodation.

Cooperative Exploration of Production Options at the Century's End

The last two decades of the twentieth century opened up new possibilities for developing and producing GM vehicles and for setting the stage for a new cultural dynamic. The expensive tooling shift to front-wheel-drive cars provided some fuel efficiencies (on the heels of the 1973 and 1978 oil crises), but the high prices, poor quality, and loss of brand differentiation were not persuasive to consumers.[183] However, four innovative "partnerships" laid the groundwork for a future that had the potential to be brighter.[184] Each partnership on its own represented a break with past patterns of resisting a changing environmental context. Two of them involved GM with either Toyota, or with former Toyota employees, while the two others engaged GM and the UAW in cooperative activity never before initiated. Working hand-in-hand with a rising competitor and establishing the conditions for building a manufacturing process based on the Toyota experience were acknowledgments that Toyota's practices and operations were better than GM's and worthy of examination. Working hand-in-hand with a union whose democratic values, seniority-based work rules, and ongoing attempts to identify new union jobs signaled GM's willingness to accommodate ideals that often had been at cross-purposes with its own. Gradually, and collectively, the four partnerships began cracking the hard shell of parochialism that GM had been reinforcing within its culture over the previous decades.

New United Motor Manufacturing, Inc.:
Little Receptivity Back in Detroit

The earliest of the partnerships involved GM, with its model of diversified mass production, and Toyota, representing the flexible and lean work paradigm. In 1984, the two companies launched a joint venture known as NUMMI, or the New United Motor Manufacturing, Inc., that was housed in an old GM plant in Fremont, California. "Cooperative business arrangements" were being advocated as a way to "catch up with . . . foreign competition—and catch up as quickly as possible."[185] The workers were represented by the UAW and managed by Toyota. In an assembly plant assessment conducted by the International Motor Vehicle Program at the

Massachusetts Institute of Technology in 1986, NUMMI's quality matched its Toyota counterpart in Japan, the Takaoka plant, and was three times better than its GM counterpart, the GM Framingham plant.[186] NUMMI also achieved the best quality of any GM plant in the United States that year,[187] demonstrating the benefits of the Toyota approach to vehicle production.

GM's adaptiveness was low. Its leaders appear to have expected to learn about and apply Toyota's "technological solutions" but unexpectedly confronted continuous improvement, JIT, and "people-oriented practices;"[188] this pattern of seeking "the quick fix through investment in hardware"[189] has been linked to American national culture.[190] GM's responsiveness was also low. The diffusion of NUMMI's knowledge and techniques to other parts of GM was limited. GM employees returning from assignments at NUMMI faced an organization with little receptivity to what they had learned or how it might be applied to GM's advantage. Moreover, GM seemed unable to transform its own existing work practices.[191] GM announced it was terminating its relationship with NUMMI as part of the bankruptcy in 2009. The proximate causes of this change included the lack of a replacement vehicle for the Pontiac (once GM decided to discontinue the Pontiac brand), a reduction in the overall number of new vehicle entries in the GM portfolio, and overcapacity in North America. Toyota, faced with its own challenges in North America due to overcapacity, overexpansion, and worldwide losses, in turn decided to close NUMMI, its only UAW plant.

Spring Hill Saturn: Decision-Making Consensus Gone Awry
Saturn, a partnership between GM management and the UAW, was an attempt at "surpassing the Japanese, not only in product and manufacturing process, but also in employee and dealer relations."[192] A stand-alone plant conceived in 1982 and dedicated solely to Saturn was built in Spring Hill, Tennessee; it had its own labor agreement with the UAW. Spring Hill began work on its small car in 1987, hired production workers by 1989, and produced the first vehicle one year later. Excerpts from the Saturn mission underscored the importance of "members," or employees:[193] "We will create a sense of belonging in an environment of mutual trust, respect and dignity . . . Creative, motivated, responsible team members who understand that change is crucial to success are Saturn's most important asset." Together, GM management and union developed the "Saturn Way,"[194] which reflected cooperative goal setting and achievement and emphasized customer relations.

There was excitement and promise surrounding Spring Hill's start-up operations. The confrontational approach that had characterized the GM-UAW relationship historically was to be replaced by a consensus model. Consensus decision making was said to work because a simple rule of thumb was followed: "If someone is 70 percent comfortable with a particular decision, he/she must be 100 percent committed to it."[195] Our interviews with current and former Spring Hill employees emphasized this new cultural response—especially in the early years of Spring Hill's operations. One interviewee commented, "I would say that my early expectations were pretty well met. We decided what responsibilities were management's, what were the union's, and what were joint responsibilities. And, when we decided something was a joint responsibility, we kept it that way and we truly involved both sides." As new waves of employees were hired, however, Spring Hill's culture shifted away from "Saturn first, then the team, then me" to "me or the team rather than . . . the customer." There was also a lack of support from GM management and UAW leaders who were not involved in Saturn's formation. Accountability surfaced as a critical issue—evident in absenteeism and lack of goal accomplishment. The consensus decision-making process was viewed as laborious and ineffective: "You had 50 percent management and 50 percent union on all decisions." It paralleled Spring Hill's early organizational structure in which represented (or UAW members) and nonrepresented (or GM) employees were paired together. One individual commented critically, "They're just like Noah's ark. They have to have two of everything, one management and one union person doing everything. That's not the way the Japanese run the business."

The Spring Hill experiment failed both due to operational and cultural reasons. Having a single brand in a dedicated plant did not take advantage of any economies of scale, nor was Spring Hill equipped to produce all Saturn models. Culturally, tensions surfaced between GM and the UAW related to productivity, as well as the consensus model; the two sides were unable to sustain the partnership in the long term. Ultimately, the Spring Hill facility was reintegrated into the company. In 2004, the special labor agreement was eliminated and the hourly employees were brought back under the national GM-UAW contract. Spring Hill's overall performance, low relative to many other GM North American plants, was a key reason for idling it as part of GM's restructuring in 2009. The Saturn brand, which suffered from lack of investment and mediocre product, was terminated after efforts to sell it to Penske Automotive Group failed in 2009. One bright spot in the Spring Hill experiment was that

GM learned that consensus decision making was not an effective way to manage. The value of consensus lay in gathering input, but that value dissipated quickly if decisions languished, if the decision making was excessively deferential, or if some took their eyes off the goal of efficiently built, high-quality, desirable products. During the Ideal Plant Culture study, a number of high-ranking manufacturing executives challenged our core finding about the importance of creating and sustaining a collaborative work culture. They heard us emphasize "collaboration" and then seemed to translate collaboration to mean "consensus," indicating that GM had tried and failed at using that approach.[196] They argued that organizations needed a well-defined set of roles and responsibilities, including individuals designated to make certain kinds of decisions when consensus could not be reached. They also indicated that despite the initial strategy to put a portion of employee pay at risk, dependent on overall performance, there was increasing misalignment between employee behavior and the end goals. These executives had internalized the "cultural" lessons of Spring Hill and were unwilling to entertain a repeat performance of that experience. As such, they demonstrated a high degree of cultural adaptiveness: they "got it," that is, they recognized that a different path would be necessary for GM's future.

Quality Network: Some Level of Rapprochement between GM and the UAW

A third partnership, known as the Quality Network, was announced in 1987 in conjunction with the GM-UAW labor contract. This GM-UAW initiative was designed ostensibly to focus on the production of quality products, an emphasis derived from the work of globally recognized quality experts including W. Edwards Deming,[197] Joseph M. Juran,[198] and Philip B. Crosby[199]—all of whom worked with GM organizations during their careers. The Quality Network quickly expanded beyond the concept of quality to highlight the advantages of a union-management partnering relationship, working-level relationships between salaried and hourly employees, and a philosophy that treated employees as valuable assets to the business. It reflects a commitment to partnership and reconciliation, away from a confrontational past.

The Quality Network created an organizational structure to mitigate perceived and actual "boundaries" between hourly and salaried employees. Pairs or groups of employees from both the union and management sides work together to achieve agreement on the "joint," GM-UAW sanctioned activities known as Action Strategies. Quality Councils are aligned with various levels in the corporate hierarchy (e.g., corporate, divisional, plant).[200] The Quality Network has been largely responsible for integrating the concepts of "teamwork" and "continuous improvement" into GM's lexicon.[201] It symbolizes an evolving rapprochement between GM and the UAW that has broken down some of the barriers to change and positioned both institutions to become more culturally adaptive—particularly with respect to external competition. It also has enabled them to band together and act as a united front on issues ranging from preventative maintenance in the plants to petitioning the U.S. government for a bridge loan in 2008. The Quality Network continues today and plays a particularly active role in manufacturing plants.

Opel Eisenach Gmbh: Incubator for Diffusion and Learning
One other partnership, emerging in Europe just prior to the Spring Hill launch, involved GM's Adam Opel AG vehicle–manufacturing operations. Opel purchased the Wartburg automotive factory in Eisenach in former East Germany with the idea of using the best Toyota methods to "out-Toyota Toyota."[202] About twenty-eight managers with Toyota experience were recruited to lead the new effort. Production workers hired from the former Wartburg operations engaged with a diverse management team (i.e., in terms of nationality, lean-manufacturing work experience) to improve upon TPS. According to one of the Eisenach interviewees, Eisenach "made the decision upfront that the team would be empowered to run the manufacturing process—like at NUMMI and at other Toyota plants. The team leaders were really the key. They took the lead and ran with it." Eisenach started up its operations with two shifts in 1992. Teamwork, standardization, high productivity, and quality products were among the important features contributing to its success.

Eisenach played a pivotal role in the development and diffusion of what would come to be known as GM's Global Manufacturing System (GMS). Its ideological roots were grounded in the notion of "common," or shared, processes advocated throughout GM's operations beginning in the 1990s. One interviewee stated, "GMS became our bible. It was the vision of where we were moving. What I did was to lock five Europeans and five Americans in a room. I gave them the outline of what GMS was at that time. I said, 'Your task is to come out with a final document, a common global system.' This was the beginning of the common approach to lean manufacturing." Much of the power of Eisenach was the hands-on experience with the production system. According to one individual who worked there, "Probably one of the biggest success factors in the greenfield [or new site] launch is that people work the line in Eisenach. They knew what the process looked like when it was finished and they had the opportunity to ask questions. The training provides the steps in making the transition to GMS."

Indeed, GM's Shanghai leadership team spent five weeks at Eisenach in the mid-1990s, including one week working on the line, one week as group leader, one week as area manager, and one week as assistant plant manager plant. A member of this leadership team reported its impact: "We came back [to Shanghai] as a team that solved things the same way. We found ourselves asking each other, once we were back in Shanghai, 'How would Eisenach do this? What would Eisenach do in this situation? What problem-solving technique would Eisenach use for this?' When we asked those questions, it got us back on the same page."

Diffusion of ideas and learning based on the Eisenach experience occurred quickly in GM plants built since the late 1990s, since the plans for four new plants were underway at about the same time. What was different compared with GM's approach to NUMMI was that there was a conscious diffusion strategy for implementing an innovative production process. Employees from later greenfields, and even from some brownfields (or older plants), traveled to Eisenach for in-plant GMS training. Eisenach, as a "benchmark facility," offered the opportunity for training consistency. This diffusion process created a critical mass of new adherents.

But then new questions arose related to GMS process standardization. Plant variation due to differences in cultural context, production difficulties, and environmental conditions would affect the consistent application of GMS. At the same time, there was strong interest in "trying to get the United States onto one [production] system."[203] Implementation of GMS in GM's U.S. brownfield facilities had been slow, sporadic, and uneven. Therefore, a large corporate effort was initiated in the mid-1990s to codify and document GMS principles. The result was that the production process was written down. Mastering an understanding of the process was now easier for GM's low-context U.S. operations precisely because it was "written down" and could be taught based on the written materials. GM leaders continue to specify the use of GMS in manufacturing plants worldwide. New ideas for inclusion in GMS are reviewed on a regular basis.

Summary

GM's cultural responses to the changing environmental context can be interpreted in different ways. With the termination of both NUMMI and Spring Hill, a reduction in the Quality Network budget and staffing, and the full benefits of GMS not yet fully realized in all North American plants, some may view the cumulative benefit of the four partnerships as a draw at best. They could point out that the NUMMI and Spring Hill experiments reflect the silo-ing conditions that have been associated with GM's strong tradition of individualism and autonomy and that neither has yielded a robust set of lessons that were both actively disseminated and implemented across the company. They could argue that the jury is still out on the long-term success of the Quality Network and GMS, since both initiatives have the potential to yield some duplication in method and approach, as well as tension on the plant floor, as GM and the union sort out how work will get done in U.S. and Canadian plants. They also could suggest that GM's internal and external relationships have taken some hard hits over the years and may have difficulty fully recovering. As a result, they could conclude that potential for future sustained success is in question.

An alternate perspective takes GM's culture (past and present) into account but views it in an evolutionary context with a window open onto the future. GM's cultural adaptiveness is now quite high given the events of 2008 and 2009 surrounding bankruptcy and corporate restructuring. Our conversations with employees suggest strongly that there is a heightened sense of awareness of the external environment, of the risks ahead, and of the desire to succeed given this "second chance." What we cannot be sure of is how culturally responsive GM will be and what specific actions GM will take. Certainly, GM has the benefit of the four partnerships behind it, with its manufacturing outlook expanded as a result. Two of these initiatives—the Quality Network and the Eisenach experience (that led to the creation and diffusion of GMS)—have the potential to have a longer lasting impact than either NUMMI or Spring Hill. Thus, GM seems to be on the path for revitalizing its manufacturing operations based on the cumulative ideas (e.g., work processes, work practices) of these two initiatives. Let us now move on to explore GM manufacturing culture from the inside out at the time that these early initiatives were getting underway.

CHAPTER 3

HELPING ORGANIZATIONS TO SEE "WHAT WAS" AND "WHAT IS"

One member of our research group, Elizabeth Briody, had the unique experience of conducting anthropological fieldwork in GM manufacturing plants at two different points in time: the mid-1980s (as a sole researcher) and the mid-2000s (as a research-group leader).[1] She did so from the standpoint of an "insider" (a full-time GM researcher) whose job was to design and conduct organizational-culture research. In each case, the research approach was exploratory and inductive. The focus was on understanding GM's manufacturing culture generally, including the ways work was organized and coordinated and the ways plant personnel perceived that culture. The methods used in the two studies were the basic research methods used in ethnographic research (e.g., interviews, observation). The plants involved were located in Michigan. Thus, there were some important baseline similarities in the two research designs.

Yet, the field experiences reveal two distinct snapshots of manufacturing culture. The contrasts emerge through the stories told by employees to describe and explain the culture in which they worked. These stories offer insight into the prevailing beliefs, expectations, and behaviors at those two points in time. The stories also allow us to link backward and forward in time. The cultural parallels between the first field study in the mid-1980s, and the historical record pertaining to the culture surrounding mass production, are striking. Similarly, the cultural themes emerging from the stories of the second field study foreshadow aspects of a potential future. We use this chapter to identify some of these contrasting cultural elements between the past and the present.

Cultural Tensions Surrounding Individualized Work

In the mid-1980s, GM manufacturing culture was driven largely by two principles: quotas and efficiency.[2] The plant in which the fieldwork occurred exhibited a number of highly visible productivity and quality issues. The hope was that the field project would result in recommendations that the plant would find useful. Much of the fieldwork focused on material handlers as they interfaced with assemblers by supplying them with parts. Their statements and behaviors came to symbolize a diversified mass-production culture characterized by uncompetitive work strategies, high levels of discord, and an inability to achieve the new quality targets while still maintaining productivity. The field data also mirrored the conflict-oriented relationships between labor and management at that time, the process of "grieving" issues rather than resolving issues, and the focus on individualized work (and blaming) and individual rewards, rather than working groups and group responsibilities and rewards. In essence, this characterization reflected the dominant cultural paradigm at that time and established the conditions for the culture described in this chapter.

Trucks were selling well in the mid-1980s in spite of the fact that a downward trend in U.S. market share for GM trucks was already in progress. GM manufacturing employees were under extraordinary pressure to achieve the quotas (referred to as "the build") for completed vehicles per shift. They also were expected to produce these vehicles as efficiently as possible in terms of worker hours. Employees feared that they might be blamed for what they considered to be the most significant problem in the plant—causing the line to shut down, which would then lower throughput. Various forms of sanctions were used to ensure productivity among salaried employees (e.g., minimal raises, the reduced likelihood of promotion, the inability to transfer elsewhere). Hourly employees faced individually focused written warnings (which became part of their record), probationary periods, time off without pay, and, ultimately, dismissal.

Operators or assemblers performed a specific set of tasks on any of several product lines housed in the truck plant. None of the work was shared, and employees did not rotate from one set of tasks to another over the course of the shift. The work was organized on an individual basis by workstation. Other employees who supported those working on the assembly lines (e.g., material handlers, repairmen) also had individually assigned responsibilities. It was rare for plant personnel to collaborate on a set of tasks unless an urgent situation emerged that required immediate attention.

With the U.S. quality movement in full swing due to the increasing success of the Asian automotive companies (launched in turn by the influence of Deming[3] and others), changes were occurring on the plant floor. A restructuring effort emerged within GM manufacturing related to "quality of work life" programs in which workers offered input into production processes and working conditions,[4] as well as product quality, leading to the institution of Statistical Process Control as a quality control system.[5] GM manufacturing was under increasing pressure to make quality improvements—driven in part by the zero-defects goals of their Japanese competitors.[6] Even with these changes, however, the segmented and individualized nature of work prevailed at the core of plant operations.

GM exhibited some level of cultural adaptiveness and responsiveness at the truck plant by training managers in the Philip B. Crosby quality program, which emphasized "doing it [the task] right the first time"[7] and requiring managerial participation in internal quality seminars. Signs focusing on the importance of quality were posted throughout the plant. Interviews with plant managers on quality appeared in plant publications. Plant audit scores were posted. The management also introduced a team-based, problem-solving approach to specific plant difficulties (e.g., paint problems, water leaks). Hourly employees were pulled off their regular jobs during particular times during the week to work on these issues. Quality became the stated plant goal—the new ideal toward which plant personnel were expected to aspire. That stated quality goal was not realized during the field period; indeed, a later study found that minimum quality levels were achieved largely through inspections and rework rather than through self-monitoring.[8]

The beginnings of a quality focus and quality control (representing an early state of cultural adaptiveness) were additive ideas to the basic ideals of efficiency and throughput. Quality and productivity not only were viewed at odds with one another but also operated in different cultural spaces with few, if any, links between them. Rewards for high productivity (and sanctions for low productivity) continued, rather than for achieving the expected levels of productivity at a high level of quality. Moreover, work was focused at the level of individual responsibility. The individual worker, particular department, or specific area of the plant (e.g., underbody, paint shop, trim line) continued to optimize its own operations rather than develop alternatives that would integrate plant roles in innovative ways within the broader plant context. The new emphasis on quality led to a more complex cultural response that continued to pit new quality ideals against long-standing productivity standards.

Blaming

The mid-1980s truck plant ethnography documented a critical behavioral response to this attempted change in orientation to quality: blaming behavior among plant personnel. Blaming stood as a symbol of the culture of the past, a past that was at odds with any kind of cultural transformation. It was clear almost immediately that blaming was endemic in the plant. A later analysis in which the frequency of blaming statements in the field notes was compared with the frequency of praising statements demonstrated that plant personnel were seven times more likely to blame than to praise each other. As one material handler indicated, "If you admit a particular thing was your fault, you have to do something about it. It shows that you are not . . . doing your job. It's so much easier to blame another individual in another department, on another shift . . . The first rule of thumb is 'cover thy ass.' If you admit you are at fault, you get knocked down in this society." A general foreman, looking at his watch, remarked, "Break was over at 1:00 and here it is 1:22, and if I hadn't come out here right now with you [Elizabeth Briody], they [these skilled tradesmen] would still be playing cards."

These kinds of blaming statements are examples of a partial or incomplete cultural adaptiveness. Plant employees knew, appreciated, and accepted the importance of quality as a new area of emphasis but found that they were unable to effect a change in plant production goals. Employees expressed a significant amount of frustration related to their inability to do a "good job," since they were constrained by production and material problems. The content analysis of their blaming statements revealed two key themes: (1) inattention to the new quality goal in the plant and (2) inadequate job performance of some plant employees. One employee remarked, "GM has spent lots of money on quality courses and working together. They have done their studies but are unwilling to implement any changes." Another stated, "There are so many repairs due to the lack of interest [by people]." A third pointed out, "There is the problem of not being able to get the proper tools that we need. We have been trying for weeks to get another air gun [tool using compressed air] and can't get it. We have told our foreman but she isn't able to do anything about it. We really like her and don't blame her. The system is all screwed up."

Blaming as a form of cultural responsiveness created significant tension in the plant and weakened the concepts of individual and collective responsibility within plant culture. The blaming behavior was patterned, mapping onto the pattern of workflow within the plant. Plant personnel blamed their peers upstream who sent them work, not those downstream who were the recipients of their work. (You would only blame those who directly affected your ability to do your work; those downstream from you in the production process have no impact on you.) For example, one employee stated, "GM wants numbers and efficiency. I will go over to Paint the next time they don't paint all the parts they are supposed to. I am sick of it. They put all the parts in a basket and paint them that way. So, a bunch are half painted or not painted at all. They are supposed to paint them individually but it is quicker this other way. Meanwhile, my department has to deal with these defective parts . . . I'm so mad I will go over there the next time and find out for myself what the problem is."

Plant personnel blamed those on an alternate shift rather than those with whom they interacted directly on their own shift. (You might need your co-workers as allies if, for example, the jobs, or trucks being assembled, were improperly sequenced and you were unable to keep up with the pace of the line.) One second-shift assembler criticized his counterpart on first shift: "When I first came in December to cab trim, the first shift guy left me one regular window and one tinted glass window ready to be put on the cab. That night, I left the first shift guy two of each. The next day, that guy didn't leave me any. After that I didn't build him up." They also blamed their own managers for work-related difficulties, not those outside their own chain of command. One hourly employee commented, "I tried to get switched to the night shift. I went to my foreman who did nothing about it. Then I went over his head to the general foreman. Right after I went to the UAW . . . Meanwhile the problem wasn't getting solved." (Someone else's foreman has no impact on you in terms of rewards or punishments.) Thus, it was not the case that everyone blamed everyone else. Blaming was not random; it was symptomatic of a cultural breakdown, and it prevented the plant from ever reaching the point of engaging in cultural problem solving.

Blame Avoidance

The plant goals of meeting production targets continued to predominate as a part of the adaptive and responsive strategies that were evolving spontaneously in the plant. Three blame-avoidance strategies emerged that helped to maintain plant functioning according to the quota principle. Material handlers were responsible for supplying the assemblers with parts. Often the parts were not delivered to the particular departments, leading to the first such strategy: the search for parts. Material handlers would use their jitneys, or motorized carts, to search for parts, with their success hinging on their detective-like skills. The parts may have been delivered to the wrong dock (i.e., delivery entrances) or the wrong department. One week, 25 percent of the field time was spent searching for parts with material handlers, as this excerpt from the field notes illustrates:

> I almost felt like we were part of a game board or race to see who could locate the parts and get back to home first. Dave says that Even when you finally locate the parts and return to your area, they [the foremen] usually have something else that they want you to go and find. The race really never ends. In fact, we went back and his foreman handed us two pieces of paper with the word "Hot" written on them. These [parts] were needed almost immediately. We located some of those parts and brought them back to the line, but had been unable to find the others. We checked in dock [X] area . . . and checked some of the trains. No luck.

If the part-search strategy by the material handlers was not successful, a follow-up strategy was used. They would search their lockers as a way to keep the line supplied, since they frequently saved or hid parts there that typically ran short. One material handler commented,

> A lot of people hoard parts . . . If you are in material and your line is about to run out of a certain part, you are responsible. And, it becomes extremely important if that part is labeled "shut down"—if you can't find it and the line runs out, the line shuts down. If the line were even to shut down for five to ten minutes, it would reflect on your foreman, general foreman, superintendent, and plant manager, and also cost GM a bunch of money. Consequently, a lot of people stock up on certain parts and store them in their lockers, [or] in the wrong stock area where only they will know where it is.

Another material handler made a similar comment: "If the material handler had set some extra ones [parts] aside from before, he wouldn't be facing this problem. Over and over I have found parts hidden in different places in the plant." Holding onto excess stock was a way to retain some control over the work process while simultaneously protecting the individual from being blamed.

When neither the search nor the hoarding strategies worked, a third strategy was used: material handlers entered the trading network. Material handlers from one product line knew those on other product lines who used the same or similar parts; there were four different product lines in the plant. Networks of these relationships crisscrossed work areas and shifts. Approximately 20 to 30 percent of the plant's parts were shared. The large trading and bargaining network on the plant floor was created to keep the line moving. One material handler described the situation this way: "A material handler could go to a guy he knows on a different line who uses that part, or possibly to [his counterpart] on the first shift, and ask if he has any of that particular part left. If the guy feels bad for you he might say, 'Well, I have only [so many] of those parts that I could give you.' This way you feel like that guy is doing you a really big favor." Another material handler stated, "Sometimes I am able to bargain with another department for . . . what I need. They may have [so many parts that] I need . . . and can't find anywhere else in the plant. I might go to them and ask if I can have [them]. They may say that they can only spare [fewer than what I need]. Well, [that] is better than none, and it makes me look better than if I had to go without any. Maybe I can even finish my shift with [them] and then I won't even have to worry about the problem."

What may have seemed like bizarre behavior in the mid-1980s allowed plant employees to cope with perceived, expected, and actual material shortages. These blame-avoidance strategies enabled employees to safeguard themselves during their shift so that the part-shortage problems became the next shift's problem. (That way, your problem becomes their problem and their fault, not your fault.) On the other hand, while these blame-avoidance strategies helped employees in the short run get through their shift, they did not address the broader issues related to material shortages, and they concealed and perpetuated the material flow problems due to excess levels of inventory in the plant. Moreover, they did nothing to mitigate or intervene in this culture of blame or to help reroute energy and attention to alternate, and more effective, ways of working. These workarounds were part of the informal, or hidden, structure of plant operations and were consistent with the emphasis on individualism. They demonstrated a lack of cultural adaptiveness to the spirit and intent of quality changes that were sweeping across the automotive industry.

Some of the key elements from the truck plant's experience foreshadow the path that GM manufacturing culture would take in the years ahead. Quotas and efficiency would continue to serve as critical markers for GM's performance. The "can-do" spirit that pervaded the truck plant also would continue to thrive as competitive pressures increased across the industry. The desire to produce a quality product would continue unabated, kindled, in part, by the quality campaign and despite initial attempts to give it only lip service. The frustration with the inconsistencies between stated goals (e.g., quality) and actual goals (e.g., quotas, efficiency) would rise, ultimately resulting in the commonly heard expression "walk the talk" and issues of management credibility.

The hoped-for cultural transformation in which quality goals were on par with productivity and efficiency goals was not fully realized at this time. The measurement system would require expansion to include elements such as quality, which were becoming increasingly important to customers. Blaming and blame-avoidance behaviors reflected a negative adaptation to the changing manufacturing environment and stood in stark contrast to a potentially viable future in which GM could compete effectively in world markets. Changing that cultural dynamic would entail reshaping manufacturing priorities and practices. No cultural transformation would be successful without a set of mechanisms that would link the work force, the production process, and the new quality goals together. Manufacturing culture's ability to adapt to the changing world had not succeeded on this round, but the overall organizational response to these types of situations paved the way for future cultural transformations.

EVIDENCE OF CHANGE IN MANUFACTURING PERFORMANCE

Before fast forwarding to the present decade, we thought it might be instructive to examine some of the key variables used by the automotive industry to measure its manufacturing performance. We were curious how the GM data on these measures would compare to other automotive firms. We also wondered what the directional trends and the current state of performance were.

Overall manufacturing performance at GM has improved remarkably. Productivity is one area that has undergone significant change. GM achieved a 54 percent productivity improvement between 1986 and 2007, as measured by Harbour data.[9] The most recent productivity figures we were able to acquire for GM (2007) are stronger than those for Nissan, Ford, and Toyota, though somewhat weaker than those for Chrysler and Honda.[10]

Quality also has improved. J. D. Power and Associates' Initial Quality Study has been the industry's standard benchmark of product quality. Included within it is the well-known and commonly used Problems Per 100 Vehicles (PP 100) quality measure. U.S. vehicle owners fill out the survey during the first ninety days of ownership. GM PP 100 dropped by 69 percent between 1989 and 2008, or 6 percent per year.[11] GM values have hovered around the industry average beginning in the early 1990s; by 2008, GM averaged 119 PP 100 compared with the industry average of 118.

Particularly since 1994 with the publication of a new health and safety policy, GM has been fully engaged in reducing occupational injuries and illnesses.[12] GM's lost workday rates in the United States, Canada, and Mexico due to occupational injury and illness decreased 98 percent between 1993 and 2008. GM had .073 lost workdays per 100 employees in 2008;[13] stated another way, GM had an annual incidence of 7.3 cases per 10,000 employees. Similarly, GM's total "recordables" rate[14] dropped 93 percent over the same fifteen-year period, resulting in 1.72 recordables per 100 employees in 2008.[15]

These productivity, quality, and health and safety measures illustrate the magnitude of changes occurring at GM over the last two decades. Organizational-culture change at GM has clearly demonstrated adaptive and responsive elements, even when (or even if) those elements are not being clearly recognized by the broader American culture. GM's cultural adaptiveness (i.e., its worldview regarding issues of productivity, quality, and health and safety) has changed and continues to change. GM's cultural responsiveness is manifested both externally (e.g., numerous awards for its vehicles) and internally (e.g., new managers assigned to work on environmentally friendly issues and products). Tracking and measuring multiple dimensions of manufacturing work provides a more balanced assessment of internal operations. Cultural problem solving is occurring. However, the automotive industry overall also has improved substantially, which has led, in turn, to increased competition in the marketplace and to a lack of recognition of the cultural changes that GM has made. GM's current financial troubles demonstrate that the company needs to improve even further if it is to survive, while it also must find ways to create an understanding that it can compete successfully in the culture of manufacturing despite the current perceptions and misperceptions.

A SHIFT TOWARD WORK GROUP EMPOWERMENT

By the mid-2000s, GM manufacturing culture had made dramatic improvements in its work practices, processes, and quality and quantity of output. The individualized nature of work had been giving way to shared work on the plant floor, typically characterized by job rotation within a defined work group or "team." While productivity and efficiency continued to be critical aspects of the production process, the organization of work had started to change. The set of work tasks assigned to the four-to-six-person work group became the responsibility of the larger work-group collective rather than a particular individual within, or supervising, the work group. Job rotation has a number of advantages over individualized work tasks (as practiced under both Ford and GM's forms of mass production), including reductions in occupational injuries, improved levels of fairness in task assignments, and more suggestions for better work-group processes and performance.

Accompanying this structural change was a change in the cultural dynamics related to job responsibilities. Empowerment in the GM context involves allowing and encouraging subordinates to provide input and make decisions about particular aspects of their work, including the work process. In an empowerment orientation toward work, ideas are welcomed. This change from a directive to an empowerment approach was designed to position those with the appropriate knowledge and experience to manage their work process. When executed effectively, responsibility is transferred from higher-ranking to lower-ranking employees who are closest to the tasks at hand. Instead of "directing" employees to take a particular action, management is to "support" their subordinates by encouraging them in their individual and collective problem solving. Empowerment has the potential to improve the quality and speed of decision making, thereby improving overall plant performance.

One story and one observation from the mid-2000s fieldwork provide a window into this transformative dimension of manufacturing. The key cultural themes reflective of the transformation include empowerment and problem solving. The excerpts involve at least one hourly and one salaried employee[16] and highlight the distinctiveness of the current manufacturing culture compared with the past.

The Story of Marking the Team Room

Tracy Meerwarth, an anthropologist in our research group, learned about this story in an interview with Don, a UAW committeeman.[17] The story takes place in a newly occupied stamping plant, still not completely furnished with all the stamping presses and other equipment, and only running one shift. The story documents how the plant manager, Davis, asked representatives of one of the skilled-trades groups to identify a location for their new team room (a place for meetings, information exchange, eating, and socializing). The team room was not to be built near the storage location of the stamped metal. Team members were excited about having a place to call "home" and were pleased they had been asked to scout out a venue:

> *Don*: So what Davis told the team was that they could go out and mark space on any part of the plant floor. Davis said they could "go out and tape out" where they wanted their team room. Well, after our boys had gone out and taped it on the floor, management came back and said, "We don't like it." I had a feeling that they didn't like it because they perceived it as hidden or out of sight—out of the main view. With all said and done, of course, we were upset about this, but now we're trying to revisit the issue. The die makers of the group will have their own team room, because they're the biggest trade group that will eventually be at this plant. The electricians and the machine repair guys will have their separate team room. I guess we're going to coordinate in the future about where the teams will go.
>
> *Tracy*: It sounds like it's being resolved, but . . .
>
> *Don*: [interrupting] Yeah, but it should have been done right the first time. It's a slap in the face to us to say that you have a choice and then no choice.
>
> *Tracy*: But, did management even define the boundaries . . . for the team room? Did they say something like, "You can't be in that corner" or "You can't be in this area"?
>
> *Don*: No, that was the problem. They gave us no clearly defined boundaries. Of course, we were careful not to put our team room where the equipment would be. But, their [the skilled trades'] feeling was that we put it [the team room] in that corner because there is a lot of noise at this plant and we wanted to get sort of off the mainstream and away from the presses. Overall, these team rooms are sort of joke, because they're not covered and enclosed. They're not very quiet. They're more of a break room.
>
> *Tracy*: So, does noise have anything to do with an ideal culture?
>
> *Don*: Well, you have to understand that we've grown up in the [automotive] industry and noise is not a huge factor . . . the only part of

an ideal culture to me is the team. The team is the most ideal. The old way at GM was this sort of perception that "Hey, I'm the new boss. This is my way." . . . My point is how, if these [guys] work on the presses every day, all day, who better to make the decisions than those folks? GM has embraced this concept [empowerment]. I've seen it work better in other plants, but we still have embraced it. We . . . will work through the problem, but right now, there is a sense of frustration. Sometimes I feel like I'm banging my head against a wall and [my words are] falling on deaf ears. I can honestly say though that we have made more improvement than ten years ago and far more improvement than twenty years ago . . . We have the very best in productivity, management, and skilled trades. We have a recipe for success here . . . in spite of our problems. In the long run, we will work through these issues . . . We tackle one issue at a time and we put things behind us. That means we can get better and stronger . . . we do have a plan to help him [Davis] in the process.

Pressure from some combination of Don, the committeeman, and the team prompted Davis, the plant manager, to reexamine his decision on the team room's location. Ultimately, the team room remained where the team had marked it.

The Observation of a Problem on A Line

There seemed to be a lot of activity going on in the production managers' office area on the plant floor as Elizabeth Briody, a member of our research group, arrived. People were moving quickly to and from the office area onto the A line, an assembly line producing GM midsize sedans. Rob, the assistant superintendent, was not in his office for the interview, though two managers and a UAW committeeman were; the tempo of their conversation seemed fast paced and its content serious. The manager next door noticed her and asked if he could help. He then contacted Rob by radio. Rob responded that he would be there in five minutes. The manager apologized saying that Rob was over at the other end of the plant and suggested she wait in Rob's office; by this time the three men who had been in there had left.

Rob's office had large windows directly overlooking A line, making it possible to observe this portion of the body shop through the windows. Shortly afterward, Rob walked hurriedly into the office and said he was sorry for being late. The interview began, though Rob seemed highly distracted. He kept looking out onto A line as he answered the questions. The line had stopped. At one point he excused himself and called someone on his radio. Several team members, visible through the window, were engaged in a discussion, apparently trying to solve the problem. Appearing quite agitated, Rob stood up and remarked, "The line has been down for two minutes!" He began pacing in his office and then used his radio again to gather information. He tried to refocus his attention as she continued her questions:

> *Elizabeth:* What are you most proud of in this plant?
> *Rob:* We have changed our focus. We are committed to team build. For years we absolutely weren't. And then we were, but no one believed us. And now the team believes us.
> *Elizabeth:* What are the advantages to team build?
> *Rob:* It's back to responsibility and accountability and one other thing— I can't think of how to say it but it's where people see their desires and input is recognized [*sic*].

Once more Rob used his radio to gather information on the problem. He continued to look out the window, appearing nervous and somewhat frustrated. Finally, he interrupted the discussion and said, "I have to stop looking at them [the team members] even though I can't do that. They need to solve this problem." The interview continued for another twenty minutes.

Evidence of Cultural Transformation

These two excerpts, seen in contrast with the blaming and blame-avoidance behavior in the mid-1980s truck plant, represent a significant change in the dynamics of plant culture. The story of Marking the Team Room highlights cultural responsiveness on the part of Davis, the plant manager. We learn at the end of the story that Davis changed his decision about the team room's location in response to team pressure. That follow-up discussion (or negotiation) called Davis's attention to the team's empowerment expectation. Davis then responded appropriately so that the team room remained where the team had marked it. This case illustrates how the cultural past can continue to shape decisions. Davis was forced to confront the past—when he was the one to make the decisions—and reconcile it with the changing orientation to empowerment. The past essentially interfered with his ability to respond in a culturally expected and culturally appropriate manner.

But this story does not end on a defeatist note. Although Davis did not self-correct (as happened with Rob in A Problem on A Line),

Davis's decision was challenged and ultimately reversed. More importantly, Don, the UAW committeeman, indicates that they will reach out to Davis (i.e., "In the long run, we will work through these issues . . . We tackle one issue at a time and we put things behind us"). The fact that Don expressed support for Davis and appeared willing to "coach" him symbolizes the importance he attached to employee empowerment. It seems likely that he would continue to encourage cultural problem solving and the transformation process generally that was underway in the plant.

The observation of A Problem on A Line is a case of cultural adaptiveness. It highlights the human struggle associated with change. Rob, the assistant superintendent, experienced a change in his worldview. He knew that his role was to enable the work group to problem solve and come up with a solution without micromanaging them. Rob did not opt to leave the interview to intervene when the line was down. In that sense, his behavior was consistent with the idea of relying on the "experts"—the hourly employees—to solve the problem. By not interfering in their problem-solving attempt, at least not in person, he symbolized the new worldview of employee problem solving. Despite the struggle within himself to go out on the line and direct the problem-solving effort, Rob successfully resisted. He understood what his actions vis-à-vis the assemblers should be. He knew that the line stoppage was not his immediate responsibility unless his work group sought his help. At the same time, Rob could not resist repeatedly contacting others by radio to get updates. Empowering the team to address the issue was not yet a routine part of Rob's day-to-day activities. This excerpt is a good example of a cultural transformation in progress where the new patterns have not fully solidified.

Summary

This chapter has highlighted key themes in the evolution of GM's manufacturing culture over a time frame of roughly twenty years. The structure and organization of work in the mid-1980s was aligned with mass-production principles of the past. The production process involved centralized control and limited worker autonomy—rather than allowing workers to contribute freely and routinely to work-process or product improvements.[18] In the first field study, we saw that individuals were assigned tasks and held accountable for their specific impact on plant outcomes. Blaming and blame avoidance emerged as symptoms and strategies, respectively, to cope with an unstable and unpredictable production process. Directive managerial styles of interaction exacerbated the tensions in the plant, singling out individuals for the plant's poor performance rather than examining plant operations holistically to explain the behaviors exhibited on the plant floor.

Significant changes are evident by the mid-2000s—both from output measures (e.g., productivity and quality statistics) and from the qualitative difference in story character and elements. Shared work is prominent on the plant floor and with it a changed worldview. There is more evidence of employees working together to address production problems. Empowerment has begun to shape how plant personnel respond to work tasks and appears to be gaining ground over a micromanagement approach. Employees appear to be applying their knowledge, skills, and experiences in ways not possible just two decades past.

But what direction is manufacturing culture taking based on this evolutionary progression? What should the next-generation plant culture be? What are its core elements? How can the cultural transformation process unfold so that GM can improve both its internal effectiveness and its external competitiveness? The next chapters of the book address these questions from the perspective of a cross-section of manufacturing employees. Employees can and have articulated a vision for the future of the firm. Their ideas frame our investigation of the ongoing process of organizational-culture change at GM.

Chapter 4

Getting Organizations to See "What Is" and "What Could Be"

Our Research Approach

Our original charge was to determine how American manufacturing culture could be transformed to take advantage of the positive relationships that had been described as working well in other GM locations, such as Mexico. Our approach was to conduct a study of GM manufacturing sites and organize our key findings, making sure they were valid and reliable. While we developed our core set of findings, we also identified general (or generic) and locally specific obstacles to organizational-culture change, along with the positive elements of the culture (e.g., ideals, processes, relationships) that would assist in transforming the culture and maintaining that transformation. Since we were investigating a complex cultural system, we chose a basic ethnographic research approach[1] for the research design. Ethnography is well suited to discovery and to the exploration of both culture as a whole and culture in particular detail[2] and has proven to be useful in organizational research.[3]

When we began our study, we were quite aware of GM's attempts to adapt to the changing automotive manufacturing environment by exploring innovative approaches to manufacturing in the United States (e.g., Saturn, NUMMI). We were also aware of, and did some investigation of, the GM manufacturing system called GMS. However, our charge and our goal were neither to focus exclusively on a particular plant or a particular aspect of plant operations nor to focus exclusively on what was but to look at what could be. We were interested in investigating and documenting views of culture and cultural change in several GM manufacturing environments in the present, as well as forward into the future. We wanted to listen to and observe those involved in manufacturing work to learn what we could about their worldview. We had been given a broad charge by our project sponsor, Troy Clarke, to develop an understanding of the past and present states of GM manufacturing culture along with the future potential and ideal. Indeed, the Ideal Plant Culture project had three primary objectives. One objective was to document the characteristics of an ideal plant culture—features that would make manufacturing work environments great places to work. A second objective involved applying the cultural insights we gathered to the new "greenfield" plant (a brand new plant) at Lansing Delta Township in Michigan. A third objective entailed developing recommendations and applications to improve the long-term prospects for manufacturing in GM's North American operations.

The theoretical basis for the project involved both a cultural-models and a comparative-culture approach that had four research and development phases: data collection, data analysis, validation, and applications development. As it turned out, the project developed into a highly interactive process during all four phases and eventually included our research group, the research sponsors and advocates, and the study participants. Since our goal was to help GM transform part of its culture, our research design was a hybrid of two applied-research approaches that accommodated our need for objectivity, empiricism, and independence in the research but also a simultaneous need for intensive stakeholder input, buy-in, and action. The research, analysis, and validation phases followed a community-based participatory research design; the research was developed and directed by both the researchers and the key stakeholders (in our case, project sponsors and leaders at the greenfield plant) in consultation with each other.[4]

The development and applications stage grew out of the research and the interactive feedback of the validation process. Here we followed an applied, or "action anthropology," design to support specific organizational-change efforts.[5] The action anthropology phase was made possible by having both GM insiders and contract/consultant outsiders as part of our research group. We consciously used the knowledge, credibility, and insider authority of the GM researchers to propose and pursue a number of actions and used the contract or external researchers to provide outsider credibility for supporting those actions. Cultures are often divided on whom they should listen to about change. Consequently, we provided our study participants with two sets of voices to address concerns from either or both directions simultaneously.

Field Research Phase

Our anthropological field work began in 2002 and continued through 2005 at an intense level and then sporadically for validation and targeted exploration through early 2009. Four plants were involved in our ethnographic study, including three assembly plants and one stamping plant, two union locals, corporate manufacturing offices, and offices of the UAW-GM Quality Network. A total of six researchers were involved in the project, though not all six were active in every phase. A combination of data collection methods was employed.

We interviewed and observed a broad cross-section of hourly, salaried, and executive employees and representatives of the UAW (both local and international). We sought out employees at their workstations, in their offices, in team/break rooms, in skilled-trades areas, in the plant clinic, in the cafeteria, in training facilities, and at union locals. The study participants we interviewed in the research portion of the project ($N = 361$) were considered typical of the overall present and future directions of the company—including those promoting cultural change and those resisting it. As part of this group, we had opportunities to interact with plant management, employees charged with planning for, building, and launching the greenfield plant in Michigan, employees with experience at greenfield sites outside the United States, UAW representatives serving in plant leadership positions, GMS management and labor-relations personnel, Quality Network personnel, and senior GM manufacturing executives.

Our interviews were focused on open-ended, in-depth exploratory and explanatory questions.[6] We did not assume ahead of time what employee perceptions of the current conditions or their view of an ideal plant culture would be like. We began by asking study participants about their daily work tasks and responsibilities. We then asked them to describe what an ideal plant culture would be like. As anticipated, they were able to offer detailed narratives of plant experiences and events that highlighted their particular perspectives on an ideal plant culture. We also were interested in soliciting employee views on what obstacles they perceived were preventing them from achieving an ideal culture and what positive elements of the culture they might access to help attain improvements in the plant culture.

We also engaged in thirty-four formal observations (e.g., training classes, team or staff meetings) and numerous informal observations, all of which we documented as part of the field records. Observing the ways in which employees interact provides a valuable orientation into their relationships, roles, and viewpoints. Observations also give us clues as to how employees spend their time—the activities in which they engage, the length of time associated with those activities, and their reaction to those activities. Observational insights can then be compared with other types of data, including employee recollections of a particular event or activity and documents specifying plant goals, job-specific procedures, or particular plant policies. Given the fluctuating environment within American and GM manufacturing, we focused some attention on changing roles and turnover as employees transferred from one site and into another. These various data sources provided a diverse depiction of manufacturing culture, the processes by which work gets done, and the relationships that exist.

Validation Phase

In addition to the interviews and observations, we set up a consistent "feedback loop" validation process. This approach is the qualitative equivalent of statistical reliability and validity checks on research data.[7] We conducted thirty-five validation sessions timed throughout the study to present preliminary results and findings to our key study participants and advocates and sponsors of the study. These validation sessions were meetings with at least two to three people and sometimes as many as twenty to twenty-five. We asked attendees to confirm, challenge, or elaborate on the findings. Later, we incorporated their insights into subsequent interviews and observations. The validation sessions were not only informative to study participants but also an important vehicle for maintaining our relationships and contact with them throughout the study.

Data Analysis Phase

Our analysis strategy was both inductive and comparative. Since the study was intended to be exploratory in nature, we allowed the patterns to emerge from the qualitative data. We sought to triangulate (or validate) the patterns using these multiple methods, different project researchers, and data collected from different sources.[8] We analyzed the data using content analysis, coding the data into thematic categories.[9] The analyses involved coding study-participant statements and stories, as well as our observation notes, into key themes (e.g., work practices, resistance to change, trust). To the extent possible, we compared within and between groups for evidence of difference or consensus. For example, we compared employee perceptions and behaviors across organizational functions, occupational groups, and plants participating in the study. The analysis process also entailed the identification of illustrative quotes pertaining to the key themes.

Applications Phase

During the implementation phase of the project, we met frequently and repeatedly with the leadership team at the greenfield plant. On several occasions, we worked with them at "off-sites," or meetings held away from the regular work site. These off-sites lasted from a few hours to entire days. Our discussions led to new questions, new suggestions for applying what the results were revealing, and new ways for us to assist in the cultural transformation process. GM manufacturing gained both active consultation and proactive action including the development of ten collaboration tools for use within the corporation (see Chapter 7).

THE CULTURAL TRANSFORMATION FROM THE "OLD WAY"

Our guiding ethnographic goal was to capture views of an "ideal" plant culture and to elicit contrasting views of the current or past plant culture. As part of this goal, we wanted to understand where the culture should and could go and how to get there. We phrased the ethnographic question in various ways:

- Describe what you consider to be the ideal plant culture.
- What characteristics make up an ideal plant culture?
- How can you reach the ideal? What are the barriers?
- What could be done to make this plant the best place to work in GM?

When asked these questions, study participants offered a coherent worldview that could be characterized by two important dimensions that help frame the possibility of achieving an ideal plant culture. First, they included an important time dimension. Study participants repeatedly pointed out that plant culture evolves. They frequently framed their examples in a comparative perspective that consisted predominantly of recollections and experiences from the past juxtaposed onto preferences and hopes for the future. Specifically, they emphasized shifts in manufacturing culture from the "old way" of doing things to a current way, or to the potential for a new (i.e., transformed) or ideal way.

Second, their worldview identified the critical attributes (and subattributes) of an ideal plant culture, elements that categorize and cross-cut various dimensions of plant life. An evaluative element was also central to most of their descriptions, with some features of plant culture highly valued and others viewed negatively and even spurned. Employees offered examples in which particular concepts, actions, or interpersonal behaviors were characterized either as valuable and positive or as problematic in some way. In some cases, the old way was identified as encompassing the past, and the present was seen as somewhat better than the old way but not yet up to the ideal. In other cases, the old was also the present way and was contrasted with the ideal way.

Typically, the old way was linked with characteristics that were perceived negatively. Employees described relationships in the old way as divisive and exclusionary, caused by a "directive" and "authoritarian" management style. For example, employees talked about the prevalence and rigidity of status distinctions between management and hourly workers. The "lines of demarcation" (i.e., status and role distinctions) constrained interaction and the development of social ties. Moreover, the quality of interaction across such culturally defined boundaries was generally regarded as poor. Those of higher status had the power and authority to enforce their perspectives without taking other viewpoints into account. Employees referenced situations in which such leaders ruled with an "iron fist" and threats were common—a trait that was consistent with the historical record on mass production as practiced at both Ford and GM. The following examples illustrate this directive approach:

The supervisor's role was very different [in the past]. He ruled with an iron hand. He would say, "Just do what I tell you to do," and give no explanation. When I hired in on the line five years ago, my supervisor scared me. I was worried about keeping a job. He used to say, "I'll fire your ass." You can't say that to people. I remember it to this day. I said to myself that if I were to become a manager, I would treat people like they ought to be treated. You really took ownership away from the people and made them feel like a number [back then]. Everybody has ideas, and who knows better than the team who's actually doing the work?

A rut is sort of the old GM. The leadership was very militant. They said, "Do it," and you did it. The feeling was "Hey, we're in a hurry. Band-Aid the problem, and just get on with it." Now, there's sort of a new regime and it's sort of like "Listen, let's get together—let's figure out who is closest to the problem and let's fix it." Part of it [the new way] is listening to people who are doing the actual job.

These descriptions of the old way also are consistent with GM's production culture at the truck plant in the mid-1980s that was captured in ethnographic record and described in Chapter 3. In that manufacturing culture, time was money. Production quotas mattered above all else. Employees had to learn the rules for operating within that culture. The notion of speed was accentuated, problems were covered up, and short-term fixes sufficed. From the previous examples, we also can see that employees were treated as "numbers" rather than as valuable resources, suggesting the parallel concept discussed in the mass-production literature—employees as "human appendages" to machines.[10] At the same time, employees used these examples to comment on the change in management behavior away from the dictatorial old way. Both quotes draw attention to the knowledge base and expertise of those individuals who are directly engaged in the work tasks. There is a sense of a shared outlook on plant life, a common purpose, and a collective "ownership"—all of which represent the new way or ideal.

Just as the old way was correlated frequently with negative perceptions, the new or ideal way was associated with positive ones, and the "present day" was often an amalgam of the two. One study participant offered this perspective: "We turned the plant from a plant of reactive to proactive people. For example, we tried to identify when equipment would fail in the future—based on hours and the cycle of the machines. What we were really getting at was determining predictability." Interestingly, she uses the word "we" three times in her example, emphasizing the role of the collective. Working as a team in a collaborative way is a key component of the ideal culture. Another individual commented, "Problem solving needs to become the first response, not the last. It used to be that the boss took care of it (any problems or mistakes), and now the teams problem solve." This study participant recognizes the role and contribution of those most closely tied to the production process. Thus, the new or ideal way involves creating an environment that supports and values employee expertise and problem-solving abilities.

Other examples offered by study participants pinpoint changes perceived as currently occurring:

Getting the press up and operating and doing throughput on the press is my specialty. I learned it from [my plant experience in] Germany and Ohio. Now, I have to impart that knowledge [to my team]. I have two operators on my press. Actually, it's our press. We had some problems with it and some troubleshooting. The other day, I said to them, "You know, we're really doing lousy on time. We're behind." But, I did this without communicating [this issue] with the people—without explaining to the guys. I just went out and did it. They told me, "You know, we know you have a lot of information, but let us come to you for help." They're actually teaching me.

This study participant relays a story about adjusting to a new set of responsibilities. He appears to have accepted input from team members graciously. He then concludes with an introspective remark about how he himself is changing. His attitude reflects the continuous improvement cycle associated with the ideal. A study participant from a different plant noted a related phenomenon: "Another difference from the past is that people are more patient now when you are learning a job." This individual thought that the change to the teaching-learning feature of the present way (away from the directive do-as-you-are-told approach of the old way) might have to do with how the work in this new plant was organized. Plant leaders had established a "team-build structure" in which all hourly employees were put together into work groups and were expected to support each other to get the work done.

Moving from the old to a new or ideal way involves significant organizational-culture changes related to how people work in a plant, how they construct and interpret relationships, and what behaviors get reinforced either positively or negatively. In the ideal or new way, work is structured to enable more shared, team-based, cooperative activities than in the past, more plant-wide problem solving, more empowerment and responsibility, and more learning. In addition, the dynamics of work in the ideal configuration entail a greater degree of unity, connection, and responsiveness, with a significant improvement in the quality of interactions compared with the past.

Our research suggested that the contrasting cultural models of the old and new ways could be visually and metaphorically represented as two different cultural "places" connected by a bridge. Our Prototype Bridge Model (see Figure 4.1) illustrates a composite conceptualization of the cultural transformation process that is situated within its broader cultural context. The old way is illustrated on the left side of the diagram, while the ideal is illustrated on the right. The Prototype Bridge Model is a visual representation of people's ideas about the past or present, in relation to the ideal, and combined with the idea of needing a cultural transformation (both adaptation and response).[11] One pillar of the bridge represents cultural adaptiveness, or the recognition that the context is now different. The other pillar, cultural responsiveness,

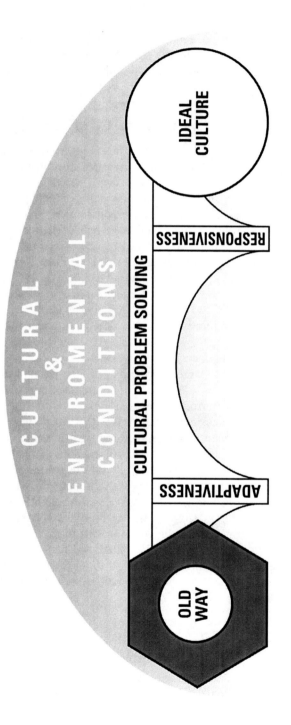

Figure 4.1 Prototype Bridge Model of cultural transformation

signals how employees have begun to process the differences between the old way and the ideal. Both cultural adaptiveness and cultural responsiveness serve as conduits to cultural problem solving and, ultimately, action.

ELEMENTS OF THE IDEAL CULTURE

The second dimension of our study participants' worldview—the elements of the Ideal Plant Culture model—emerged during our conversations, discussions, and interviews with them. Referring back to the time frame, study participants reported that some of these features were already active in the manufacturing environments in which they worked, while others were desirable and describable but not yet in place. We grouped their statements into four topical areas, or content categories. Information and elements grouped under Plant Environment emphasized the physical structure and the technological features of an ideal plant. Features that clustered under Work Force included the personal qualities, skills, and technical competencies necessary, and desirable, for salaried and hourly employees. Elements under "Work Practices" were derived from comments on the parameters for getting manufacturing work done, including *what* the work practices were and *how* those work practices were to be employed. The Relationships category was constructed from a cluster of comments emphasizing the development and maintenance of relationships.

Each of our study participants provided us with what they identified as crucial elements of an ideal plant cultural environment. There was considerable overlap in what they told us and some remarkable consistency in their viewpoints. They typically told us stories or provided examples of their experiences at work that were highly congruent in terms of the view of the ideal, while varying slightly based on their position in the plant culture. In one-on-one conversations, updates to manufacturing personnel, off-sites with plant and union leaders, and in observations on the plant floor, we first confirmed and then validated the basic cultural consensus about the ideal and its potential as an alternative to that past. The composite result was the Ideal Cultural Model (see Figure 4.2).

THE IDEAL CULTURAL MODEL WITH COLLABORATION AT ITS CORE

We constructed a four-quadrant model based on the four components of the ideal plant culture that study participants articulated. As we

Figure 4.2 Ideal Cultural Model

continued to examine study-participant hopes, expectations, and recommendations for the ideal plant culture, we noticed a salient theme that cross-cut the entire data set. Collaboration was viewed as essential to the ideal. Indeed, the ideal culture was symbolized by a unity of vision, effort, and cooperation. Collaboration acted as the integrating theme for the model, increasing the strength of the collective dimension of the culture and reducing the impact of the individualism aspect of the culture.

Collaboration is advocated by hourly, salaried, and executive employees, reflecting the importance of this theme to all plant personnel. One source of evidence for this pattern is the frequent repetition of terms and phrases about the ideal plant culture, such as "fully engaged," "teamwork," "empowerment," "working together," "proactive," "consensus," "people oriented," "open," "trying to do our best," "honesty and integrity," "making a difference," "responsive," "solving problems," and "good communication." A second indicator of the strength of collaboration is its presence in each quadrant of the Ideal Cultural Model. The prevalence of collaboration throughout the model gives some indication of its importance to employees.

A third indicator of the impact of collaboration is the presence of specific prescriptions surrounding the ideal. Salaried statements tend to emphasize trust, openness, and empowerment:

- "You work to understand each other's needs."
- "You need a willingness to be open. You need open lines of communication."
- "You have to trust . . . that I'll do the best I can, and you have to focus on the issue when something goes wrong—not the person. And there has to be some fun to it . . . also, teamwork."
- "You need to trust team members to do the work. They need to be empowered in problem solving."

Hourly employee statements often stress the importance of management listening to their concerns and taking the time to become familiar with their work. In some ways, their statements are a mirror image of the call for trust and empowerment by management. Consequently they reinforce collaboration as a cross-cutting theme of the model:

- "If I can walk up to someone and tell him or her I have a problem, and know it will be taken care of, then that would be ideal."
- "Management listens to input from guys on the line about how to do things and tools we need."
- "Mangers [have] experience on the line so they'd know what operators go through."
- "Managers . . . come out on the floor once in a while."

Similarly, the local shop committee captures the expertise and practical knowledge of hourly employees. For example, one representative commented, "People need to be respected and they need to have input into how things are done. Their input needs to be listened to." Another remarked, "If there's a way to . . . make them [hourly employees] feel they are important, and that they can give input and make a difference, [that is my ideal]."

Taken together, all plant personnel focus on establishing the conditions that would result in stronger working relationships and improved overall integration. Notable about these phrases and comments is how closely linked they are with work activity and not with personal relationships or friendships. Salaried employees offer "cultural rules"[12] for their relationships with their subordinates, including how they should interact with them. Comments from hourly employees and the shop committee also are phrased in the form of rules. However, their rules are not self-directed (as the salaried rules are), but rather target their management's behavior—behavior that reflects some aspects of the old way and, perhaps, the current way.

A fascinating aspect of this cultural ideal of collaboration is that it represents a consensus view of all employees. There is no evidence of differentiation across status and role boundaries. Expecting or assuming, for example, that GM executives would express an opposing vision of the ideal compared with UAW members would be a mistake. All employees, regardless of role, have articulated a cooperative orientation to their potential future, not a conflict orientation that so often dominates the news as well as business and scholarly publications.[13] This emphasis on collaboration also is consistent with union ideology as exemplified by the Quality Network. Indeed, collaboration is an aspect of manufacturing culture that both union and management agree on and support in the telling of the cultural transformation story. The features of each quadrant reflect the views of all study participants.

The collaborative working relationships stressed by both hourly and salaried employees differ in kind and in quality from previously described plant-floor relationships. Ford saw no need for relationship building in his plants and tried to keep that kind of interaction on the plant floor to a minimum. Indeed, he expressed concern that relationships would interfere with getting the job done (due to favoritism or employee unwillingness to improve plant efficiencies). Toyota did not purposely target relationships for focused attention, except for supervisors and their direct subordinates. GM employees, under diversified mass production and, later, in the blaming and blame-avoidance culture, followed the every-man-for-himself strategy. Individuals acted autonomously and independently, since there were few identifiable ways to connect with others in those cultural environments. The individual union-management relationships associated with the Spring Hill experience were not sustainable due to the lack of clarity surrounding decision-making roles and responsibilities and the increasing misalignment between day-to-day activity and the achievement of end goals.

The collaborative ideal from the Ideal Plant Culture project is a fresh idea with a sound empirical foundation. However, it can be criticized from two angles. One criticism of a culture of collaboration is that it has the potential to become an end in itself rather than a means to an end. For example, plant personnel might concentrate so much on trying to work well with one another that they lose sight of achieving plant goals. The response to such a critique is that plant goals (e.g., productivity, quality) are the target toward which the energy of the plant should be directed. These goals are partly a function of the cultural and environmental conditions (e.g., competition) in the manufacturing industry and partly a function of company and plant expectations for performance levels. An organization's goals, whether stable or evolving, are part of the workplace culture. The end point (e.g., achievement of certain goals) and the means (e.g., culture of collaboration) can and should be framed together, with an alignment between end and means maintained throughout the process. The danger arises if the ends and means are decoupled and the balance disrupted.

A second criticism of the collaborative ideal is that it is too hard to achieve and sustain. Production pressures intervene and the top-down, directive patterns of the past reappear. The response to this critique is that cultural transformation requires ongoing vigilance and attention to ensure that the ideal stays in focus or is recast as a new ideal. Cultural drift, an obstacle to cultural change described in Chapter 5 becomes an active force in working against change, even as changes are implemented. Particularly in American culture where the task is core to the American worldview and work ethic, slippage can easily set in. The ideal can and will remain in focus if it is constantly reinforced throughout the organization through multiple mechanisms and by all members of the manufacturing community. We describe some useful mechanisms for reinforcing the ideal in Chapter 7.

Structuring the Plant Environment for Workplace Effectiveness

The consensus elements that were derived from the comments pertaining to the Plant Environment quadrant of the Ideal Cultural Model revealed how the physical environment, equipment, and technology should be structured to encourage plant collaboration and effectiveness. Several statements pertained to a "better ergonomic layout" in which "the plant has to be set up ergonomically." One individual stated, "I'd like to have it be where we say, 'OK. You guys tell us where you want it [your workstation] and how the whole area should be structured.'" A salaried employee remarked that the plant should be "an enjoyable place to work. I think that if you like where you work, you'll do a better job, and I'm talking about . . . climate-wise. Those of us who work in offices take all of these things for granted and we don't think about people working out in the plant." An hourly employee made a similar comment: "It would be good to have climate control for the people and for the equipment." Some of the points made by study participants stressed the importance of preventative maintenance of the equipment: "Machinery has to be maintained" so that plant personnel can be most effective.

Other attributes of the physical plant were identified in an effort to improve plant performance and enhance the overall ambience of the plant. "Better lighting and signage," "visual . . . everything color marked, color coded for visual management," and "sunshine" (i.e., "windows") were features mentioned repeatedly by study participants. "Bathrooms closer to the line" would lessen the burden currently experienced by remaining work group members when an individual has to temporarily step away from his or her job. Several comments related to the importance of social interaction. One hourly employee suggested, "A community center in the plant where people can get together for cards and meals [or] a picnic area outside." Others advocated having team rooms located farther away from the mainstream noise of the presses so that they were more conducive to social interaction.

Engaging a High-Performing Work Force

Comments that related to the Work Force quadrant identified a common view of the key employee skill sets and personal attitudes. Hiring individuals with "people skills," who exhibited a "willingness to share knowledge," were "cooperative," and possessed a clear "understanding [of] their role" were viewed as critical in the ideal plant culture. Such selection criteria applied across job descriptions. One plant manager mentioned a recent hiring experience as close to the ideal: "We tried to pick [those with] qualities that could work well with the union [when we picked] our first-line supervisors . . . We [were] looking for enthusiastic, open, and honest people." Finding managers that could get along (e.g., understand worker perspectives, communicate) was a desirable quality. Technical skills were a necessary but not a sufficient condition, as this manager pointed out: "When I was involved in the hiring process here, I had to make hard decisions. I was hiring for technical roles. Although we would get the best technical people [to apply], some people suffered in [lacked] the people-skills component.

They were horrible. I knew that if I hired an engineer that was an intro-vert, we would be in trouble."

Being able to perform one's role effectively—both in terms of tech-nical abilities and attitude—was important too. Employees should rep-resent an "engaged, well-trained work force," stated one individual. One manager stated, "Your goal [as manager] is to maximize their level of contribution." Another manager suggested, "You really want people who are happy with what they are doing." Hourly employees reiterated, "[and] people that appreciate the work," and "people that come to work"—a reference to the absenteeism rate in this particular plant. Another individual emphasized that "ownership by each person for the plant, or for his department" is an essential part of the ideal culture. Work ethic was highlighted, along with appropriate, timely, and sufficient training. In short, study participants valued a positive attitude toward the work and plant personnel, complemented by the necessary work-related skill sets.

Accomplishing Plant Goals through Cooperative Work Practices

This quadrant of the model was constructed from the data that focused on study-participant views of working together to accomplish goals. A salaried employee stated, "I don't believe in being passive; I believe in participating." The following is an excerpt from our field notes: "We noticed that for three to four minutes there was an opera-tions meeting. They would take a conference call and take that to the floor level where the TCs [team coordinators][14] would hear the latest issue[s] from the night before, what [they] could expect to encoun-ter that day, and little stuff that would help eliminate the confusion [between shifts]." The process of meeting and sharing information is a critical part of a collaborative culture, serving as a bridge between the two shifts. Within a shift, problems often arise. Hourly employ-ees stressed the importance of "being able to identify and remove roadblocks" and as such, "concerns [can be] addressed and accom-modated." One supervisor told us, "I'd like the manager to learn all the jobs . . . [so that he or she would understand the demands of those positions]." One of the clinic nurses suggested, "Don't always think of [the] medical [department] as a recordable. We can be more help-ful. We can cascade to the staff to keep our arms around a situation in the plant from the standpoint of ergonomics and safety . . . We are here for occupational injuries." Thus, sharing information, offering to help, and addressing the difficulties head on were viewed as enhancing plant performance significantly.

Another aspect of the Work Practice quadrant involved maintaining consistency between words and actions; it is encapsulated in the often-heard message "walking the talk." One salaried employee stated, "The people on the ground are the experts . . . It kills motivation when you teach the way of trying to solve problems on their own and then it's sabotaged—that's awful. We want people to come up with their own problems and solve their own problems." A parallel view was expressed by an hourly employee: "There would be open and honest accountability for employees and supervisors." When there are "common goals," according to one salaried employee, it makes it easier to be focused. Intrinsic to the Work Practice component was its impact on plant outcomes and relationships.

Cultivating Strong, Healthy Relationships as a Basis for Plant Success

The Relationships component of the model was identified and elaborated on by numerous stories about the benefits of and preferences for strong, healthy relationships and interactions—whether among co-workers, between supervisors and subordinates, or between GM plant management and UAW local leaders. One of the managers offered this example as an ideal: "I was part of a start-up plant [where] the plant manager would explain what had happened that day, and what was going to happen the next day. He really got people involved." An engineer commented, "I am here to assist. It helps cement the marriage between the groups." An hourly employee held a similar opinion: "This is what makes it work—our union-management relationship. Everyone supports it." His co-worker agreed by saying, "Union and management are married and divorce is not an option." The comparison to marriage is powerful analogy implying a committed partnership. Related statements about the ideal included "People getting along at work"; "Everybody makes a contribution because they have a contribution [to make]"; "The new place [plant] needs to be people friendly, worker friendly"; and "More interdepartmental and intradepartmental cooperation."

Another priority was the creation of a plant culture characterized by trust, open-mindedness, and respect for one's competencies and contributions. Frequent interaction enables personal exchanges of information and support that make people feel connected to one another and integral to the plant's success. The visibility and accessibility of management in this ideal plant culture are highly valued attributes as expressed in this comment: "[The new plant manager] needs to go out in the plant on a regular basis in his jeans and work a job for a day. Have him bring his [staff] . . . Have them interact [with us] on a regular basis." Overall, the foundation for collaboration in the Relationships quadrant is valuing people. One salaried employee reiterated, "Dignity and respect [matter]. A ten cent cup of coffee and a thank you goes a long way." Another employee remarked, "We need to maintain a stable environment here and work on communication skills and [focus on] the fact that people are our best assets."

VALIDATING THE IDEAL CULTURAL MODEL

Once we began our analysis of the data and synthesized our participants' responses into the Ideal Cultural Model, we began conducting a number of high-intensity validation sessions. We sought opportunities to test and gather feedback on our ideas. We relied heavily on "cultural experts" (i.e., knowledgeable individuals willing to share their viewpoints) to comment on our emerging findings, perspectives, and explanations. Later, given our interest in implementing our results, recommendations, and applications, we sought feedback from a broader set of individuals who had neither prior knowledge of the study nor an understanding of the powerful impact of culture on plant operations. Validation also entailed comparing and contrasting field observations and interviews with documentary data (e.g., GMS documents, Quality Network materials).

One aspect of the validation entailed an assessment of the conceptual and visual portrayal of the Ideal Cultural Model. Comments ranged along a continuum from strong agreement to sharp disagreement. Sometimes the model evoked positive comments. For example, one plant leader stated, "We [the plant staff] can have a huge impact on relationships and work practices." A senior executive remarked, "The storytelling, the relationships, the collaboration is so much more important to people compared with the high-level words like teamwork, values, and mission statements. We are building our own history and the history gets better because you relate something each time you tell the story. You are pulling out these values and positive elements."

As we were developing the notion of the Ideal Cultural Model, we linked an early version of it with the Bridge Model. One excerpt from the field notes captures the exchange of ideas between the researchers (Elizabeth Briody and Tracy Meerwarth) and a plant leader with the pseudonym John. He offered his feedback on the way we illustrated the Ideal Cultural Model:

John: I think in your conceptualization of the bridge you should not use the phrase "old way" but rather "current way."

Elizabeth: That's interesting—so that you get at the idea of the current state or what's happening in real time.

Tracy: We were trying to use the wording that people use.

John: I just think that that's a very important distinction.

Elizabeth: Maybe you could have the "old way," then the "current way," and then the "ideal way"?

John: Maybe somewhere under the bridge, like Ann [another manager] said, you could put the "current way"?

This discussion helped focus attention on the progression from the past to an ideal future. At the same time it explicitly acknowledged the current state.

A few months later we received other helpful feedback. We showed the Ideal Cultural Model with four equal quadrants. We then linked it to an illustration in which quadrant size reflected the number and importance of study-participant comments. Consequently, the Relationships quadrant was larger than the others. Interestingly, this illustration was perceived as taking away from GM's focus on manufacturing vehicles because it emphasized relationships. In this excerpt, the senior leader (with the pseudonym Len) disagrees with the portrayal of this illustration. Elizabeth Briody and Bob Trotter (the researchers) and Elizabeth's boss (with the pseudonym Sam) explain the rationale.

Len: What are you saying about the ideal culture? What you need are the four parts and balance. And [yet] you're showing that you need more emphasis on relationships.

Elizabeth: What this slide is attempting to show is that much more emphasis on relationships needs to take place . . .

Sam: Really what this second new model [with a larger quadrant for relationships] is showing is the measure of energy of what they need to change to achieve that balance. [More discussion ensues.]

Len: The relationship side should be small.

Bob: Well, the ideal is the balance. But our model is a dynamic one . . . we will give you the diagnosis but then you want to come back to the balance.

When all the researchers got together later, we discussed Len's feedback and agreed with the merits of his argument. We subsequently revised the Ideal Cultural Model to contain the word "collaboration" at its core. We emphasized the importance of achieving and maintaining balance among the four quadrants. We also discussed how one or more of the quadrants might require more effort and energy as organizational and environmental conditions change and new challenges materialize.

PLACING THE IDEAL CULTURAL MODEL IN COMPARATIVE CONTEXT

The Ideal Cultural Model represents a perspective and consensus worldview of an ideal future and of the organizational-culture changes that must occur within GM's manufacturing culture to realize that ideal. It was developed in a particular historical context that is very relevant to the present and future. Production work at GM had already begun its shift away from the diversified mass-production paradigm. Innovative manufacturing approaches had emerged within parts of GM as a result of Toyota's influence (e.g., at NUMMI, through GMS), the impact of the UAW (e.g., Quality Network), and an ambition to reinvigorate GM and improve its competitive performance. At the same time, our data indicated that the adoption of those approaches was both partial and silo-ed (though the dissemination of GMS has improved in the late 2000s). The Ideal Cultural Model reflects elements of these and other innovative approaches to manufacturing, while it also points out that the old way–new way contrasts mean that the relationship dimensions of the cultural transformation are highly desirable but incomplete.

Comparing the Ideal Cultural Model with Other GM Models

At about the midpoint in our field research phase, we found it useful to compare and contrast the Ideal Cultural Model with three of the manufacturing-related programs that were frequently mentioned in our conversations with GM plant personnel. The comparative method is a useful and powerful approach to cultural analysis. It is frequently used in cases where members of the culture can discuss, describe, comment on, and evaluate the important cultural elements of competing views, processes, or values within their own culture.[15] The resulting analysis provides an explanation for both the similarities and the critical differences in competing worldviews and cultural processes associated with GM's manufacturing culture. It also provides important insights into the competing conditions that might be obstacles to achieving the ideal.

The three comparison models for manufacturing culture we explored represent the incremental transition points to the model and include the Quality Network, GMS, and Star Point; they emerged roughly in that chronological sequence.[16] GMS introduced a structured and rigorous approach to vehicle production, while Star Point reinforced the conceptualization and effectiveness of production team activities. GM pushed for the implementation of GMS in the United States, despite significant resistance in the plants. Much of this resistance came from the UAW (both local and international), since they perceived GMS as a competitor to the Quality Network. Unlike GMS, Star Point was never proposed for adoption and therefore did not face any active resistance in U.S. plants. All three models offered opportunities for new thinking and experimentation as competitive pressures were rising. However, the changes initiated on GM's international periphery—particularly those embedded in GMS—ultimately penetrated GM's core operations, affecting GM's autonomy.

The Quality Network

The Quality Network program demonstrates an important evolution in the UAW's view of plant relationships and processes. This view is much different from the conflict orientation surrounding organized labor and its employers during a significant part of the twentieth century. On a broad cultural level, the Quality Network signals significant changes in the dominant values of the American culture in relation to work, individualism, conflict, and cooperation. Its mission statement reads as follows: "The Quality Network is the process of institutionalizing GM's 'people, beliefs and values' to achieve total customer satisfaction through people, teamwork, and continuous improvement." The set of "beliefs and values" was developed from interviews with both union and managerial leaders. The interview data repeatedly demonstrated employees' desire "to be respected, trusted, and involved" and served as the basis for "a set of guidelines for successful relationships."[17] Sixteen specific "beliefs and values" are highlighted, representing a set of core ideals.[18] Interestingly, ten of these sixteen elements focus on the relational aspects of employee interactions and the GM management-UAW leadership interface:

- Invite the people of GM to be full partners in the business.
- Recognize people as our greatest resource.
- Demonstrate our commitment to people.
- Treat people with respect.
- Never compromise our integrity.
- Build through teamwork and joint action.
- Take responsibility for leadership.

- Make communications work.
- Trust one another.
- Demand consistency in the application of this value system.

The remaining six elements direct attention to aspects of continuous improvement. They include the following: "make continuous improvement the goal of every individual," "put quality in everything we do," "eliminate every form of waste," "use technology as a tool," "accept change as an opportunity," and "establish a learning environment at all levels." The similarity of these six elements to the well-publicized features of TPS is remarkable.

The beliefs and values are linked with numerous Quality Network Action Strategies, which consist of conceptual, methodological, and practical tools to achieve customer satisfaction. Each Action Strategy describes a set of objectives, key roles, implementation guidelines and examples, and measurement suggestions. The Action Strategies are categorized according to similar characteristics. For example, the Environment Action Strategies direct attention to the sociocultural dimensions of the settings in which employees work. These Environment Action Strategies are closely aligned with the Relationships quadrant of the Ideal Cultural Model and, particularly the ideals of cooperation and support. They include "Support for the Employee," "Communication," "Cooperative Union/Management Relations," and "Top Leadership Commitment and Involvement."

At the same time, the Environment Action Strategies exhibit a key difference in comparison with the Ideal Cultural Model. Explicitly and implicitly, they emphasize the institutional relationship (UAW-GM) and hierarchical relationships in the plants (manager-employee, leader-employee). By contrast, the Ideal Cultural Model does not target relationships between specific roles but rather focuses generally on the quality of relationships among all plant personnel. The Ideal Cultural Model, applicable to all relationships generally, is appropriate for vertical relationships (e.g., between supervisors and those they supervise) as well as horizontal relationships (e.g., among peers).

The Quality Network's emphasis on people, teamwork, and continuous improvement has helped raise awareness of the hidden "people" potential within GM's U.S. operations. It has stressed the value of employee problem solving and decision making, attributes that are central to the Work Practices quadrant. It has advocated mutual trust and respect, qualities that exemplify the Relationships quadrant. Its logo consists of a curving white line representing the "journey to continuous improvement" and positioned between the UAW and GM logos.[19] The symbolism of the "journey" aligns well with the Ideal Cultural Model, which looks to a potential, brighter future for GM manufacturing.

GMS

GMS developed out of an effort in Eisenach, Germany, to create a single GM approach to manufacturing and is now GM's official system for organizing, executing, and evaluating GM's manufacturing processes and products. GMS shares innumerable features with TPS, due in large part to the team of former Toyota leaders that GM recruited to craft GMS. GM has incorporated key elements, such as team structure and the *andon* cord, into the way it manufactures its products. Borrowing and adapting methods, practices, and processes from other manufacturers is commonplace in the automotive industry. Toyota "borrowed" key ideas and techniques from Ford in the past, just as Ford had borrowed from earlier industries.

The GMS logo is illustrated as an atom. Orbiting electrons encircle the nucleus and represent the five GMS principles: Continuous Improvement, People Involvement, Standardization, Built-In Quality, and Short Lead Time. These five principles consist of thirty-three elements that target particular arenas for action. For example, the principle of People Involvement is designed to "engage the work force" by focusing attention on eight elements including Qualified People, People Support/Team Concept, and Shop Floor Management. Within the element of People Support/Team Concept, the arenas for action include job rotation, team member and team leader roles, empowerment, and accountability. Team Concept is specified further as small groups on the plant floor that share common goals and assist each other in the performance of common tasks. These aspects of GMS align well with the Work Practices quadrant of the Ideal Cultural Model. GMS is clearly focused on the structural and process-oriented dimensions of production work.

The GMS approach is consistent with the emphasis in both GM culture and American national culture on work—working hard, working efficiently, and working until the task is completed. Structures and processes are considered both necessary and sufficient conditions for organizing the work and accomplishing it, as is indicated in the GMS Mission Statement: "The Global Manufacturing System is a single, common, competitive manufacturing system, consistent with Quality Network Principles, that uses best processes, practices, and technologies to support General Motors' Vision of World Leadership and Global Customer Enthusiasm." The mission statement explains the ways in which GMS achieves its goals: by using "best processes, practices, and technologies." Yet, processes, practices, and technologies cannot operate without people. The crucial role that plant personnel play in the day-to-day work activities is not emphasized. It is as if the people are incidental to the work rather than core to work activity. Moreover, there is no acknowledgment of the importance of strong, healthy plant-floor relationships and interactions as the critical mechanism for ensuring the work is done as effectively and efficiently as possible. While the mission statement does capture other important elements of the production process—including an emphasis on a "single," global system, GM's market awareness, and an alignment with the Quality Network—it falls far short of the commonly heard aphorism in GM that "people are our greatest resource."

Star Point
Star Point is the name of the production system developed for use at GM's vehicle assembly, engine, and stamping facilities in Silao, Guanajuato, Mexico during the 1990s. The success of Star Point was not only an important precursor for the development of the Ideal Cultural Model but also a key element in GM management's sponsorship and impetus for our study that resulted in the model. One of Star Point's most recognizable features has involved creating and sustaining high-performance work teams. Silao hired a consulting firm to help the plant configure and optimize this team-based work design. Star Point builds on the sociotechnical systems approach to production in which the work group is self-regulating, multiskilled, and complementary to the production machinery.[20] It also applies the lessons from research on group dynamics and development and planned change through group decision making.[21] Silao has won numerous awards for product quality, manufacturing processes, and health and safety records, among others.

Team members and team leaders are selected carefully and then trained. Among the training themes are the principles of the Silao Production System: making the difference, valuing differences, participating in meetings, obtaining consensus with teams, and resolving conflict. Expectations target work process and performance, with special attention to continuous improvement. Roles and responsibilities are described and documented on a roles and responsibilities matrix. Significant emphasis is placed on the concepts of trust, commitment, empowerment, and participation. These training themes echo the features associated with the Ideal Cultural Model. Employee selection and training are key features of the Work Force quadrant. Moreover, the expectations presented during Silao's training sessions underscore the value accorded to role effectiveness and employee involvement.

Teams are evaluated on their performance during a "team check up." Sets of behavioral characteristics define four stages of team development. Newer teams are more likely to be classified in an earlier stage of development (i.e., forming or storming), while teams with more experience working together are likely to be classified in one of the later stages (i.e., norming or performing). What is fascinating about the Silao approach is the attention to the teams' ability to work well together. Silao has moved beyond the organization of work using teams to specific, targeted efforts to maximize the teams' potential to be successful. Effort and attention are devoted to poorer-performing work teams through hands-on coaching. The objectives of the coaching are to improve the teams' collaborative abilities and to help them achieve higher levels of performance. Teams are recognized for their levels of achievement. Silao's logo brings into sharp relief the focus of team efforts. It consists of a five-pointed star in which the GMS logo is embedded. Each point of the star, translated into English, represents a goal: S for Safety, Q for Quality, R for Responsiveness, C for Cost, and P for People.

Silao represents one path for developing work-group effectiveness, a path worth exploring in the realization of the ideal. While this kind of approach was never articulated by our study participants, it is not inconsistent with what they envision. Teamwork and team concept (i.e., the organization of individual workers into work groups) are important features that are captured in the Work Practices quadrant of the Ideal Cultural Model. While Silao's focus and energy are on the plant-floor production teams, the Ideal Cultural Model emphasizes teamwork for all plant employees. Thus, salaried employees can and should engage in team-based cooperative activities reflecting the broader collaborative orientation of the ideal plant culture. Teamwork in the Ideal Cultural Model is not restricted to a particular work role (e.g., hourly employees) but is inclusive of all work roles in the plant.

What the Combined Precursor Programs Tell Us about the Ideal Cultural Model

The salience of collaborative relationships is a critical part of the ideal at GM. We found that a culture of collaboration is internally consistent with the primary foci of "people" and "teamwork" in both the Quality

Network and Star Point. By contrast, collaboration is not an explicit part of either the GMS mission statement or its People Involvement principle, though many associated with the GMS organization assured us that its focus was implied. Unfortunately, the low-context nature of American culture favors explicit conditions and diminishes or ignores the implicit conditions. When things are not made explicit in a low-context culture, particularly in writing, they do not get the attention and focus they deserve. By contrast, in high-context cultures, implicit conditions are often the driving force.

When we conducted a content analysis of the features of the GMS People Involvement principle (the principle most likely to include an emphasis on strong, healthy relationships), we found that GMS emphasizes work structure and work process—including the importance of goals and objectives, a structure for the coordination of work including roles and responsibilities, and a patterned set of work practices. Relationship conditions were missing. By contrast, the Ideal Cultural Model specifies the importance of building and maintaining relationships as a foundation for collaboration. Study participants repeatedly indicated that working cooperatively, being listened to, feeling respected, and contributing to solutions to work-related issues were what mattered to them.[22] Creating a culture of collaboration positions work groups and organizations to enhance their effectiveness and efficiency.

The GMS focus on work structure and work process, on the one hand, and the collaborative-relationship emphasis in the Ideal Cultural Model, on the other, are complementary and necessary in a competitive global market. Making collaboration an explicit part of the production-work paradigm is particularly important for GM's operations in low-context cultures. By contrast, the Quality Network and Silao programs are explicitly oriented to the welfare of the group. The Quality Network focuses on relationships, while Star Point emphasizes work-team training and coaching. Both the Quality Network and Star Point would be considered higher context relative to GMS.

A solution to this cultural issue for GM's low-context U.S. plant cultures where GMS is in place is to focus more time and effort on relationship building and maintenance while simultaneously attending to plant work goals, processes, and practices. Collaboration must be viewed as necessary and critical to GM success, rather than simply incidental. Documentation related to plant operations has to highlight the importance of collaboration. Otherwise, the information conveyed in that documentation will not get the attention it deserves. Metrics have to be developed to track indicators of a collaborative work environment, including patterns of work-group effectiveness, cooperative problem solving, and quality of co-worker interactions. Plants have to be measured and recognized for creating a culture of collaboration. They also would have to continually reinforce the importance of strong, healthy relationships in the plant's daily life. Strategies such as documentation, measurement, and reward will level the playing field for low-context cultures so that they can reap the benefits of collaboration in this competitive world.

Congruency with GMS and the Quality Network

During our validation sessions, study participants also focused on the extent of congruency between the Ideal Cultural Model and either GMS or the Quality Network. In some cases, attention was simply called to the comparison: "I like that there is no conflict on this [presentation] slide with GMS. It shows a consistency with GMS." In other cases, the Ideal Cultural Model was evaluated negatively. In this exchange, one senior manufacturing executive (with the pseudonym Lowell) defends standardization,[23] a key GMS principle:

> *Lowell:* Did standardized work come out?
> *Elizabeth:* It was there [in the data], but it was not as important as some of the other issues.
> *Lowell:* But it should be the bedrock of the company. We get the lowest score on standardization. It takes hard work.

Lowell's implication was that standardized work should be highlighted in the Ideal Cultural Model.

In still others cases, the Ideal Cultural Model captured little interest because it was viewed as redundant. One senior leader commented, "Doesn't GMS tell us what to do and how to do it? We have a host of elements under People Involvement that drive the right behaviors. Do we really need this 'culture initiative'? [a reference to the Ideal Plant Culture project] My opinion: No." Another indicated, "I may be terribly insensitive, but as far as I'm concerned, being collaborative—simply translated: working together—is a given in a GMS environment."

The redundancy argument also appeared in comparisons with the Quality Network model. One Quality Network leader told us, "If you [researchers] take the time to go back to the Quality Network Action Strategies, there are avenues for achieving what you are talking about [i.e., collaboration]. There are Action Strategies to address People Involvement." Our research group had already examined the Action Strategies at that point and found that they were in varying stages of development, with significant work required to make them practical and useful. However, we thought that the Action Strategies represented a potentially fruitful area for the future.

The range of reactions to the Ideal Cultural Model is primarily a commentary on the stake that manufacturing leaders had in ongoing GM and UAW initiatives. Leaders frequently become defined by the programs they sponsor and the decisions they make—whether as individuals or as members of a larger collective. Their status and role are affected by the impact that they have on the organization based on their association with particular initiatives.

The Ideal Cultural Model was neither management driven nor union driven. It was aligned with no one (in particular) and everyone (simultaneously). It represented a worldview, a conceptualization of the direction that GM's culture could and should take (as expressed by our study participants). It had an identifiable end point—a culture of collaboration—that was independent of any organizationally planned change efforts. Indeed, no leader (or anyone else in the organization) was aware of this worldview until our research group made that worldview explicit.

The Ideal Cultural Model clearly specified the focus and direction of any cultural-change efforts as part of GM's continuing cultural transformation. Based on the cultural-transformation model we described in Chapter 1, progress had been made through the first few stages (or subprocesses) of change (e.g., recognition of the need to change, identification of the direction for change, establishment of the focus of the change). But the transformation process was far from complete. We now move on to the next cultural-transformation stage in which the Ideal Cultural Model interfaces with cultural forces that resist it.

CHAPTER 5

OBSTACLES TO CULTURAL TRANSFORMATION

Our research group used the classic and current "cultural change" or cultural transformation literature as a starting point to create a framework for understanding the obstacles that GM would encounter in the process of moving from the "old way" to a more ideal plant culture model.[1] Any form of cultural change, from sweeping cultural revolutions to small changes in material culture, always meets some level of resistance. In general, people automatically resist change and favor continuity even when the new way may be more beneficial to them. The resistance can be mild and can be overcome by simply learning about the new way, or it can be vehement and virtually unchangeable, requiring the strongest tools of cultural change to encourage the adoption of the new way.[2] Mild forms of cultural change are often called "evolutionary change" because they follow a step-by-step (i.e., small or incremental) progression from the old to the new. More sweeping and abrupt forms of cultural change are sometimes labeled "revolutionary change." Those changes usually signal a significant break between the old and the new, especially in terms of the ideology or philosophy that is guiding the new way of doing things.[3]

The cultural change literature is useful for identifying significant obstacles to deliberate cultural transformations or innovations in organizations by identifying and focusing on the processes of change.[4] A process approach allows us to understand the key conditions needed to create effective change and to identify the possible barriers to completing those processes. There are four primary cultural processes that are relevant for framing the obstacles to cultural change that are embedded in our study. They include the following:

1. The acceptance of (or the resistance to) the concept of culture as changeable or needing change (the ideology of change)
2. The process of learning a new culture (acculturation or enculturation)
3. The process of identifying with a particular culture where individuals in a culture believe that their way is the right way to live and the best way to live compared to other ways or other cultures (cultural identification and ethnocentrism)
4. The process of accepting cultural norms or cultural consensus as the appropriate way to interact with others (a normative approach to culture)

These processes have seven corollary obstacles to cultural transformation that must be addressed to achieve some or all of the ideal culture goals for GM:

1. *Having to learn a new culture* is a barrier to cultural change because there is always some level of resistance or effort necessary to get someone to learn something new.
2. *Ethnocentrism* is an obstacle because it is the belief that the old way is the right way and perhaps the only way (based on the individual's current identification with a particular culture), so why change?
3. *Cross-cultural conflict* becomes an obstacle to change when people perceive that their culture is being challenged by another group with a differing culture (e.g., union-management conflicts, old way–new way groups), and the conflict itself acts as a barrier to change.
4. *Resistance to change* is an obstacle that occurs because people have adopted certain cultural rules, norms, and behaviors and are automatically resistant to changing what has always "worked" in the past.
5. *Cultural dilemmas* become barriers to change because individuals are capable of holding two competing values (e.g., the need for standardized work and the need for constant improvement) and using each one to resist change toward the other or toward a new way of doing things.
6. *Cultural contradictions* are obstacles to change because they reflect inconsistencies in the culture (e.g., stated goals vs. actual goals) that lead to mixed messages and ambiguity.
7. *Cultural drift* can be unconscious or unrecognized resistance to doing something a new way because the old way is more comfortable; it is a gradual lessening of the process of adhering to the new rules and procedures.

THE CHALLENGES OF CULTURAL CHANGE IN ORGANIZATIONS

Throughout the course of the Ideal Plant Culture project, we never ran into a person who ever suggested that change was easy. Indeed, we experienced quite the opposite. Study participants often commented on how difficult it was to change the culture—to do things differently, to try innovative methods, to access new technologies, to work with people one did not know, or to explore alternative approaches. They repeatedly stressed the amount of effort and energy required to make such changes. Some spoke of successful outcomes but warned of the challenges that had to be overcome. Others commented on a reversion back to the ways of the past—a sign that the desired change had not been sustained.

Elaborating on the Cultural Obstacles

We describe the cultural obstacles—the barriers to attaining the ideal culture—in terms of the seven primary challenges that organizational members face as they attempt to move in new directions and away from past practices and traditions. These obstacles work to impede or arrest the cultural transformation process. We build on the Prototype Bridge Model from Chapter 4 by incorporating cultural obstacles as a key element (see Figure 5.1). In addition, we added some of the key themes associated with the old way (e.g., individual work, distrust) and specified the four key components of the Ideal Cultural Model.

We found that employees were able to express culture-change difficulties they encountered in everyday language, even if they did not recognize or articulate them as cultural issues or as the more specific processes and barriers that we identified above. They were able to articulate the crucial barriers to change that could be addressed by the Ideal Culture Model and by the appropriate cultural change processes (called enablers and discussed in Chapter 6) that can be used to overcome the cultural obstacles to change. One employee commented, "The Flint people that come here just don't want to do the type of work we do." Another stated, "People are very individual focused. They are self-centered. They are competitive. It is really the opposite of team." A third remarked, "We have a majority of hard workers here. The old school guys tell us that the jobs are overloaded. Typically these guys are on the first shift. On second shift, you have the younger guys. The younger guys, I feel, really want to make the numbers [production quotas], and the old school guys really hate

Figure 5.1 Bridge Model with obstacles

that. The day shift is fighting to add two jobs [to their line] and night guys want to remove jobs." Study participants expressed their interest in and expectations for getting as close to the ideal as possible despite these and other difficulties. The following sections offer an elaboration of the seven primary obstacles to cultural change and also an understanding of the need to incorporate an obstacle-removal or obstacle-avoidance process in our Bridge Model metaphor.

Having to Learn a New Culture

This cultural obstacle was particularly evident when employees changed roles or changed work teams, work areas, work shifts, or plants. Typically, another person working in the same location was available to assist the "newcomer" in acculturating. However, when large numbers of individuals were being hired or transferred, the acculturation problem was more complex, since more "teachers," "trainers," or "mentors" were required simultaneously. The impact of this obstacle was felt both by the newcomer and by those linked with that newcomer. The following quotations exemplify this cultural obstacle:

- "In the new plant, they [the employees] need to learn the process. So we have this exercise to teach them. That way, people are not learning and doing [work on the line] at the same time."
- "Some people are not as engaged as you'd like them to be, but others are strong."
- "And, I also think that the issue is with our contractor and per diem managers. These people don't know processes and they make our job tougher [by stepping in where they don't need to be]."

Ethnocentrism

This cultural obstacle has to do with the imposition of a particular point of view on others without being able to see the value of alternative perspectives. In a manufacturing environment, plant personnel may believe that their approach is the only way or the best way. Moreover, they may insist on the superiority of their ideas rather than considering other options. An individual acting in an ethnocentric manner typically has a narrow, limited orientation to the culture and little tolerance for the differences within it. Examples of ethnocentrism in employee comments include the following:

- "People believe they have the best of what there is [at their plant] because they don't look at what other places are doing."

- "[That group] thinks it has the right way to do it and that's why they don't listen."
- "When they say that 'You are the most profitable plant in GM,' that really does not mean anything. GM does not need to be benchmarking themselves against themselves. GM needs to be benchmarking themselves against the best in the world . . . They need to ask themselves, 'Are you [GM] really that good? Are [we] really that good when we compare ourselves to others who are world class?'"

Cross-Cultural Conflict

Tensions are a part of culture. Cultures can fragment as those with different roles, experiences, and beliefs maintain distinct viewpoints. In a manufacturing context, the fragmentation might appear along job-classification, job-function, and production-location boundaries, for example. In the mid-1980s culture-of-blaming environment, employees blamed those upstream from them in the workflow as well as those on the previous shift. Conflict also may arise due to characteristics of a particular employee or group of employees (e.g., plant location, ethnicity, age, technical competency, worldview). The characteristics of the plant, the job, or the individual may combine to produce divergent groups within the plant population, such as younger employees who are more open to GMS, salaried employees who do not value all union work rules, or workers in one part of the plant with limited manufacturing experience. Examples of this cultural obstacle include the following:

- "There are questions on our hot-button issues like the inside view versus the official line."
- "Flint has always been different. They have a different work ethic here [in Lansing]. We have people from Detroit, all different characters. The guy from Detroit was fired. He was on a DO [disciplinary layoff]. He changed the date on a drop slip the first day he was here. He was here one day and gone for a month. The Flint people that come here just don't want to do the type of work we do. They feel like they're working too hard for their money."
- "There is pushback from the unions on changing the culture."
- "Their work ethic is kind of low. They work their shift and take their lunchtime and that's it."

Resistance to Change

This cultural obstacle targets comfort with routine and discomfort with differences. Resisting change often is perceived as easier than trying something new. When resistance is high, learning is low. We noticed resistance around work practices such as job rotation and standardization. Sometimes resistance also appeared around plant policies. One plant had a dress code and another had a no-smoking policy, which some employees found difficult to accept. The following quotations are examples of this obstacle:

- "First, people had to accept the fact that they weren't changing for the sake of change."
- "I'm not a big fan of GMS. I truly believe that you need to take what's done in the job and personalize that approach. As long as you have your own standardization and have a comfortable way to process it [things works fine]. They'll say, for example, that GMS is supposed to do it this way and do that second and do that third. For me, it may be easier to do three first and two third. That way I can double-check my work. I think that the process should work whatever is best for each individual [*sic*]."
- "I hope that [the union local] grows up and matures, or they will be the nemesis of the whole program. They are different . . . They go to the same churches and they buy their food together at Meijers [an area store]. But, it has to do with the growth and running of GM's business versus being a thorn in everyone's side."

Cultural Dilemmas
This cultural obstacle appears when opposing cultural themes (e.g., innovation vs. standardization; hierarchy vs. empowerment; individualism vs. group focus) have the potential to clash and create tension within the culture. The tension emerges because of the expectation that both themes will operate simultaneously and in concert. The boundaries between the contrasting themes are often ambiguous, leaving the gray areas open to interpretation, as in the following:

- "You can be creative and make things work for the long haul, but there is also a rigidness. You have to do it this way."
- "There will be a lot of complaints. Those complaints would get mentioned to the plant manager and they would get handled. This wasn't great for those in middle management because they didn't have the power to handle the complaint in the first place. But, since the plant manager asked for it all of a sudden, you know, the issues got resolved. So what needs to happen is that the plant manager needs to push down those kinds of decisions to his superintendents."

- "People are concerned about their careers here. People that are seventh and eighth levels, they are looking for the next promotion rather than dealing with the issues . . . I had a project that I presented information on. I got a mark on me because I disturbed the waters. I took a risk."

Cultural Contradictions

All cultures have contradictions and inconsistencies that cause ambiguity and frustration. This cultural obstacle is easily recognized when someone says one thing and then acts in a completely different way. Those behaving in ways contrary to what was said risk losing credibility. Those affected by the contradiction may become jaded and skeptical of future actions such as "getting on board" with new programs (e.g., quality initiatives) or trusting co-workers or leaders, as in the following.

- "We've been through I don't know how many hours of training where they say, 'I don't care what it takes. We won't send out cars that are below our quality standards.' Then we get back on the line and the first thing they say is, 'No, we don't have the time to stop the line and solve this problem. We have to keep going.' So, what kind of message is that sending?"
- "And then there's the issue of *takt* time. It may take . . . 90 seconds for a car to get through your station [but] another car may take 110 seconds. So our foreman . . . says, 'You know what we're going to do? We're going to pitch and *takt*' . . . So now you are allowed to start ahead of your station to compensate when you have these tasks that take 110 seconds. We are getting away from our GMS process."
- "The team concept should have been reiterated. As a team, you share the effort and it's a joint effort. The PMP [production and maintenance partnership] is a partnership. I didn't feel as if the group leader was utilizing the team concept very well. He kept saying, 'You go down there and take care of this' and 'It's all your fault.'"

Cultural Drift

Cultures have the tendency to revert to patterns that are older and well established, and easier and simpler because they are known and understood. Cultural drift often happens when employees are faced with stressful events or decisions at work. Reverting back to old behavior is comfortable, automatic, and something employees could align with more easily than facing the more difficult task of adhering to the new way. This cultural obstacle represents the deterioration of ideals or the slippage associated with those ideals. Cultural changes necessitate constant reinforcement and relearning to remain anchored to the new way, or cultural drift sets in. The following quotations exemplify this obstacle:

- "We'll see some slippage. I am not sure how you guard against it. We will have new people."
- "It's both communicating and walking the talk. There are a lot of tough challenges ahead. There will be an immense amount of training and some of it will be repetitive. We have to follow through, and if we don't, we'll be a failure."
- "The question is: how do you keep the culture elevated so that you're stepping along?"

The Trail They Leave Behind and How to Track That Trail

The obstacles to cultural transformation are revealed in many ways. They leave a trail in employee statements and stories and in employee behavior that reflects their viewpoints. These forms of evidence provided us with clues about the particular difficulties faced in a manufacturing environment, the ways in which those difficulties are manifested, and the impact that they have on the employees and work done in that setting.

Stories serve many functions in a culture, including raising awareness about a particular issue, assisting in the discovery of cultural explanations (e.g., for beliefs, behaviors), reinforcing ideals, solving problems, and improving decision making. Stories transmit vital knowledge as employees share stories with each other or with others (e.g., our research group). The imagery that "stories become knowledge-flow facilitation devices"[5] was useful to us as we uncovered the obstacles associated with organizational-culture change. The concept that stories can "provide a framework for the future"[6] had parallels with our cultural transformation process.

One of the great advantages of the stories we heard and the storytellers with whom we interacted was that we were exposed to a diverse set of organizational experiences. And yet, since the stories were part of a particular type of cultural environment, they shared certain characteristics and themes reflecting those milieux. We were able to detect and extract cultural obstacles from the stories we were told and then analyze them to understand and explain the culture-change processes associated with manufacturing culture.

IDENTIFYING OBSTACLES IN THE CULTURE

Our analysis of the field data combined with reflections on the culture-change literature positioned us to describe the key obstacles associated with cultural transformation in organizational settings. Organizations interested in transforming their culture should take the time to review and understand these obstacles. One of the easiest ways to learn about the obstacles is to read through fieldwork data. In this section we present the data in the form of "story snippets," which we define as short narratives or accounts of some aspect of work life. We view them as high-impact stories pertaining to cultural transformation because they involve experiences or events in which a particular work-culture theme predominates. Typically, the teller of the story contrasts how things are (or were) compared to how they are supposed to be (or could be). Snippets are persuasive. Indeed, they are used as strong rhetorical devices, and there is almost always an emotional "hook" to help readers/listeners understand the story conditions and values that the storyteller is trying to convey. Snippets may focus on cultural obstacles to change or enablers for change (as described in Chapter 6); they normally suggest some follow-up action. When they emphasize cultural obstacles, the follow-up action usually entails modifying behaviors so that those behaviors are consistent with the desired cultural ideal.

Obstacles Related to Managing Performance

Our first example of a snippet tells the story of Janie, an assembly line operator, who had been given limited training and on-the-job practice. The story was told by the employee who trained her. Because she was being trained for only one set of tasks, we can assume that this part of the line was not organized into teams and therefore did not involve job rotation:

> Janie was put on a job and trained on it. But she made a mistake that caused an alarm to go off... When the first alarm went off, I went down and tried to help her again understand how to do what she was asked to do. But then the alarm went off a second time within a two-hour

period. The second time it went off, several other people came down [to her work station]—the MC [manufacturing coordinator][7] came, the superintendent, and [one other individual]. I was still trying to defend her. I told them we were still in the process of training her. There was no one to train her. We only had twenty minutes to break her in.

One obvious barrier theme in this snippet is the insufficient exposure that Janie received to the tasks she was expected to perform. She was not allowed to acculturate completely; that is, the time she spent in training was insufficient. There were two indications that Janie made a serious error. First, the production managers appeared by her workstation when she made the mistake for the second time. Such behavior reflected what would be described as the old way of micromanaging work activity—behavior that often increased the levels of nervousness and tension and did little to resolve the problem; it could be seen as ethnocentric adherence to the old way. Second, the alarm sounded and the line stopped each time Janie made the mistake; using the *andon* cord (that sent both an auditory and visual signal to indicate that help was needed) was a rarity in this plant at this time. Therefore, if the line ever stopped, it meant that the problem had to be fixed immediately rather than being tagged for repair and that a delay had occurred that put at risk the plant's ability to achieve its daily quota. The snippet also highlights the divisions within the management chain (cross-cultural conflict) as evident in the use of the word "defend"; the trainer makes clear that he was siding with Janie.

This snippet describes the cultural conditions that act as barriers to movement toward the Ideal Cultural Model in a culture that encapsulates incomplete acculturation, ethnocentrism, cross-cultural conflict, and cultural contradictions. The management chain exhibited little tolerance for any line stoppage even when a newly trained employee was involved and seemed unconcerned about their collective impact on the assembler. Productivity was favored over proper training, creating a cultural contradiction. Cross-cultural conflict paired the employee serving as trainer and the assembler together in opposition to production managers in the plant; the latter appeared disinterested in the trainer's explanation. In addition, nowhere in the snippet is there any reference to the foreman, whose role involved mitigating issues between hourly and managerial employees.

Obstacles Embedded in "Walking the Talk"

We heard this next snippet from a tool-and-die maker at a stamping plant.[8] He indicated that plant employees had received GMS training so they knew that the *andon* cord should be used to stop the line if a problem arose:

> I have to say one frustrating thing is the double talk from management . . . You've got GM's GMS, and if they [management] want it to stick, they have to back themselves up. It's like . . . we signed up for this and then they fall back and contradict themselves . . . David [a manager] found out that he needed a die maker. Instead of calling him with the *andon* cord, which is what we were taught, he called one of the guys on his two-way radio that he had. We were told not to use radios but to use the *andon* cord . . . We got the die maker over to him [but] I'm not sure if it [the fact that he used his two-way radio] was ever addressed.

This incident captures the stamping plant in the throes of change. While its production process (i.e., GMS) was new, its employees were still accustomed to work practices associated with an earlier time. The die maker singles out David for having violated the very GMS principles he advocated. Managers are expected to serve as role models and "walk the talk," that is, follow through on any new work-related expectations. Advocating a particular work practice and then disregarding it represents a key cultural contradiction. In addition, some cultural drift and resistance to change seem to have set in since the GMS training occurred, perhaps because the training was not consistently reinforced. The credibility of plant leadership, as well as the credibility and relevance of the new production process, was damaged when the new expectations of using the *andon* cord in lieu of the two-way radio were not consistently followed and advocated by management. Cross-cultural conflict emerged, evident in the "us versus them" statements expressed by the die maker. Interestingly, the die maker does not critique himself or his co-workers for not asking the manager to explain his reasoning for using the two-way radio—despite the fact that GMS advocates employee empowerment.

Obstacles in Making Your Contribution

This story snippet examines role perceptions in an assembly plant. An assembler comments negatively on the role of skilled tradesmen to his foreman: "When I was working A line, I would often see these three guys sitting across from where I was stationed. One was a millwright[9] and one was an electrician and one was [another tradesman]. I would say to my foreman, 'Look at those three guys just sitting over there,' and they were all sleeping. They made twice as much money as me, and they get weekend work [i.e., overtime]. But how do we want to get the car to the customer with the least amount of time and work put into it and high quality?"

The key cultural obstacle expressed in this story is cross-cultural conflict. The assembler calls attention to job classification differences related to workload and work expectations. He points to three trades-men who are sleeping on the job and indicates that they also make more money than he does and are able to get additional work on the weekends at an overtime rate. The assembler is upset because he has none of these opportunities. The assembler also asks how GM can be competitive if tradesmen are not pulling their weight. Whether or not the interpretation of the story snippet is appropriate, it illustrates a commonly held perception that "sleeping on the job" does not exem-plify the American work ethic. Such sources of tension reinforce rather than break down barriers across job classification lines.

Obstacles Linked with Demonstrating Team Support

This story snippet involves a work group of assembly-line workers in the body shop (the portion of the line assembling the vehicle body). The plant was in the process of changing how production was orga-nized. This work group participated in a modified form of job rota-tion. Two assemblers, Joel and Kurt, always worked together when performing a set of tasks. Then, every hour they switched to the other set of tasks for which their work team was responsible. They offered succinct perceptions of the two co-workers who were part of their team of four. The issue Joel and Kurt complained about involved building up stock for use at their workstations. It was clearly a sore subject because they only infrequently spoke to their co-workers.

Joel: We fill up the studs for them, but they won't for us.
Kurt: We rotate too! How were they brought up?

This example highlights four obstacles: ethnocentrism, cross-cul-tural conflict, cultural dilemmas, and resistance to change. Ethno-centrism appears in Joel and Kurt's comments; they believe that the other pair in their team should reciprocate with them and keep the parts restocked. This same issue creates cross-cultural conflict within the team because there is no agreement on the work process. There is evidence of a cultural dilemma related, in part, to the shift from individualized work to shared work. Should Joel and Kurt only take care of their own stock or be mindful of the team's stock? Finally, there also seems to be some resistance to change by Joel and Kurt's co-workers. As GM plants implement GMS more fully, more problem solving discussions, not fewer, will be required. In this example, attempts to reach agreement had been tabled.

OBSTACLES TIED TO AN
OBSERVATION ON THE PLANT FLOOR

Another fruitful way of identifying and understanding obstacles to change involves observing workplace interactions. While observing, one has the benefit of using one's senses to experience a situation. The description below is based on an observation of the breakage and repair of a plant stud gun.[10] The description reads like a story, so we refer to it colloquially as the "Stud Gun Story." It provides a much more complicated and in-depth view of the surrounding context than a snippet would. The overall sequence of events included employee reaction to the stud gun failure by those present before the repair began, the conflict emerging between the electrician and the contract maintenance supervisor over the particular technical reason for the failure, the electrician's explanation for the stud gun's failure, and the subsequent repairs to the stud gun.[11]

Failure and Repair of the Stud Gun

At the beginning of afternoon break, a stud gun breaks and falls on box of studs, which scatter on the plant floor. Tracy Meerwarth, from our research group, is in team room with Rose, an assembler, when they hear a loud hissing sound. Rose says, "Oh, that is a problem with the air gun." They leave the team room with another team member, Joe. All of them walk to farthest back section of the plant where one of the underbody lines is located. They see that the air gun pipe is not attached to the stud gun, a metal box that held the studs for the air gun is tipped over, and studs are all over the floor. Rose says, "I have never seen something like this before."

The team coordinator (an hourly group leader) appears and calls the pipe fitter and electrician on his two-way radio. Within two minutes, two electricians arrive on their cart. A pipe fitter arrives shortly afterward. Everyone who enters the robot cell "locks out."[12] The pipe fitter, Greg, turns off the stud gun. In the meantime, Tracy asks Rose how long it will take to do a repair. Rose jokes, "At least two weeks" but continues, "actually about a half hour or so."

Ned, an electrician, assesses the problem. He concludes that (1) the auxiliary (or back-up) stud gun cannot be used in place of the broken stud gun and (2) the air line system to both the broken stud gun and the auxiliary stud gun must be fixed, requiring that the line be shut down. Next on the scene is Al, a contract maintenance supervisor. With limited observation and no discussion with Ned or Greg, Al says, "Bypass it! We are in the business of making cars." By this comment, Al directs Ned to use the auxiliary gun as back up. Ned replies, "Stay out of the way because you do not know what you are talking about. You do not understand the problem."

Ned walks over to Joe who is standing near Tracy and Rose and says, "I have been telling them [management] that it has never been a safe operation here. I have two years of notes on this equipment." Al comments that the studs on the floor need to be cleaned. Rose explains to Tracy that the studs have to be cleaned before they can be reused. Then Al says to everyone standing nearby, "We need to clean up those studs. That is my profit sharing!" Al leaves. Sam begins to pick up the studs, while Ned and another electrician work inside the robot cell on the equipment.

To get the back-up stud gun working, the air flow has to be restored. Ned knows that he has about fifteen minutes of break time to work on it. It takes another fifteen minutes after the line starts up to get the air flow moving to both the stud gun and the auxiliary stud gun. The stud gun breakdown does not cause a problem as far as the line went because the banks[13] are full. Once Ned and the other electrician get the air line fixed, they are able to bypass the broken stud gun and use the auxiliary gun. At this point, the line starts up again. By the end of the day, Ned repairs the broken stud gun.

Key Obstacles in the Stud Gun Observation

This vehicle assembly plant was scheduled to "cease operations," or close, at the time the stud gun observation occurred.[14] Plant personnel were aware of this pending change, though no date for the plant's closure had been communicated. Plant personnel also knew that a site was being prepared nearby for the construction of a new assembly plant; employees understood that they would be considered for positions in that new plant. In addition, the plant had taken some steps in becoming compliant with GMS. For example, the team structure was in place along some parts of the assembly line, and some plant personnel—especially plant leadership—had received training in GMS principles. Both of these transitions had an impact on the way in which equipment repair proceeded.

Ethnocentrism

The first indication of conflict during the observation appeared as Al, the contract maintenance supervisor, commanded Ned, the electrician, to use the auxiliary stud gun. His authoritative style and tone of voice left little room for discussion on the part of the repair team. He imposed his assumption on them about the cause and solution to the equipment problem. He neither considered any other alternative possibilities to explain the stud gun failure nor solicited input from the technical experts present. He did not engage in any problem solving with the team coordinator, skilled tradesmen, or anyone else on the scene. In short, he made an uninformed, unilateral judgment. His response to the equipment failure ran counter to the problem-solving approach advocated by GMS as well as the Ideal Cultural Model. Moreover, he conveyed an attitude of superiority toward those he supervised, neither acknowledging their skill sets, nor understanding the value of strong working relationships.

Cross-Cultural Conflict

Ned's response to Al confirmed and then exacerbated the tension when he confronted Al in a similar commanding verbal style. In fact, Ned called attention to Al's lack of knowledge of the particular situation, though his words suggested derision of Al's general knowledge of such matters. Ned did not respond appropriately to his supervisor—at least from a collaborative standpoint. He treated Al just as he had been treated—as an adversary, rather than as a source of support. The tension reflected a divided manufacturing culture in which management and labor were on opposing sides.

We learned or confirmed two other dimensions of cross-cultural conflict in our follow-up interviewing. First, Al's title was contract maintenance supervisor. Because Al was not considered a full-time GM employee, it was easier to question his authority; contract employees were not treated as full members of the GM team. Second, we discovered that Al was not an electrician, yet he was supervising electricians. At least part of Ned's outburst can be explained by the contradiction between Al's presumed authority and Al's lack of electrical expertise.

Cultural Contradictions

Ned's statement to Joe about the long-standing equipment problems signaled the potential for cultural contradictions—a point later confirmed in our follow-up interviews. The issue for Ned and other skilled tradesmen revolved around insufficient preventative maintenance on plant equipment. As Ned stated in the follow-up interview, "Everything at [the plant] is worn out. We need more work to keep ours [tools] going." At the same time, Ned reported that the skilled trades were expected to keep the aging equipment in good working order. He said, "You [can't] work overtime but you're supposed to have high grades on preventative maintenance." He continued his line of reasoning by making two related points. First, he focused on the reduction in skilled tradesmen despite the apparent need: "The better we keep our areas [in the plant] going, [the more] they [management] start eliminating the guys. The harder you worked, the more guys they would get rid of." Ned also commented on the contradiction between the plant's stated goal of quality and its actual goal of quotas: "Quality is just that—talk. The number one priority is jobs off the end of the line. If I can bypass it [a problem situation], then I should."

These themes of quality versus quantity and ongoing preventative maintenance versus attention to equipment only after a malfunction are consistent with the diversified mass-production paradigm—particularly in recent decades. The findings from our 1986 fieldwork in a GM truck plant, for example, highlighted the discrepancy between the stated plant goal of quality compared with the actual plant goal of quotas.[15] Cultural contradictions have noteworthy implications for work cultures. They can damage credibility, put a damper on morale, lead to distrust, and reduce employee effectiveness, among other impacts.

Cultural Drift

The deterioration in preventative-maintenance schedules seemed to correspond with both the decision to terminate operations at the plant and the decision to hire temporary contract employees to fill the increasing number of open salaried positions. Ned indicated that he had "two years of notes on this equipment." This shift away from a work practice that skilled trades perceived as valuable was at odds with the skilled trades' ideal. Preventative maintenance was an important dimension of their job, trade, and identity at work, as well as being a way to increase their level of income (i.e., through overtime). But we also learn another dimension of what was behind Ned's frustration when he said, "I have been telling them [management] that it has never been a safe operation here." Ned linked the failed stud gun with the potential for a safety issue. While safety in the plant environment has been paramount at GM for decades, the drift away from preventative maintenance in this plant, according to Ned, had the potential to affect plant safety.

This particular equipment failure reveals the difficult situation facing management of this plant. They were eager to control costs—particularly preventative-maintenance costs on equipment. Because most preventative maintenance on the robots took place during non-scheduled work hours, it required overtime. Justifying such a line item would have been difficult given that the plant was going to close. Plant management also sought to control the costs of skilled labor under these changing manufacturing conditions. Ned's comment about "eliminating the guys" is a reference to the reduction in the headcount of skilled trades on the plant floor. Thus, management appeared to be trying to balance its production costs in the context of a transition, while the perceptions associated with those decisions took a hit just as the aging equipment did.

Having to Learn a New Culture

Another obstacle becomes apparent later when we learn about the immediate production environment of the breakage. Two elements of the environment are relevant: the stud gun broke when "the banks were full," and when this portion of underbody was on one of its breaks. Al's strong reaction to the stud gun failure suggests a lack of familiarity with these kinds of manufacturing details; he had not been fully acculturated into plant culture. This portion of underbody had a sizeable cushion against a line shut down. Yet, as we knew from our general fieldwork, the plant had only started hiring contract employees to replace the permanent salaried employees who were interviewing for jobs at other GM sites.

Another dimension of cultural learning that Al had not yet absorbed related to his interactions with the work groups reporting to him. We do not know if Al had been formally exposed to GMS training as his full-time colleagues had. Regardless, he would have heard about concepts such as teamwork and empowerment—as evident from the numerous references to these concepts by study participants from this plant. Yet, Al's relationship with skilled trades suggested that even if he had been aware of this new orientation to manufacturing work, he opted for an approach that represented the old way. Al could only have known about the old way if he had experienced it on the plant floor. We knew from our fieldwork in the plant that the old, autocratic way still existed. Thus, Al, as a newcomer, learned enough about plant culture to perform his supervisory role. He knew that quotas and cost reductions were vitally important to a plant in transition, and he worked to ensure plant performance on the basis of these measures.

Stud Gun Observation Outcomes

An interesting note about this incident was that all of the energy was tied up in a few brief exchanges between Al and Ned and between Ned and those standing by the robot cell. The culture was revealed cogently and vigorously; then its power and strength seemed to become latent as the air line and stud gun repairs were made. The outcome of the repair was documented, but it is almost as if it were an afterthought.

There was never a hint of doubt that Ned would be able to fix the problem. He had the technical capabilities to perform the repairs and the access to additional support (e.g., from the other electrician, from the team coordinator) if he needed it. Ned also seemed motivated and engaged in his trade. He was responsive, arriving at the robot cell "within two minutes" of being called. Once Al left the area, Ned got right to work on the repair. He reported that he was able to fix the airline within thirty minutes and the broken stud gun by the end of the shift. The outcome, from a technical standpoint, was successful. In fact, all the skilled tradesmen appeared to perform their jobs well and in a timely fashion. The repairs were made and production quotas were maintained.

But culture is not just about technical outcomes. It is about relationships, roles, perceptions, expectations, and rules. In the cultural environment of this plant—a plant in transition to teamwork and empowerment—this incident represented the past rather than the future. Nothing about the interaction between Ned and Al suggested a hopeful outlook or a progression toward the ideal. The interactions illustrated a directive and divided culture in which listening was not the norm, information was not shared, and lessons were not learned. The old way seemed to have reasserted itself, much to Ned's dismay. Relationships had been damaged and any collaboration across the "lines of demarcation" had not yet become the way of the present. Cultural drift, with respect to preventative maintenance, had set in with little evidence of movement toward the ideal. The cultural transformation process had stalled.

Barriers Can Be Overcome:
Transformations in Spite of Obstacles

Organizational-culture change toward the ideal takes time and requires the implementation of strategies to cope with the cultural obstacles encountered along the way. We worked with the GM community to uncover both general and specific strategies to overcome or avoid the seven primary cultural obstacles in ways that should eventually lead to a plant culture that is closer to the anticipated ideal.

One example occurred during an off-site with a plant leadership team. Our research group presented the Stud Gun Story and story snippets within the context of a discussion of what could be done to overcome identified barriers to the ideal. The strategy we used consisted of a number of interactive "what-if" scenarios and discussions. An attendee sought our perspective on alternative actions by plant personnel. He asked, "What could the contract maintenance supervisor have done differently?" In the second type of question, a different attendee questioned the behavior of plant personnel. He commented, "I'm surprised that the team coordinator wasn't involved much. The team coordinator wasn't Tracy or Rose, was it?" Toward the end of this off-site, new questions were raised leading to other ideas for alternate what-if scenarios:

- Why did Al direct Ned to bypass the stud gun rather than ask Ned to explain the situation?
- Why did Ned get so angry with Al?
- What if Ned engaged Al by offering an explanation for the equipment failure?
- Why did Sam, the team coordinator, choose not to intervene?
- What might have been the most effective ways of responding to the escalation in conflict?
- What impact did the equipment failure have on the culture of the work group?

What-if scenarios help demonstrate how an organizational culture could change based on modifications in the behavior of participants in that culture. Instead of focusing solely on "What happened?" they eventually were able to speculate and frame their questions in terms of "What could have happened?" Envisioning a different future represents an important step toward that future. In this case, the what-if scenarios led directly and indirectly to the identification of both "fixes" and the overall discussion of enablers, which are presented in Chapter 6.

From Obstacles to Enablers

This chapter explores the linkages between basic cultural change and transformational theory through snippets, stories, and what-if scenarios. It leads to a critical understanding of key elements of the transformational model, which includes obstacles (in this chapter), enablers (Chapter 6), and tools (Chapter 7). We find both specific and more generic obstacles to change, depending on whether we are looking at a sector of the organization (such as the plant floor or the manager's office) or on a more general level (GM as a whole); we list and provide examples of the seven primary obstacles.

One of the "whole-organization" conditions that is an obstacle to change is GM's complexity. That complexity is expressed in several ways. We found, at the time of our research, that GM had what was seen by most people at all levels of the organization to be an outstanding work force interested in change (as evidenced by the NUMMI, Eisenach, and Silao experiences). Yet, at the same time, the champions (or internal change agents) supporting those changes encountered persistent cultural flaws, conflicts, and divisions in the existing GM culture that prevented a full transformation to the ideal culture from any of the existing starting points or from the starting point of GMS.

One condition that is consistently mentioned as an organizational-level obstacle to cultural transformation is the mixed hierarchical and highly compartmentalized structure of GM, sometimes called the GM "silo-ing effect." That structural complexity makes it hard for a cultural transformation to travel smoothly through the organization as a whole. The result is pockets of transformation vying with pockets of resistance or both vying with an alternative cultural consensus (e.g., GMS vs. Quality Network, union vs. management). The end result is that subsets of the organization change relatively easily, but the organization as a whole is remarkably resistant to cultural change on a large scale even when that change is desired, sponsored, and reinforced.

Therefore, realizing that we were working in a complex environment that was both supportive (locally) of change but also resistant (globally) to change, we began to explore those elements of the existing cultural system that support, allow, or expand the process of cultural transformation. We began focusing on the positive elements of the existing culture (enablers) to move the process of incremental, evolutionary change along. This focus was our version of "think global, act local" within the realm of desired cultural change. Chapter 6 provides strong evidence that the culture of GM has sufficient, positive processes in place to achieve an incremental evolutionary change.[16]

CHAPTER 6

RELIANCE ON CULTURAL PROCESSES DURING CULTURAL TRANSFORMATION

The literature on deliberate or planned cultural change, development, and innovation provides a valuable set of guidelines for identifying both the barriers to innovation and change (as demonstrated in Chapter 5) and the conditions or processes that increase the probability that directed change will achieve its goals successfully.[1] Some of the key elements of planned change depend on the definition of culture being used to direct the cultural change (e.g., a focus on behavior vs. a focus on ideas),[2] while others depend on the interplay between cultural change and the psychology of change.[3]

In all cases, planned change must be acceptable and sustainable.[4] The acceptability of change depends on establishing a "perceived need" for the change[5] and a willingness or empowerment to change.[6] Acceptability depends heavily on appropriate levels of engagement by the individuals most impacted by the change.[7] Sustainability of the change is always a challenge,[8] though a number of the important lessons learned come from our understanding how culture is transmitted to both children and adults[9] and how that transmission supports cultural change and cultural stability.[10]

Many of the key elements of directed organizational-culture change can be summarized when Romer's Rule[11] is applied to the overall concept of social change: "Systems theorists, paleobiologists, and social scientists alike have used Romer's Rule to predict and explain change. The general lesson is that the goal of stability is the main impetus for change. Evolution occurs incrementally as gradually changing systems keep on attempting to maintain themselves [as they gradually change]."[12]

The basic principle here is that evolutionary change in social systems favors stability over instability, while it also allows change to occur. Evolutionary change normally occurs in an incremental fashion, since incremental change is less disruptive than abrupt change to an existing system. Abrupt social change (such as revolution) often produces highly unstable social systems, at least during the revolutionary changeover period. Thus, it is possible to predict both the obstacles to change, using Romer's Rule, and the ways of overcoming those obstacles. It is possible to make change incremental, appropriate for the local environment, and directed at issues that activate "community" (e.g., plant culture) values. Community members have "down-to-earth and specific objectives" and can be contrasted with abstract "planners' values," such as "learning a better way," "progressing," "increasing technical know-how," "improving efficiency," or "adopting modern techniques."[13]

The down-to-earth and specific objectives that make up the enablers in the ideal plant culture fit with this interpretation of Romer's Rule. As a consequence, after identifying obstacles to change linked with the ideal plant culture, we also began to look for key elements in the culture that would promote or sustain cultural change. These positive elements of cultural change are an important part of the cultural transformation process. They create an appropriate and sustainable environment for change. They represent the possibility of transmitting the new cultural ideal and reinforcing it. They identify consensus about the direction or goals of change. In short, they help people learn the "new way."

Enablers for Cultural Transformation

Organizations grapple with many questions about change: what to change, under what circumstances to change, and how to change, among others. These questions help frame some of the important decisions related to the change process. Our study participants in the Ideal Plant Culture study revealed their interest in transforming manufacturing culture. Their statements, stories, and behaviors indicated that they wanted the change to be as widespread as possible—across job functions, levels, and classifications—and to occur as quickly as possible. However, they also suggested that they did not know how to change. Therefore, in this chapter, we focus on dimensions of the culture that can facilitate the cultural transformation process.

As we began our fieldwork, we heard the word "enablers" and realized that it was used to describe cultural processes that help influence the direction and speed of organizational-culture change. We soon incorporated the term into our interview questions and found that study participants readily responded to it, as captured in the following example:

Question: "What would be the enablers for this kind of ideal plant culture [you have just described]?"

Response: "The leadership; team building; spend[ing] time together; develop[ing] the relationships."

The elements in this response are both specific and positive in support of cultural change. Other examples included "I see the ideal culture as a huge enabler [to becoming even better than we are]," "You can give me the [collaboration] tools, but if I don't have the enablers, I can't get the work done," and "The [project] . . . is on collaboration as an enabler for performance."

Thus, the term "enablers" refers to the processes within the existing culture that support cultural transformation. Enablers have the potential to be useful both in planning for change and in guiding the organization toward a particular end point—such as the cultural ideal. In the GM case, a collaborative culture represents the target for cultural transformation. Numerous enablers are part of GM manufacturing culture and can be tapped to assist in the change process. These enablers temper the impact of any obstacles that arise to prevent, delay, or slow cultural transformation. They can be invoked to help plan for anticipated roadblocks ranging from everyday challenges to major crises. Similarly, they can be used to help address those roadblocks directly by initiating possible counteractions. Their activation during a particular event or incident can serve as a positive counterweight to those obstacles preventing progress toward the ideal. Figure 6.1 illustrates the Bridge Model with the addition of the enablers. With the addition of the enablers to the Bridge Model, we have a composite conceptualization of the time element and key components of the cultural transformation process from the perspective of our study participants.

Our analysis of the GM-specific enablers provided an important enhancement to the basic cultural transformation model. There were a significant number of specific enablers that employees directly associated with the Ideal Cultural Model, both as a whole, and with specific quadrants of the model. Some of the general and specific enablers are activated repeatedly in the culture. Others appear less frequently, though they have an important impact when they become active. We also found that each quadrant of the Ideal Cultural Model could be associated with both generic (cross-quadrant) and particular (quadrant-specific) enablers. In the following sections, we describe the enablers by quadrant, recognizing that many of them cross-cut the model.

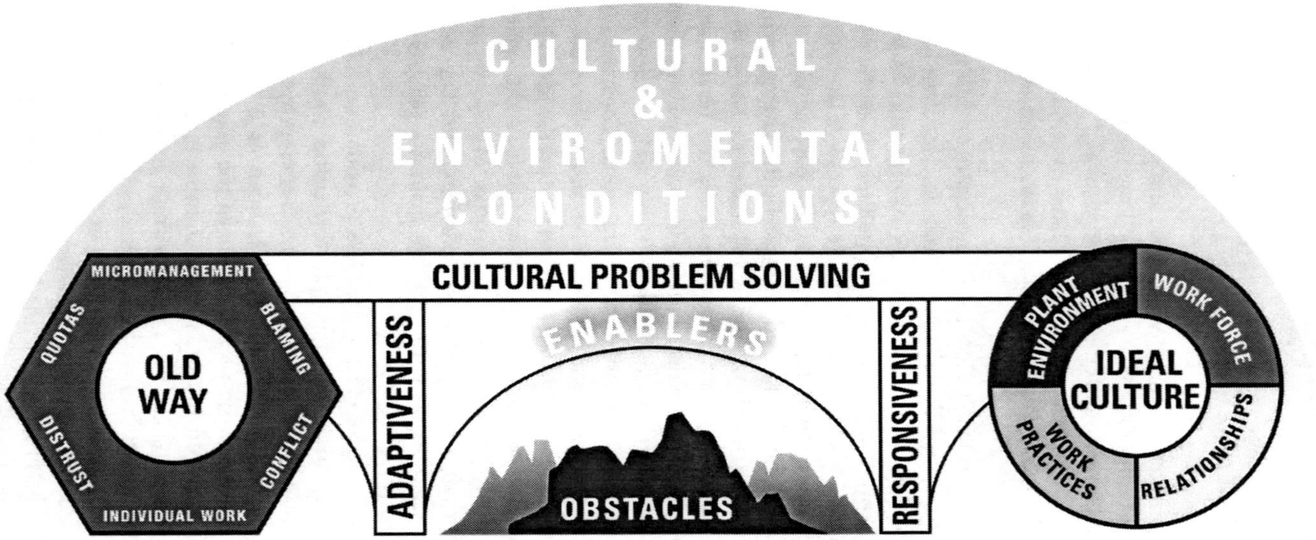

Figure 6.1 Bridge Model with enablers

The list of enablers we present is not exhaustive, but it is instructive. We describe the ones that appear prominently in study-participant descriptions of their experiences or in our observations of them at work. We view this set of enablers as a "living document," in which additional enablers could be added to the set over time, and other enablers could become less important. Organizations, generally, will have to identify their own set of enablers and then decide how and when to apply them to the cultural issues that they face. Moreover, any cultural transformation needs to accommodate agreed-upon goals and possibly non–agreed-upon goals (which have the potential to become barriers to change).

Plant Environment

The enablers for the Plant Environment component of the Ideal Cultural Model emphasize processes related to the physical structure and the technology that nurture collaboration. These enablers can help employees transition away from the "old" plant design and layout associated with physical discomfort (e.g., occupational injuries) to new interiors and technology that are ergonomically designed to enhance comfort and ease of use. The rationales for the enabling processes are embedded within the descriptions. Each could be expanded to provide additional detail. For example, designing comfortable workstations could be expanded to include situating restrooms close to the workstations to reduce the stress of being at a distance and enable employees to enjoy the majority of their break time in conversation, reading the newspaper, or enjoying a cup of coffee; employees often identify very specific processes they would like to see in a potential future, as is the case in the following:

- *Designing comfortable workstations* involves arranging the workspace with input from employees, thereby taking advantage of employee expertise and maximizing employee effectiveness.
- *Providing areas for community building* entails creating specific places in which employees can meet to gather and share information and create a community feeling on the plant floor.
- *Improving ergonomic standards* refers to keeping equipment updated and arranging it so employees can perform their work tasks efficiently and effectively, without injury or accident.
- *Consistently using preventative maintenance* focuses on the regular inspection and upkeep of equipment so that it is kept in good

working condition and employees can do the work they have been assigned to do.

Overall, the enablers pertaining to this quadrant of the model help to create and sustain an environment that is conducive to employees' physical and emotional health. Employees are more likely to act in a collaborative and cordial way when they are comfortable in their work environment, doing their work, and around others who are part of their work community.

Work Force

The Work Force enablers represent the processes that support the vital "people" component of our collaborative model. Enablers for the Work Force quadrant focus attention on acquiring people skills and technical competencies to help to create a highly effective culture. The ability to collaborate is compromised unless there are enablers that reinforce work-related competencies and individuals who serve as role models. The processes that follow encourage all plant employees to "check in" and see to what extent their actions support a collaborative ideal:

- *Showing proficiency as a qualified and skilled work force* involves demonstrating the appropriate knowledge, expertise, and experience on a consistent basis to position the plant for success.
- *Serving effectively in a given role* emphasizes the importance and relevance of both technical and relationship skills.
- *Exhibiting a people-centered orientation* shows the importance of employees in achieving plant goals and objectives.
- *Demonstrating involvement and commitment* consists of employee engagement in the work of the enterprise including work-group or plant-wide problem solving.
- *Providing appropriate and sufficient training* involves instruction and practice in relevant areas of plant operations so that proficiency is ensured and employees are exposed to new practices and processes.
- *Cultivating work ethic and pride* refers to the interest, energy, and effort devoted to the accomplishment of work goals.
- *Ensuring the availability of experts* involves staffing the workplace with sufficient numbers of knowledgeable employees who can be tapped to perform both routine and nonroutine work.

- *Responding to tasks quickly and effectively* involves a fast and competent reaction to emerging issues so that they are handled accurately, completely, and efficiently.

A culture in transition from the old way to the new struggles with balancing a demanding production schedule with the appropriate levels of quality and productivity and sufficient attention to the people who make the organization function. This set of enablers makes explicit certain preferred behaviors (e.g., hardworking and well-trained individuals, critical people skills) regardless of job position or role. As these enablers become more closely associated with the work force, it will signal that cultural transformation is underway.

Work Practices

Work Practices, tackling work tasks, developing new ideas and processes, and engaging with others in problem solving are part of the everyday work and focus of employees. The enablers that support Work Practices present daily, ongoing opportunities to move toward the ideal culture of collaboration. Work Practice enablers frame how the work gets done through such means as sharing information, working together, recognizing success, and empowering. These enablers include the following:

- *Setting clear expectations* involves clarity of expression about work goals, objectives, and assignments as a way to minimize ambiguity and misunderstanding.
- *Participating in job rotations*, defined as involvement in multiple kinds of work tasks on an alternating basis, increases the likelihood that ideas are exchanged about the best ways to complete the work and that work-related issues are addressed promptly.
- *Encouraging work-group problem solving* emphasizes the investigation and resolution of work-group issues by the work group.
- *Maintaining leadership visibility and accessibility* involves linking plant personnel together by reducing status and role barriers and encouraging camaraderie, interest, and understanding across roles.
- *Empowering employees* is the process for encouraging employees to offer input and make decisions about key aspects of their work assignments.
- *Following standardized work* involves completing work tasks according to a best-practice standard so as to reduce errors while ensuring high levels of performance.

- *Accepting accountability* entails taking responsibility for a particular set of work tasks.
- *Rebalancing the work pace* refers to organizing the work tasks on a sustained, yet comfortable, basis within a specified *takt* time.
- *Sharing responsibilities* refers to the process of dividing up the work tasks or duties to enhance both a culture of collaboration and successful outcomes.
- *Sharing and using lessons learned* involves creating systems of knowledge sharing and use as part of the work process to hasten problem solving and innovation based on learning from past experiences.
- *Providing support* consists offering encouragement, resources, or assistance through one's own labor, expertise, and efforts.

These enablers have an important role to play in cultural transformation because they are part of the regular work activity. Each of the individual Work Practice enablers is at a different stage in the cultural transformation to a collaborative culture—with some in the early stages (e.g., sharing and using lessons learned) and some in the middle stages (e.g., participating in job rotations, encouraging work-group problem solving).

Relationships

Employees view Relationships as the glue holding the organizational culture together. The Relationships component of the Ideal Cultural Model is filled with stories that advocate strong, healthy, collaborative interactions and working relationships. The enablers for the Relationships component of the Ideal Cultural Model are aligned with these stories. The Relationship enablers include the following processes:

- *Maintaining healthy relationships* is defined as cultivating supportive and collaborative relationships through mutual exchange or reciprocity.
- *Providing clear, honest, timely communication* consists of relaying information that is straightforward, truthful, and prompt.
- *Exhibiting trust* is defined as a process of instilling confidence in the integrity of a person, group, work system, and the like.
- *Showing respect* involves acting in a way that conveys a feeling of high regard, honor, or esteem.
- *Displaying job empathy* entails putting oneself in another person's shoes by understanding and appreciating his or her feelings or experiences.
- *Recognizing effort* is the act of acknowledging and praising the efforts of others.

- *Creating a win-win orientation* involves valuing and seeking benefit for all involved.
- *Taking time for relationship building* refers to initiating and cultivating rapport and understanding with others.
- *Proactive listening* involves concentrating and reflecting on what is being said so as to gather accurate and complete information and enhance problem solving.

Work is a social and cultural activity. In a collaborative work culture, there are expectations that employee behavior be outwardly directed to create a community of people working in concert toward organizational goals. According to our study participants, the Relationships quadrant of the Ideal Cultural Model is the least developed of all the quadrants. Given the long-standing emphasis on work task and work output, this assessment is not surprising. Significant time, effort, and energy will need to be devoted to building and maintaining collaborative relationships to achieve the collaborative ideal.

Identifying Enablers in the Culture

We were successful in identifying and then validating enablers in different GM environments. Based on our experience, we recommend that each organization going through some form of planned transformation take the time to search out and utilize their own set of enablers in addition to identifying the barriers to change that they face. When the enablers are culture specific rather than generic, they are more valid, credible, and useful to the organization during cultural transformation.

Our process, which can be replicated, was to compile study-participant examples and experiences into groups. We refer to these brief descriptions as statement snippets. Each group of statement snippets reflects a common theme viewed as a desirable feature in the ideal plant culture. As with the story snippets described in Chapter 5, these statement snippets were gathered on the plant floor. We examined the statement snippets for evidence of key enablers that could help in cultural transformation.

Enablers Linked with Supervisory Success

Employee perceptions of their work culture are directly affected by their relationships, particularly by those with their supervisors, subordinates, or both. We selected the snippets that follow because they contrast negative and positive examples of this hierarchical relationship. Often, individuals are judged in terms of the quality of interactions in which they engage. The oral tradition of manufacturing culture demonizes those who treat plant personnel harshly. Because these examples of the old way are durable—that is, they circulate in cultural memory for a long time—they likely present a higher hurdle for the organization in search of change. Numerous examples of the old way reflect not only the inattention to relationships but also the abuse of those relationships as well. Employee recollections have highlighted the inappropriate ways in which employees were treated, especially under conditions when production pressures were high. Under these circumstances, trust and respect plummet along with plant performance indicators. Dan, an engineer, described one situation in which he was involved:

> At one point, I had three different breakdowns happen at the same time. I went to the first one and the skilled-trades guys were taking care of it. I went to the second one and they [the skilled trades] took care of that one. And I got to the third one and everybody was there—my boss, my boss's boss, the production guy's boss, and his boss's boss. There were so many people there that my tradesman couldn't even get close to fix the problem. And the MC [manufacturing coordinator] just unloaded on me. He was screaming at me and asking me why the heck I wasn't there. I had had enough. I said, "You're in the way; let him get in there and fix it." After that incident occurred, I was advised to go to third shift.

Such recollections of the old way compare poorly with statements about the ideal. The following is one hourly employee's perspective of his salaried supervisor. Jim's portrayal is consistent with many of the features of an ideal plant culture. His description was unsolicited; one day he just started talking about her.

Jim: Beverly is one of the best supervisors I have ever had. You should go over and speak with her.
Elizabeth: What characteristics make a good manager?
Jim: She listens. She treats us like people. She takes what we say and puts it together. She doesn't need someone telling her how to run her area. She knows how to do it. She also doesn't say, "I'm the boss. You're the employee. Do what I tell you." She's the right person to work in that position. She would ask me to help her with something, and I would ask her to do favors for me. It wasn't, "Give me. Give me."

Jim's comments reveal the degree to which he admired and respected his supervisor. Several enablers are evident from this passage. Beverly's behavior is linked with maintaining healthy relationships, exhibiting trust, showing respect, and proactive listening (the Relationships quadrant). She seems to act in an inclusive way that welcomes input and suggestions. She also engages in reciprocity by doing things to help those around her. Jim's account highlights processes such as serving effectively in a given role, exhibiting a people-centered orientation, and demonstrating involvement and commitment (the Work Force quadrant). Thus, Jim views Beverly as both technically and culturally competent—important attributes in the ideal plant culture. Beverly also appears to be one of those supervisors who maintains visibility and accessibility (the Work Practices quadrant). His praise of her crosscuts the three different quadrants of the Ideal Cultural Model: Relationships, Work Force, and Work Practices. Interestingly, Jim's evaluation of his supervisor was not negatively affected by the gender and ethnic differences between them.

By contrast, Dan's account of the leadership at his plant delineates a chaotic situation in which tempers were frayed and problem solving was weak. The MC's accusatory wording and the equally negative counterresponse by Dan suggest the lack of cooperative activity across departments (i.e., engineering and production) and across roles. Even Dan's own boss does not intervene in the exchange to mediate, or mitigate, the situation.

It is useful to compare the two descriptions. In Jim's example, the enablers help in identifying those aspects of the current and ideal culture that are valued. The enablers focus on what is happening within the current culture and, at the same time, reflect what should be an integral part of the ideal culture. The particular enablers in Jim's discussion tap into multiple dimensions of the Ideal Cultural Model, providing a fairly robust distribution of cultural processes that are part of the cultural ideal. Despite similarity in content, we see no evidence of enablers in Dan's example (other than the fact that the skilled trades had apparently responded to the breakdowns quickly and effectively). His example simply tells us about the kinds of cultural processes that are not valued and that should not play a role in the ideal culture.

Enablers Related to Hands-On Work Experience

Issues often arise on the plant floor for those work tasks tied to the pace of the assembly line. We selected these two sets of statement snippets because they contrast divergent views of the expectations and responsibilities surrounding work roles. Assemblers may indicate that the set of tasks they have been assigned contains too much "content" or has been allocated too little *takt* time. In the old way, assembler views may not have been addressed or addressed adequately. In the new or ideal culture, assemblers seek confirmation of the difficulties they have experienced by asking salaried employees to "try out the job" to see how they (the salaried) fare. Engaging in the actual work tasks becomes a mechanism for understanding the work tasks holistically, the parameters or constraints surrounding those tasks, the level of proficiency required to complete them efficiently and effectively, and the ability to know how to do the tasks well enough to train someone else to do them. The following statement snippets are those that we grouped together related to gaining hands-on experience:

- "They brought engineers in as line supervisors. These engineers had to call other engineers to fix their problems. This was really good on GM's part [since the engineers serving as supervisors got a better understanding of the issues facing those on the line.]"
- "Let foremen do the line job for six weeks. Then they'll know what it takes to run the job."
- "When the supervisor worked on the line and did problem solving with the team, a collaborative and cooperative atmosphere was created, which team members appreciated."
- "How can I tell you what's wrong with the door if I don't know what I'm talking about?"
- "How is the supervisor expected to communicate if he doesn't know [anything about the job]?"

Numerous enablers are linked with these statement snippets including encouraging work-group problem solving, maintaining leadership visibility and accessibility, sharing responsibilities, and providing support (the Work Practices quadrant). The symbolism of a higher ranking individual working hand in hand with those tied to the pace of the line (e.g., assemblers) plays an important role in the culture of the plant. Such activity symbolizes enablers as demonstrating the involvement and commitment of salaried employees in problem solving and serving effectively in a given role (the Work Force quadrant). Finally, the impact of the hands-on experience is likely to generate a positive reaction across the work group for those particular salaried employees who experience work on the line, which include the enablers of showing respect and displaying job empathy (the Relationships quadrant).

During an off-site with one of the plant leadership teams, we paired the set of statements about gaining hands-on experience with a different set of statement snippets about remaining at an arm's length. The comparison was intended to emphasize the ideal behavior while identifying those actions considered undesirable. We used an overarching quotation to introduce this paired comparison: "The further you are removed from the plant floor, the harder it is to understand the roadblocks." The statement snippets below underscore those processes that would have no place in the ideal plant culture.

- "Sometimes management is really trying to help. The engineer might come by and he might try out what you're doing on the workstation and say, 'Oh, this is OK. You can do this.' But when you're doing that seventy-three times an hour for nine hours a day, then it becomes much more difficult to perform the task. It is too heavy. Maybe the engineer should just do it for an hour and then see how he feels?"
- "Some [members of the skilled trades] are willing to listen to your ideas and opinions, but others are not. [Yet] an operator knows that machine. If the skilled trades would listen, they could help."
- "[The contract supervisor said the job had to be done according to the specifications and did not listen to counterarguments from the team. Dawn, an operator, said,] He didn't know anything when he started working here. We trained him—showed him how it is done. [The supervisor proceeded to write up, or create an official record of, the team member's actions.]"

These statement snippets, though written from a critical point of view, parallel those related to gaining hands-on experience. By comparing the two sets, we can identify processes that distinguish them. In the "arms-length" snippets, proactive listening (the Relationships quadrant) emerges as an essential part of the ideal collaborative culture. Moreover, those same snippets reveal a set of outcomes perceived negatively by hourly employees. None of the reported outcomes illustrates a long-term solution developed through a collaborative approach. Even the statement involving the engineer indicates dissatisfaction on the part of the assembler and the potential for an occupational injury at some point in the future.

A small group of leaders with whom we worked at an off-site engaged in a discussion of the "hands-on" versus "arm's length" strategies associated with the paired statement snippets. They subsequently offered their reactions to a guideline (or "recipe")[14] we proposed, summarizing the contrast: *increase sensitivity to production pressures and difficulties faced by operators by having other plant personnel work the line on an occasional but regular basis.* One salaried leader advocated "supporting the operator" just as GMS specifies. Another salaried leader suggested, "The focus should be on the root cause of solving the problem. This is a process issue." A union attendee took a different approach. He chose to highlight a role model from the past—one of the relatively few positive recollections from the old way. He commented, "There was a former plant manager . . . He had the respect of the worker and their trust. They [the workers] went the extra mile because they wanted to please him. He tried to reinforce the positive. He never gave up." This particular union view reflected the importance of the Relationships quadrant of the model, unlike the salaried view that emphasized reliance on the Work Practices component.

As this leadership discussion shifted toward particular action items that the new GM plant would try to put in place, the theme "walk in their shoes" emerged. The group indicated the importance of displaying job empathy for the human element in plant culture (the Relationships quadrant). As one attendee stated, "All managers have to understand what is going on on the floor. They have to schedule time to understand it." Therefore, the group agreed that the first-line supervisors (referred to in the past as foremen) should be proficient in all the jobs in their area of responsibility, calling to mind the sharing-responsibilities enabler (the Work Practices quadrant). At the same time, supervisors should be trained in empowering employees to solve problems (the Work Practices quadrant); that is, those "closest to the problem" should be the ones trying to address the issues rather than the supervisor working in isolation. The attendees also emphasized serving effectively in the role by receiving appropriate and sufficient training in the work processes (the Work Force quadrant), taking time for relationship building (the Relationships quadrant), and being aware of what is going on in general so that they understand "why we didn't get our quota out." Moreover, all plant roles and responsibilities should be positively and consistently reinforced.

This leadership group discussion was consistent with the Ideal Cultural Model generally, as well as with key enablers in three of the four relevant quadrants: maintaining leadership visibility and accessibility (the Work Practices quadrant), demonstrating involvement and commitment (the Work Force quadrant), and displaying job empathy (the Relationships quadrant). Discussion of the action items involved an emphasis on work practices and processes—as we would have anticipated given the heightened role of GMS. However, the discussion also stressed care in relating to employees—particularly when help is needed across job functions (e.g., engineering and production) and job types (e.g., salaried and hourly). The ability to put oneself in someone else's shoes—displaying job empathy (the Relationships quadrant)—has the potential to reap significant benefits, including improved problem-solving rates and a reduction in status and role boundaries among plant personnel.

Problem Solving as an Enabler

One of our data collection experiences involved capturing and documenting a set of events pertaining to an ergonomic/health and safety issue on the plant floor. The example, which we refer to colloquially as the Hoist Story, demonstrates the critical role of work-group problem solving (the Work Practices quadrant). We learned about this issue and the way in which it was addressed over the course of two interviews with Dan, a plant engineer. Dan told us his recollections in his office; he also showed us the original blueprints to explain some of the difficulties encountered by the operators when they tried to use a hoist—an apparatus for raising something heavy into position. About two weeks later, we conducted a follow-up interview with him to clarify and refine the accuracy of our notes and gather additional detail. At that time, Dan took us out on the plant floor to show us the hoist and introduce us to the operators.

It is important to distinguish between Dan's recollections—which we have labeled a narrative essay—and snippets. Narrative essays differ from snippets in many ways including their length, complexity, diversity of cultural themes, and presence of multiple obstacles and enablers. The recollections take the form of a story in that they align with the various conventions used in storytelling (e.g., character development, setting, sequence of activity, conflict). Dan narrated his recollections to us from his point of view, based on his particular perspective of the events.

We thought it would be instructive to examine a compilation of the two interviews with Dan, rather than a shortened, paraphrased version. When people tell their stories, they often look more like these raw notes than a polished account. The text below represents a composite of the two interviews. Text concluding with the number one (#1) represents the first interview while the text concluding with the number two (#2) represents the follow-up discussion.

I have to come in this weekend. There was a problem out on the floor of people lifting the hoods by hand. They weren't using the hoist. (#1)

There was a medical concern. We got a recordable.[15] (#2)

I asked them [the operators] to explain why they weren't using the hoist. They said, "It's cumbersome, it's not fast enough, and it adds sixteen steps to the job." I said that I would try to work with them to help figure out a solution. I came up with something and I said, "These are my ideas." [At this point, Dan pulled out a blueprint to show how the original rail supporting the hoist was configured, and how the new rail could be configured.] Then I came up with a fix and went out and talked with the guys again. I asked, "Do you think it will work?" (#1)

I . . . got their input. As a group we came up with the most . . . cost-effective [way] to solve the throughput issue, and then the ergonomic issue goes away. The next step was redoing the plan and getting management to buy-in. After getting management buy-in, we placed the order. (#2)

The cost was about five thousand dollars. (#1)

The normal process [from my experience in other GM locations] is to have the operator, maintenance, ergonomics, and safety [departments] buy-in prior to shipping from the supplier to our facility. That is called a buy-off. That was something the [plant] management saw as unnecessary . . . We were not allowed to go down there [to the supplier's location] . . . They [the supplier] shipped it [the ridge rail] in and we had eight tradespeople from two shifts and two operators to install it. After installing it, we found out by measuring the [physical] forces [needed when using the hoist] that there was a problem with [both] the design and the build [of the new ridge rail]. They [the forces] were just within our ergonomic limits but not acceptable because we felt as a team they should be a great deal better. The forces were twenty-two to twenty-four pounds of force. (#2)

We needed to get a new one [ridge rail]. The [senior] manager told me that he was dissatisfied with what I had done. He said, "You told me that this tool would satisfy their [the operators'] problem but it hasn't." I replied, "But you wouldn't let me go down to do my buy-off." (#1)

We got the supplier . . . [to come to the plant. Their design engineer] came in with an attitude that "We've built a hundred of these [ridge rails], and there has never been a problem." After the team convinced the design engineer to use it [the hoist] for himself, after loading three hoods he said, "This is too hard." For me . . . I gained credibility with the team since I didn't leave it [the ridge rail issue] alone. Then the supplier agreed that there was a problem and that they would work with our design suggestions. They had some major design flaws . . . The supplier said they would build us a new one [ridge rail]. Actually they said they would build some new components. I told them I wanted a whole new one. They needed the whole unit back so they could analyze what they did wrong . . . After going through the whole build process I asked the management staff, "Do we go into an official buy-off this time?" The comment was, "Why wouldn't it be right this time?" The team responded, "The first one [ridge rail] wasn't right so do we want to take a chance, or do we want to do business the way we should and do a formal buy-off? If there are any issues or concerns, they'll be taken care of before it is shipped." (#2)

The manager said, "Go and do the buy-off." So I finally got permission to go . . . I took nine people with me, both day and night shift, salaried and hourly. I took people who do measurements etc., and we did go through the buy-off. Each person signed off. This kind of thing will save money in the long run. It's them [the team who worked on solving the ridge-rail problem] that are pulling the culture along. It turned out that there were still four items, which were a problem [on the supplier's second ridge rail]. I got them [the supplier] to write down in writing that they would correct each of these problems. (#1)

After we got the new one [ridge rail], the force varied from four to seven pounds and only momentarily it jumps to seven pounds due to our design suggestions. This helped them [the supplier] improve their overall design . . . During installation we had the actual maintenance and production [departments] involved on the weekend. From what we learned in the supplier's facility, it took half the time to remove and install it than the first one, and with half the manpower. We learned some tricks [from the supplier] and applied them here [at the plant] . . . So, we ended up with a 400 percent reduction in forces to move it [the hoist] . . . So therefore, it was not a throughput issue anymore and not an ergonomic issue . . . [To conclude] the only suggestion I've got is, there's no "I" in team . . . I'm just here to assist. They [the team] did it. It helped cement the marriage between different groups like production and maintenance. (#2)

The narrative of the Hoist Story documents the achievement of an important milestone in the cultural transformation of GM manufacturing. The recordable happened in a GM plant that only exhibited a limited number of features associated with the Ideal Cultural Model. Indeed, from a cultural perspective, Dan told us that he and his team were "pulling the culture along." The passage reveals Dan as a man with a mission, trying to correct an occupational health and safety issue and support the team members so that they could be as effective and as safe as possible in their work. Dan spent most of his career in other GM facilities. The culture associated with his most recent job was inclusive, cooperative, and open to change; Dan seemed to have transferred those expectations to his current position. We identify the specific enablers associated with each of the key interactions in the narrative.

Enablers Present in Engineer's Interactions with Team Members

Dan activated the encouraging work-group problem-solving enabler (the Work Practices quadrant) to frame his approach with the team members; it was the core enabler that guided his approach. For example, he actively solicited ideas and feedback from all appropriate plant departments (e.g., ergonomics, maintenance) and from the individual operators who opted not to use the hoist. He exhibited the following enablers: demonstrating involvement and commitment, exhibiting a people-centered orientation, responding to tasks quickly and effectively, and serving effectively in his role (the Work Force quadrant). Dan knew that there was misalignment between the operator's work tasks and use of the hoist. Consequently, he wanted to focus attention on improving ergonomic standards through the use of a more appropriate tool (the Plant Environment quadrant). He was successful in empowering the employees and in getting them interested in sharing and using lessons learned in the design of the ridge rail (the Work Practices quadrant). In doing so, he exhibited proactive listening, creating a win-win orientation and showing respect for them (the Relationships quadrant).

Enablers Mitigating the Obstacles in
Engineer-Team Interactions with the Supplier

Together Dan and the team worked out a solution, which they proposed to the supplier. The narrative explains that the supplier "came in with an attitude" in which he expressed some key obstacles, including resistance to change, ethnocentrism, and cross-cultural conflict. Despite initial resistance, Dan and the team members won the supplier over by coaxing him to try out the ridge rail. They also engaged in setting clear expectations, sharing and using lessons learned from past experiences (the Work Practices quadrant), showing respect, and creating a "win-win" orientation to the possibility of a redesign of the ridge rail (the Relationships quadrant). The team was able to get the supplier focused on demonstrating involvement and commitment in the problem-solving discussion (the Work Force quadrant), improving the ergonomic standards (the Plant Environment quadrant), and, ultimately, in framing the solution in terms of sharing responsibilities (the Work Practices quadrant). As a result, cultivating work ethic and pride (the Work Force quadrant) emerged from the story due to the joint problem-solving activities.

Obstacles Dominating the Engineer's Interactions with the Manager
Initially, Dan had no difficulty in getting the production manager's budget to cover the purchase of the new ridge rail; thus, he was successful in applying the enabler securing support (the Work Practices quadrant). But in the remaining interactions with the manager, he was embroiled in conflict with him. He proposed using the "buy-off" process, invoking the enabler setting clear expectations (the Work Practices quadrant). Immediately, he collided with the same three obstacles he had encountered with the supplier: resistance to change, ethnocentrism, and cross-cultural conflict. The production manager denied the request. The conflict reemerged later when it became clear that the installed ridge rail did not address the health and safety issue and that a second ridge rail would have to be ordered and installed. Dan exacerbated the situation by blaming the manager for the manager's earlier decision. While the manager's response was in line with the old way, Dan's rebuttal was equally of the old way. Ultimately, relationships between Dan and the manager were damaged, with no reconciliation occurring by the end of the story.

A Key to Successful Cultural Transformation: Using Enablers from
Multiple Quadrants of the Ideal Cultural Model
The comparison between Dan's interactions with the manager, on the one hand, and Dan and the team's interactions with the supplier, on the other, is instructive because Dan faced the same obstacles in each case but responded differently. With the manager, there was no engagement in problem solving. The two enablers that Dan used with the manager in the initial interactions were limited to the Work Practices component of the Ideal Cultural Model. Cultural transformation requires flexibility and adaptability. Dan made no attempt to frame the discussions in ways that tapped into any of the other quadrants despite the fact that he had options open to him. For example, he could have suggested that by using the buy-off process, they could solve the

health and safety issue, enhance the ergonomic standards (the Plant Environment quadrant), and prevent future recordables. He could have proactively listened or shown some level of job empathy for the manager's role and decision (the Relationships quadrant) in the hopes of understanding the issue better from the manager's perspective. He could have tried to engage the manager in a problem-solving discussion about the pros and cons of a buy-off (the Work Practices quadrant). He could have appealed to an enabler such as cultivating work ethic and pride (the Work Force quadrant) to encourage the manager to focus on the longer term impact of the buy-off decision on plant culture. Or Dan could have tried some combination of these enablers to reduce the negative impact of the obstacles on cultural change.

In contrast, the strength of Dan's approach with the team members and the supplier lay in his ability to access enablers from multiple quadrants of the Ideal Cultural Model. Indeed, he used enablers from all four quadrants, often in quick succession, to mitigate the effect of the obstacles. He engaged in outreach by involving all the "experts" (e.g., team members, the ergonomics department, the supplier) in the problem solving and the discussions of alternatives. With all of the key players involved, providing input, and evaluating results, the entire group had a stake in the outcome. Moreover, the problem-solving process had a direct impact on the partnership, leading to an empowered and effective set of decision makers. His approach not only increased the likelihood of a successful technical solution (i.e., a solution to the recordable) but also established the conditions for a flourishing cultural solution (i.e., strong, healthy relationships).

Narrative essays like the Hoist Story illustrate both strategies and pitfalls for operating within an organization that is engaged in a cultural transformation. When obstacles appear that can derail a cultural transformation, a multipronged approach is best. If the initial enablers selected to address the obstacles do not yield the anticipated results, it is useful to consider other enablers that tap into different dimensions of the cultural ideal. In that way, the enablers are more likely to temper the impact of the cultural obstacles and help the organization move in the direction of the desired change.

Dan reduced his chances of a successful interaction with the production manager by only accessing enablers from the Work Practices quadrant. Fortunately, when it came time to interact with the supplier, he was able to invoke a variety of cultural processes from all four quadrants to drive home the point that collaboration mattered in addressing the health and safety issue. With the supplier, unlike the manager, the Hoist Story is a success story. It not only symbolizes both technical and cultural successes in the problem-solving effort but also reinforces the desired or ideal state. A set of enablers working together, rather than a single enabler in isolation, is the key for getting as close to the ideal as possible.

Conclusions

This chapter elaborates on an important piece of the overall Bridge Model for moving from the old way (i.e., a directive, authoritarian approach to manufacturing work) to the new way (i.e., a collaborative approach). It ties together the theory (the framework for constructing the bridge and transition models) to the critical issues that would have either negative (obstacles) or positive (enablers) impacts on an organization going through the cultural-change process. The general theory frames how we should proceed. The barriers and enablers frame the processes needed for success. The theory, barriers, and enablers come together in the construction of environmentally sensitive, locally targeted tools that merge the three in a systematic way. The next chapter provides a detailed look at the overall process for constructing cultural-change tools for manufacturing culture, as well as ways of validating and deploying those tools within a complex organization.

Chapter 7

Tools to Aid in Cultural Transformation

The Ideal Plant Culture project was a highly interactive process engaging our research group, the research sponsors and advocates, and the study participants. We shared what we were learning with the newly appointed plant manager of the greenfield plant and his Joint Leadership Team. In exchange, we received feedback and new directions for the research, which was compatible with a community-based participatory research approach[1] in which researchers and manufacturing-community members are partners in the research. As the feedback process intensified, our research group began developing prototypes of applications, or tools, that could assist manufacturing leaders in conceptualizing and planning for the culture of the new plant. The development of these tools, or "actions," was aligned with the tradition of action anthropology.[2] Manufacturing leaders from both the greenfield plant and from a senior group of U.S.-based manufacturing managers worked with us intensively to test and implement the tools.

Thus, both the community-based participatory-research and the action-anthropology approaches were used throughout the Ideal Plant Culture project. These combined approaches strongly supported our view that the set of tools we were creating should be used routinely as part of the day-to-day life of manufacturing plants rather than being used only for specialized interventions or training. Therefore, flexible formats would be important so that the tools could be used in a variety of settings from one-on-one conversations, to team-staff meetings, to informal problem-solving opportunities on the plant floor. Tools suitable for individual study and learning, as well as group discussions, debates, and decision making, would be necessary.

Because employees' overwhelming preference was for an effective work culture that would enable them to achieve their various productivity, quality, and efficiency objectives, our goal was to embed an emphasis on collaboration throughout the tools to reinforce the centrality of collaboration to the work of manufacturing. Thus, the tools directly target the following cultural dynamics on the plant floor:

- Improved understanding of collaboration and its integration into work activities
- Implementation and ongoing use of collaboration metrics as a mechanism for gauging cultural change
- Reduced frequency, duration, and severity of conflict
- Faster, more effective problem resolution due to improved trust and communication
- Increased levels of job satisfaction among plant leadership and team members

Finally, it was essential that the tools be perceived as complementary to the GMS process (which was becoming increasingly integrated into plant-floor operations) as well as to Quality Network activities. GM manufacturing culture would be more effective if the work processes, procedures, and practices of GMS and the Quality Network philosophy of "people, teamwork, and continuous improvement" were combined with the ideal plant culture's emphasis on cultivating, strengthening, and sustaining a collaborative culture. As one senior GM executive stated, "The whole thing might be about getting the culture right."

Collaboration Tool Development

We ultimately developed ten tools that are part of the cultural-transformation process described in Chapter 1 and the GM depiction of that transformation process (i.e., Bridge Models) described in Chapters 4, 5, and 6. Each tool relates specifically to the Ideal Cultural Model and is targeted at known barriers to transformation in organizational settings. Each tool also serves to reinforce the ideal and has the potential to move the transformation process closer to that ideal. The tools provide employees with opportunities to learn how to apply the cultural ideal in their own work lives. In that sense, we view the tools as linking the cultural problem-solving, adaptiveness, and responsiveness processes with the end point—cultural transformation (see Figure 7.1). Without the availability or repeated use of such tools, it becomes more difficult to achieve the ideal or to sustain it in the long term.

Seed ideas for the ten collaboration tools emerged in preparation for, or during, a series of five off-sites that our research group

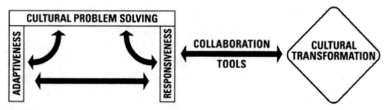

Figure 7.1 Collaboration tools as a reinforcing mechanism during cultural transformation

developed for the Joint Leadership Team mentioned above. The framing and content for the initial four tools—the Ideal Cultural Model, Cultural Toolkit, Story Packet, and Recipes for Cultural Success—stemmed from the first two off-sites held about two months apart. At the first one-day off-site, we introduced the Ideal Cultural Model, the concepts of cultural obstacles and enablers, and several sets of snippets. The second off-site, involving small-group brainstorming and synthesis sessions, was built on and shaped by the reactions of the participants to the first off-site. It led to continued development of the four tools, both in terms of content and commonality of format, and ultimately to working prototypes of each. Thus, these collaboration tools were developed iteratively and in partnership with the very group of plant personnel who would ultimately test the tools and incorporate them into plant operations.

Study participants in general seemed to be seeking some set of mechanisms that would draw them into the "organizational conversation" about change and about the future. For example, one study participant stated, "If you don't air out [your concerns] you will not get any better . . . If you practice something [like using a structured format for problem solving] long enough, you get used to the new way and it doesn't bother you anymore." This individual's point was that if there is a routine established with new processes, it has a greater potential to become regular practice. Another study participant commented, "I spent one day at Lordstown (last week) and it reset my reference point. People are starved for someone to ask them what they think . . . We are already here and just have to make the next step." This study participant emphasized the variation in collaborative behavior across manufacturing facilities, indicating that his plant was more open to soliciting and listening to employees than the Lordstown plant. Another individual commented that using the tools on a regular basis would help to reinforce the collaborative ideal: "Actions speak louder than words . . . Reflecting on our core values once a week brings people up to the same level of understanding."

Three other tools were based on ideas generated during the Joint Leadership Team off-sites, as well as during discussions with plant employees responsible for implementing innovative work practices, training, and team development at the new greenfield. Our research group had completed some analyses for this leadership team, which then resulted in some direct requests. In one case, we were asked to expand upon a series of cultural dilemmas that we had presented to them earlier. The Cultural "Hot Spots" tool was finalized with this additional detail. In a second case, our documentation and analysis of the Stud Gun observation led to an interactive discussion of what-if scenarios and the possibility of combining both the observation and the what-if scenarios into a learning game. Ultimately, the *Explore-PlantCulture* computer game resulted. Of all the tools, Workplace Disagreements resulted from repeated periods of intense engagement with the manufacturing community. Our research group gathered the Hoist Story during two interviews, created a story script from it, and passed it along to the Quality Network trainers in the greenfield plant. After using the script in a training session, the reaction was so positive that the trainers decided to make a video of it and create a set of conflict-resolution exercises for it. Subsequently, our research group developed the tool using the video as the centerpiece.[3]

Our research group crafted the last three tools and then sought feedback on them from the Joint Leadership Team. The core idea for the Collaborative Questions tool was based on our observations of plant personnel interaction styles (both negative and positive). We believed that the training provided in this tool (i.e., on how to ask neutral, objective questions) would be useful in fostering cooperation and sensitivity to others. The two other tools evaluate the cultural dynamics of manufacturing culture both qualitatively and quantitatively. From our observations on the plant floor, it was clear that there were many metrics for work activity and work output but none that focused on collaboration, conflict, or other dimensions of plant floor relationships. With no metrics, it is difficult to understand the current cultural state or how and why the culture changes over time. Moreover, in a low-context culture, metrics have value. With no emphasis on cultural metrics, the organization could neither track cultural changes over time (based on some set of baseline indicators) nor benefit from the insights that such metrics (and the organizational discussions associated with them) generated. Consequently, we decided to develop two sets of metrics—one for work groups and the other for individuals.

Interactive Tools

As the tools began to emerge, our research group matched them against the elements of the Ideal Cultural Model and against the basic goals we identified for improving plant culture.[4] Nine of the ten collaboration tools were developed to include self-contained study guides that emphasize cultural problem solving. Each tool directs attention to a particular dimension of organizational culture, utilizing a similar structure and flow (see Figure 7.2). First, background is furnished on the particular cultural problem that the tool targets. Second, a description of the tool is offered, including the goals with respect to that cultural problem. Third, in-depth information for addressing that cultural problem is provided. Finally, each tool includes a set of exercises for gaining practice in addressing that type of cultural problem. The exercises are designed to engage employees in small group discussions. This kind of focused interaction has proven fruitful in identifying sources and consequences of cultural issues and in utilizing employee energies and efforts to develop effective counterstrategies for issues emerging in the workplace.

These collaboration tools provide specific support for the cultural transformation process because they fortify the direction of the change and assist in the progression toward the ideal. We grouped the tools into types based on their primary function: understanding collaboration, practicing collaboration, and measuring collaboration. These three groupings provide some guidance to users in terms of the primary focus or area of transformation that is targeted and the potential sequence in which the tools might be used. Since the tools can stand alone, the sequencing element can be optional or ignored.

Tools for Understanding Collaboration

Four of the tools focus on understanding collaboration within a plant context—that is, with respect to developing and maintaining work-based relationships, coordinating and completing work tasks, and achieving plant goals. They incorporate and build on the Ideal Cultural Model as a mechanism for promoting an awareness and appreciation of collaboration and its impact on plant outcomes. These tools follow a progression that begins by helping participants visualize and implement a successful model for their ideal.

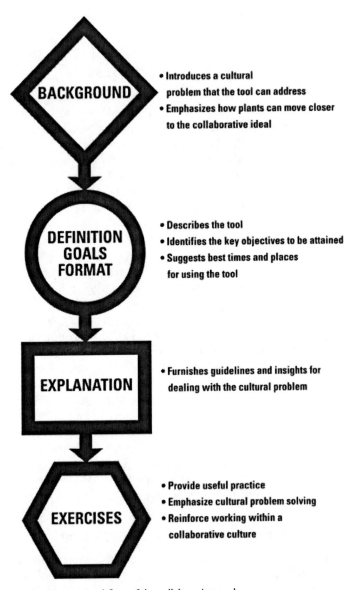

Figure 7.2 Structure and flow of the collaboration tools

Ideal Cultural Model

This tool provides a conceptual view of the cultural ideal as expressed by GM employees. It consists of four quadrants—Plant Environment, Work Force, Work Practices, and Relationships—into which all features of the ideal plant culture can be categorized. Each quadrant is defined and described, and the overall model can be used to discuss the relative balance of the four quadrants in an actual plant environment. At GM, this tool embodies a culture of collaboration as its ideal, though in other organizational contexts the cultural ideal may be expressed somewhat differently. On one occasion, when we were introducing the model to a plant leadership team participating in our pilot, we asked them to try out one of the exercises. They were asked to rate their plant's emphasis on each of the four quadrants. Because they rated the Relationships component of the model lower than any of the other quadrants, they decided to figure out why. The exercise took them into a discussion of their local union agreement—a discussion that lasted the better part of one hour. Gina, president of the union local, stated, "In order for GM to be successful, the walls need to be broken down." In response, Elizabeth Briody from our research group asked, "Well then how would you want to frame it (the relationship between union and management)?" Gina replied, "You need to reinforce that we are all in this together." In her response, Gina emphasizes the centrality of the collective and the desire for plant unity and cooperation. Though they did not settle their differences that day, the local agreement was signed about a week later. This extended discussion around a troubling and difficult labor agreement suggests that the Ideal Culture Model, particularly the Relationships quadrant, resonates with study participants and can be of great help in trying to understand and resolve issues.

Cultural Toolkit

The Cultural Toolkit describes the obstacles that prevent or slow the cultural change process and the enablers that can help position the culture to move in the direction of the collaborative ideal. The exercises associated with this tool encourage participants to identify obstacles to collaboration in their work lives and connect them with possible enablers that can serve as counterweights. As part of this discussion, employees offer specific recommendations and follow-up action items as a starting point for changing the situation. We created this tool to help encapsulate two key elements of the cultural transformation process: the obstacles to cultural change and the enabling processes that could facilitate that change. During the pilot, one manager told us that the tool's strength was useful in "generating discussion of the current state of the plant versus the ideal state." The cultural obstacles identified in the Cultural Toolkit can be applied directly to the issues faced in workplaces beyond GM. The enablers, however, require modification to capture the culture-specific features of those organizations.

Story Packet

A key aspect of the process of understanding collaboration is being able to portray the current state in relation to some future or ideal state. Storytelling is a way to move beyond simple description to illustrate appropriate and inappropriate behavior in relation to the ideal. The Story Packet contains stories on a variety of topics and issues related to achieving the ideal plant culture. We created the Story Packet tool to enable comparison of the current (or past) with the ideal, thereby identifying the direction and target of the cultural transformation. Some of the stories exemplify the ideal, others are more reflective of the old way, and still others represent something in between. In other organizations, the stories of the cultural-change process would be different, but the mechanisms in the Story Packet for exploring their meaning could be used. For example, the exercises are designed to facilitate cultural learning and evolution toward the ideal by providing examples of desired behaviors contrasted with "warning" stories from the current (or past) plant culture. The exercises also use the Ideal Cultural Model to suggest ways of moving toward higher levels of consistency between stated ideals and actual behavior. GM study participants have found the tool valuable because of the teaching moments it creates and the cultural learning that occurs.

Recipes for Cultural Success

An important progression in the process of understanding collaboration is to reaffirm the collaborative ideal using a variety of strategies; repetition helps to solidify the cultural transformation process. The Recipes for Cultural Success tool offer guidelines for incorporating a collaborative orientation toward work tasks and relationships. The core of this tool is a one-page reference card of preferred behavioral qualities in effective plant cultures; in other organizations, the recipes would reflect the guidelines for success found in their settings. The Recipes are useful in helping employees cope with change and in understanding the value of and expectations associated with a culture of collaboration. One of the exercises for this tool is to select one of the recipes (e.g., "Follow through on expectations for desired behavior by 'walking the talk'"), identify successful examples that illustrate that recipe, explain why those examples are successful, and discuss how the successful indicators could be applied to other situations. We used this tool successfully during a plant leadership off-site to gather feedback on a key insight (or recipe) emerging from a paired comparison of two story snippets or two sets of statement snippets; the leadership revealed their perspectives and their suggested solutions for addressing any obstacles in those snippets. With an analysis of ten snippet pairs, we generated a set of guiding principles linking collaboration and workplace effectiveness. Taken together, these principles offer a broader view of some important cultural areas to target during the cultural transformation process.

Tools for Practicing Collaboration

Cultural change takes time, energy, and effort. "Practicing," or engaging in the activities associated with that cultural change, helps to establish and solidify new patterns of thought and behavior. The virtue of formally practicing the tools with others sensitizes employees to the ways in which plant decisions and behavior are consistent with the ideal. The three tools in this set focus attention on actual behavior, including how to generate ideas from co-workers, make better decisions, and mediate conflict. They encourage employees to experiment with alternative collaborative approaches with their co-workers, supervisors, and subordinates. These tools build on the collaboration tools associated with understanding collaboration.

Collaborative Questions

This tool provides training in techniques that employees can use to ask questions pertaining to workplace problems and their potential solutions. It is relatively easy to collaborate in a relaxed work environment where things are going well. But when work environments are under pressure to perform, interactions among plant personnel change. It can be difficult to hear and respond in ways consistent with the ideal when individuals perceive that their work or issue is a priority. Without effective strategies and coping skills, such as those described in this tool, communication with others can be compromised. This tool emphasizes the importance of learning to ask questions in a neutral, objective way, as well as asking to learn. On one occasion when this tool was used, it enabled a first-line supervisor to practice her collaborative skills: "I was very frustrated with one of my employees . . . She could not do her job properly. I had tried everything and finally

I said, 'I'm going to try one of the tools.' So, I worked with her for twenty minutes. I'm going through the job with her. I did it first and then she did it. So I listened and tried to be honest, and it worked, and I haven't had any trouble with her since. So I think that was a big success." With this approach, more complete, detailed, and accurate information can be obtained, better decisions can be made, and improved collaborative interactions can occur. Though this tool was developed for GM employees, it has widespread applicability to many other American workplaces.

Cultural "Hot Spots"

In any culture, there are a number of conditions where there is potential for conflict or competition between two positive ideals or between the "lesser of two evils." The Cultural "Hot Spots" tool provides a procedure for opening up discussion on known cultural clashes in the work environment so that potential solutions to those clashes can be developed and the positive elements of the ideal culture can be reinforced. This tool is particularly useful when groups of plant personnel uncover and address ambiguity at the intersection of two opposing themes (e.g., empowerment and hierarchy, standardization and innovation). Teamwork and cohesion may be themes that an organization emphasizes in its vision, mission, and corporate values. Yet, how do those themes square with individual performance among salaried employees when annual evaluations, raises, and bonuses come around? One plant manager told us, "Well, looking at this graphic of the hot spots, I've used them. I've used the standardization and continuous improvement example and also the hierarchy and empowerment one. Some of those conflicts just come up in my discussions." Many of the exercises assist plant personnel in getting input from other employees on their proposed solutions to these cultural dilemmas, thereby enabling them to contribute as effectively as possible to the work culture. Because the clash of ideals is a common occurrence in American workplaces, this tool can be applied in many organizational settings.

Workplace Disagreements

A case-study format is particularly useful for practicing collaboration when it reflects compelling accounts of past events. The Workplace Disagreements tool is designed to help individuals and work groups strategize as to how to address conflict so that any damage to plant relationships, processes, and work output can be addressed quickly and effectively. This tool incorporates a video of the Hoist Story described in Chapter 6. One of the Quality Network trainers working on the video production told us, "What makes this story great is that it is so realistic." He later described a training discussion in an e-mail to us: "People could easily relate to the characters and the behaviors, which provided the basis for some robust discussion and learning." Other exercises in this tool ask participants to place themselves in the position of the actors to decide appropriate courses of action in conflict situations. We developed this tool to assist the plant trainers both in the cultural analysis of the Hoist Story and in the enhancement of the training exercises. American manufacturing organizations generally will find this tool useful as they seek to engage their work force in cultural-change efforts.

Tools for Measuring Collaboration

Progress toward a collaborative ideal can be measured—both from the perspective of work group members and from an individual's own self-assessment. The following tools help chart the movement of groups and individuals toward a culture of collaboration. Work groups and individuals can compare their current abilities to work effectively with others against their desire to move in the direction of the ideal.

Work-Group Relationship Effectiveness Metrics
The seven features that are measured in the Work-Group Relationship Effectiveness Metrics tool—trust, respect, cooperation, job empathy, communication, fairness, and conflict—are tested and established indicators of work-group success. These seven features can provide an overall sense of collaborative health at GM; other organizations may want to modify or expand this list of features depending on the salient cultural themes in their workplace settings. A baseline can be established on any of these features, with changes monitored over time. Each of the seven attributes can be explored separately or in conjunction with other features to generate insights, causes, and recommendations. The exercises provide a process for identifying which elements of within-group or between-group relationships are perceived as positive (for reinforcement) or negative (and needing change). Similarly, the exercises suggest ways of strengthening the positive metrics and reducing the impact of the negative metrics. As organizations change, some of these features may need more attention than others—for example, if cultural drift from the collaborative ideal occurs or if a work practice or process change is perceived negatively by some or all of the work force. One reaction to this tool was the following: "I came in here before this meeting and I felt alone. There was a lot of

candidness [as we assessed how well we worked together]. It (the tool) was easy to use. Helpful? Useful? Well, it was helpful because [among us] we got to common ground. It helps to know that there are three of us out there and we are not alone [in our views]." Work groups and larger workplace entities (e.g., departments) can use this tool to chart their progress toward their cultural ideal or to examine aspects of the cultural-transformation process as it affects them.

Individual Relationship Effectiveness Metrics

In American culture, we place value on individual actions, creativity, and expertise. An increased awareness of how individuals perceive their own interactions with others is an important step in any change process. The Individual Relationship Effectiveness Metrics tool focuses attention on three important areas of relationship dynamics: engaging in positive interactions, working together on work tasks, and finding ways to connect with those in other roles and jobs. These three areas of relationship dynamics are broadly applicable to any American organization. This tool is designed to help individuals measure and then either reinforce or improve their workplace relationship dynamics. It serves as a self-assessment or introspective examination of one's collaborative abilities and behaviors along with the actions the individual can take to create and sustain strong, healthy relationships at work. As one individual stated, "Sometimes a tool like this can be effective by simply getting people to think about how their behavior can affect others." Individuals can use this tool to examine aspects of their own everyday actions and activities and track changes in their behavior over time. Individuals who use this tool will find that they have a role to play in the cultural-change process and can exert influence on those around them through their own expectations, assumptions, and behavior.

Validation and Testing for the Interactive Tools

Collaboration Tool Assessment

Over the course of two years, our research group, with the help of a senior group of manufacturing leaders, validated, refined, and tested the collaboration tools. As part of the validation, we worked with six salaried and hourly employees from three different plants to assess the content and the format of the tools. The senior manufacturing managers chose these plants because of the differences in the products they produced, their perceived collaborative abilities, their existing work processes and practices, and the strength of GM-UAW relations at those sites. For the assessment, we were especially interested in the perceived strengths and weaknesses of the tools in terms of their content and advice on using the tools in a plant environment. We held three lengthy meetings during a one-month period to discuss the nine tools, and asked that each of the six committee members complete a formal assessment that we designed.

While this advisory committee offered specific suggestions for improving the tools, which we took into account in refining them, their comments represented an enthusiastic endorsement. For example, one participant stated, "In theory, I think these collaboration tools will work." Another remarked, "Thank you for allowing the open communication. I think there were a lot of eye openers. To think that we are all GM plants and how different we operate was amazing." A third indicated, "The subject matter is very interesting and is in definite need of implementation." One insight resulting from this assessment process was that some of the collaboration tools were viewed as useful for cultivating collaboration (i.e., Ideal Cultural Model, Cultural Toolkit, Recipes for Cultural Success) while others for maintaining collaboration (e.g., Collaborative Questions, Cultural "Hot Spots," Workplace Disagreements, Work-Group Relationship Effectiveness, Individual Relationship Effectiveness); the Story Packet was perceived as effective for both developing and sustaining collaboration.

We also gathered the advisory committee's advice on implementing and using the tools in the plants. Their statements foreshadowed some of the general issues related to cultural transformation as well as some of the particular difficulties we would face in moving the validation and testing phase of the collaboration tools forward. For example, one participant commented, "I think we need to start from the top—even above the plant managers—[in getting them to understand the value of collaboration.]" This comment is a reference to the importance of initiating change in various parts of the cultural system. Another individual indicated, "If you came to our plant, they would laugh us out—the idea of letting supervisors and skilled trades work the line. They would say, 'That's a way for management not to hire more people' and that's what I would believe." This comment emphasizes the belief in and strong adherence to existing work rules as negotiated in local labor agreements. Cultural transformation processes would have to confront a range of cultural rules, beliefs, and values in an attempt to create a different manufacturing culture.

Collaboration Tool Pilot Test

Soon after the assessment was completed, we designed a five-month pilot test to see how the collaboration tools would be received in plant settings. Two plants were selected by the same senior manufacturing leaders—one perceived as highly collaborative and one considered much less collaborative. Three work groups in different areas of the two plants participated in the pilot study. The composition of the groups ranged from only hourly, to only salaried, to mixed groups (e.g., hourly employees with salaried supervisor). Our research group worked with the pilot participants in sessions that took place in plant conference rooms. We provided an orientation to the nine tools and then asked the work groups to "try out" the tools (i.e., use the tools among themselves) as we observed them. We also sought verbal and written feedback on the tools and ideas to address potential implementation issues in a plant.

We encountered difficulties in planning the pilot sessions and in completing them once they started. On some days it was difficult for either hourly or salaried employees (or both) to be relieved from their usual work duties; operational issues on the plant floor took priority. On other days, individuals would only be able to participate on a limited basis. At one point in the pilot process, one of the local UAW unions would not commit to completing the pilot; the stated issue related, in part, to the lack of formal endorsement by the international UAW.[5]

Yet, despite these difficulties, the pilot was completed and participants provided feedback, reacting just as positively to the tools as the advisory committee had. In fact, there were no differences in the type or quality of comments from the two plants. The following statements were offered by participants from the plant perceived to be more collaborative:

- "[They are a] good exercise for coming to a group decision."
- "[The tools are] not threatening."
- "I could definitely try [the tools] with our ergonomics group."

Participants from the plant considered to be less collaborative expressed similar comments:

- "It was a chartered method to categorize your issues and work through them . . . It was easy to follow, well laid out."
- "The tools . . . open up doors in really good ways. They need to be done on a daily basis . . . five minutes a day in a meeting."
- "I think it is a lot of great stuff and we can use it."

Pilot participants were able to articulate some likely implementation issues when the collaboration tools would be ready for widespread dissemination in all U.S. plants. They offered recommendations for addressing the obstacles head on. For example, the more collaborative plant indicated that both corporate and plant management would have to support the collaboration tools "110 percent" to signal their importance in cultural change. The less collaborative plant emphasized that disseminating and using the collaboration tools in a plant environment should be given the same level of planning and commitment as key corporate initiatives. Participants from both plants also articulated key enablers that could assist during the tool implementation process. The more collaborative plant suggested using informal leaders in the plant as "role models" as plant personnel were being exposed to the tools. The less collaborative plant discussed ways of reducing potential conflict across status and role boundaries as the tools were being disseminated.

A Gaming Tool

The tenth and last tool completed, *ExplorePlantCulture*, is a customized video game designed to help plant personnel learn about the impact of their decisions on plant culture.[6] The game is based on an observation and some follow-up interviews related to the breakdown and repair of a stud gun (described in Chapter 5). It incorporates a powerful use of what-if scenarios to explore appropriate and inappropriate cultural interactions and relationships on the plant floor. This tool did not follow the same development process as the nine tools discussed above but rather a general game format that uses avatars as characters to recreate the actual interactions among the characters—including a serious personnel confrontation (see Figure 7.3).

Once the basic story is understood, the player advances through the equipment repair by making decisions for the characters; these decisions result in a better (or worse) outcome than the original incident produced. Character actions and inactions, and their corresponding impact on plant culture, affect the score. Immediately after each decision, players are able to observe changes in two 10-point scales. One scale illustrates attention to relationships, while the other emphasizes work process.[7] Players also receive a cumulative score, and the explanation for that score, at the end of each game. Based on the decisions the players make, a subset of the nine interactive collaboration tools appears on the screen. Players can click on those tool icons and review them immediately.

Figure 7.3 Screenshot of the repair of the stud gun in *ExplorePlantCulture*

ExplorePlantCulture can serve as a decision-support tool and as a learning tool. It can be used by a single individual or by a group making decisions based on consensus. The game also has the potential to be highly interactive—particularly when discussion precedes or follows a player's decisions. It offers a window into plant culture—both as it was and as it could be. It is designed to get players to think about their own work culture (including what the assumptions, beliefs, values, and expectations are), as well as to explore how those cognitive elements affect behavior in the plant. The game can heighten cultural awareness and sensitivity in a variety of ways including learning and practicing tips related to conflict resolution, identifying and predicting cultural issues so that players are positioned to take preventative or remedial measures, assessing and improving collaboration skills, and serving as a foundation for learning from best practices.

During the development of the computer game, our research group asked numerous employees to offer feedback and ultimately evaluate how well the game worked. In the early stages, we asked for reactions to screen shots of the plant environment, character actions, and robotic equipment—all adapted from plant photographs and layout schematics. We also sent demos electronically to interested employees so that they would get a sense of the game and forward their comments back to us. In later stages, we sought feedback pertaining to the choices at each decision point, gauges (which illustrated how well a player made a particular decision), and scoring. During testing, we gathered feedback on the visual and sound effects, decision-tree functionality, and usefulness of the narrator in providing contextual information, among other factors.

Once the game was ready for evaluation, we observed users as they played the game. We took notes on their facial expressions, ease or difficulty of use, and comments. Some users had never played a computer game before, while others played them regularly. One fascinating aspect of the evaluation concerns player decision making. Players choose between two options such as this one: "Have Al provide a solution to the problem" or "Have Al stand behind the robot cell and view the problem." While we did our best to disguise the better option, one user commented, "It seems pretty clear what the right choice is." Interestingly, we found that once users played a round or two of the game, they often made intentional decisions to select what they perceived to be the worst choice. They seemed eager to watch interactions where the disagreement or conflict escalated. When asked about their choice, we learned that the more contentious option allowed them to explore the boundaries of inappropriate or unacceptable interactions and expand their knowledge base of the range of collaborative and less collaborative behavior. By playing the game in this way, the player is able to see the contrasts with the cultural ideal and the direction of the cultural-transformation process toward that ideal.

COLLABORATION TOOL
DISSEMINATION AND IMPLEMENTATION

The simple development of cultural-change tools would have been sufficient for consultant-based change projects but are insufficient for our project approach. Since we followed a combination of action-anthropology and community-based participatory research approaches, we designed and implemented a dissemination-of-innovation strategy for the Ideal Plant Culture project. This strategy required (1) culturally validating the collaboration tools, (2) implementing a dissemination process that included both manufacturing community buy-in and "elite" (i.e., senior leader) endorsement, and (3) our own active participation in the dissemination process. We introduced the collaboration tools to various groups over a three-year period that partially coincided with the study's data collection phase. We met with and presented to a cross-section of leaders charged with manufacturing processes. This group included GM corporate executives, executives with responsibility for multiple GM plants in the United States, GMS leaders, and Quality Network leaders. Our ability to interact with many of these individuals resulted from the strong relationships we had been able to create with the senior GM manufacturing leaders. These leaders were able to champion the study's message as well as its applications.

The meetings for raising awareness about the tools had a particular structure. We reviewed the key finding—employees' hope for a next-generation manufacturing culture based on collaboration. We discussed the collaboration tools, describing the range of cultural issues that the tools were equipped to address. We provided the strong, positive feedback on the validation and testing processes that the tools had undergone. We also demonstrated the alignment of the tools with both GMS principles and Quality Network Action Strategies.

Emerging Patterns of Acceptance and Advocacy

One pattern that emerged was that the more an individual learned about the tools, the more likely he or she was to become an advocate for them. Nowhere is this pattern more evident than in this passage from the researcher field notes of a meeting with one of the most senior GM corporate executives:

> For approximately the first one-half hour of the meeting, [this executive] seemed not as focused. He appeared uncomfortable. He shifted his weight in his chair. He did not ask many questions. He did not really engage in the material. And then at about the midpoint of the meeting, he began to talk more and by the end of the meeting he was extremely animated. He was offering suggestions and identifying individuals that we should speak to. He indicated that he could help us. He wanted us to speak to another set of global leaders. He talked about some of his own career history at GM and his involvement as plant manager in four different plants and his work with the international union.

We experienced a similar level of advocacy when we presented to the large group of senior manufacturing executives for the first time. At the end of the meeting we requested a "champion" from the group who would be able to facilitate introductions for us elsewhere in the company. Five hands in a room of about fourteen people suddenly went up.

A second pattern was the testimonials. At the same large-group meeting mentioned above, our key contact introduced us by stating that some might be surprised that he was focusing attention on the "soft side of manufacturing," since he was known as the kind of guy "who is mostly interested in getting on with the job and getting the job done right." His comments were made all the more compelling when he reported the reaction of the president of a union local (viewed by some as difficult to work with) who emphasized the positive impact of the cultural study and the tools. His remarks ended with the following: "We are not trying to write GMS all over again," but we "want to get it set up right, not just go and get it done."

At a later meeting of the same group, feedback was requested from the two plants that participated in the pilot study. The plant manager of one of the plants made the following comments:

We did it [the review of the collaboration tools] with our key four.[8] And we were pretty honest. We could look at our culture, not the one we want to have but what is. You have to be realistic. We warmed up . . . The tools work well on you and on your work group. You have to integrate [the tools] with Quality Network. There is a way for a peaceful passage . . . [and] opportunity for combining [the tools with Quality Network] . . . What the tools taught us to do is where are we strong and weak. You can drive collaboration more. How would you know when you get there? Look at your SPQRC measures.[9]

He ended his remarks in the following way: "We got feedback from the Professional Managers Network Group like 'Hey, it requires total buy-in' and 'makes you look at yourself' and it makes us 'walk the talk.'" A project manager at the other pilot plant also offered feedback:

I have to be totally honest with you. We were all supervisors and at first it was another tool-of-the-month club. But we found it refreshing that someone was asking us [our views]. It's kind of like looking at a mirror. It makes you focus on how you treat one another . . . The Story Packet builds real-life stories; you can discuss it, and this opened our eyes. The video game opens your mind to how you [impact others] . . . This would be an outstanding [set of material] as we are training for GMS, and they were an outstanding research team . . . But, it's like my treadmill. I have a great treadmill, but if I don't use I don't get the benefits. We still use these tools today.

A third pattern that emerged from the assessments was that the tools were perceived to be aligned with both GMS and the Quality

Network. Prior to the development of the collaboration tools, these two organizations maintained their own focus, mission, and products and had limited interaction with each other. With the availability of our collaboration tools, many suggested that they could serve as a bridging function, connecting the two organizations together. Moreover, the tools' content was sufficiently different from the documentation associated with GMS or the Quality Network that it had the potential to build in a relationships component to GMS and revitalize the underdeveloped Quality Network Action Strategies.

Forms of Resistance

As we considered options for how the collaboration tools might be deployed, we made a decision to conduct a formal evaluation of the effect of the tools on plant culture. Our thought was that with the appropriate kind of evidence, the tools might be more compelling from an impact standpoint, and we might be able to jump-start a widespread implementation of the tools across GM's U.S. plants.

We had interacted with the GMS organization through interviews and presentations for a number of years. Lower-ranking GMS personnel, both in the plants and in the central GMS organization, had been eager to find ways to implement the collaboration tools within GMS. GMS executive leaders, however, behaved differently. They never appeared convinced of the value of the tools, though it was pointed out, "There is nothing in the material that you presented that has any conflict with GMS." Indeed, their acceptance of the tools seemed at least partially contingent on their perceived usefulness in the plants. One GMS leader stated, "The bigger issue for me is for the personnel directors. How does that personnel director see it integrated into the [GMS] People Involvement Strategy, moving into their overall plant?" With respect to the evaluation, they candidly reported that they had no resources to support it. GMS leaders also seemed uncomfortable working with the Quality Network: "We do not implement GMS jointly; GMS is strictly a management activity." When asked if they would consider modifying GMS documentation to incorporate the tools, one GMS executive stated, "I was not thinking of that," though in a follow-up statement he conceded, "If we hear feedback from the International [UAW] Union, 'Hey this is working well; we are seeing some no-kidding bottom-line business results,' well, we will be close enough to it [the collaboration tools] and we would consider it for inclusion [in GMS]." In the same meeting, they seemed to contradict themselves by stating that the collaboration tools should not be part of GMS because "This work that you have been doing is not global and GM-GMS is a global operation—a global process." Their comments represented a combination of cultural obstacles including cross-cultural conflict (vis-à-vis the Quality Network), ethnocentrism, and resistance to change. Their disinterest and reluctance suggested that they were not willing participants in the cultural-transformation process.

Resistance took a different form with the Quality Network. The UAW considered our research study and the applications we developed to be a management initiative rather than a "joint" initiative in which they participated in the study's data collection and analysis. Quality Network leaders in the plants had tipped us off to this issue even as we were gathering our early field data, though it was never a problem for us then. We also experienced some UAW resistance from one of the two pilot plants during the pilot phase of the collaboration tools, though we were able to deal with that situation.

But at this point, we wanted to scale-up our efforts to include a large proportion of hourly employees in an evaluation of the collaboration tools at a demonstration plant. We learned that involving union employees in what was considered plant floor "training" would necessitate buy-in from the Quality Network (a part of the International UAW). This excerpt from our field notes focuses first on this problem and then on the solution arrived at by George (a Quality Network leader) and James (a GM manufacturing leader):

> *George:* For our membership, it [the collaboration tools] needs to be part of Quality Network. You've bypassed the joint arena. This is outside the joint arena, and this is different from what our [UAW] vice president wants done . . . Many of our Action Strategies do exactly what your tools do. You are trying to run out in front of us and this is creating a problem—a political problem for us. We would only want to participate if it were joint.
>
> *James:* If we go beyond the two [pilot] plants, we want to be of the same mind-set [as the UAW].
>
> *George:* We would send out a joint team to the plants [to do the training]. If it's good for the membership, we should do it . . . Let's look forward. I think we can get there. Let's put a team together [to expose employees to the tools] . . . And it should be done, absolutely.

This interface with the Quality Network arm of the International UAW was part of our introduction to the UAW as an institution with its own cultural rules, expectations, and activities. The same obstacles that appeared in our interactions with GMS (e.g., ethnocentrism, resistance to change, cross-cultural conflict) now appeared in our interaction with the Quality Network. Ultimately, this "negotiation" resulted in an agreement for our research group to train Quality Network employees in the use of the collaboration tools so that they, in turn, could train work groups in the demonstration plant to use them.

With the Quality Network trainers ready to begin work on the evaluation, we were advised of a potential plant that might be willing to serve as the demonstration plant for the evaluation. We made two visits to this plant with our new Quality Network advocate and his GM management counterpart. There we met with the plant manager, personnel director, and a few other plant leaders; not present were the shop chair or the president of the union local who were part of the plant's key four. Strikingly similar forms of resistance (e.g., ethnocentrism, resistance to change, cross-cultural conflict) again emerged as we talked about the possibility of conducting an evaluation of the collaboration tools. The plant manager did most of the talking. Over the course of the eighty-minute meeting, he gave us a list of reasons why his plant should not participate.

- "We have aggressively been implementing team concept."
- "The up-coming contract is hitting us in the very near future."
- "We are spread thin with resources."
- "And then we questioned why this was a good idea for us. We have a plant that works together here. We have a partnership process that is unique. All of the managers are keyed up with the shop committee. We have [had] a working understanding of that process for twelve years. We have restrengthened the partnership process [recently]. One question is, why study a plant that works well together?"
- "Whatever happens here, it has to be blessed by the UAW and GM."
- "We have a portion of the plant now under construction."
- "We are bringing in a new [product]."
- "We have teams that are being severed and then reconvened in other forms. How would all of this [restructuring] affect the evaluation?"

We were asked to return to the plant the following day to review the evaluation proposal with the key four. This time reaction came almost exclusively from the union. The content of their statements, tone of voice, and insistence that the discussion not exceed thirty-five minutes came across to our research group as hostile. The managers were relatively quiet.

- Skilled trades representative—"Union and management work hand in hand [here]. We talk about it all. We have team concept. We have been working towards it for years. We are having tremendous success. So where are we at? You are trying to change the terminology, and we are having tremendous success."
- Shop chair—"We are doing this stuff already. We couldn't commit. We need to do this stuff. We don't have time for it."
- Group leader—"We do it all now. I mean no disrespect to you, Elizabeth [Briody]. But we could have written these tools."

The second half of the meeting revealed a plant culture that might have benefited from the collaboration tools. As several people indicated during the meeting that they would have to leave the meeting early, one of the Quality Network leaders said to us, "You have only got one shot at this and this is a hard sell." This passage from Elizabeth Briody's field notes summarizes the remainder of the meeting:

I asked which tool they would like to see. Several people started laughing and said the one they could use was the Workplace Disagreements [Collaboration Tool] and they wanted to see the video [of the Hoist Story]. I said we didn't have enough time to show the video because the video is fifteen minutes long [because of the stated time constraints]. But I can take you through the tool itself. I then proceeded to take them through the tool . . . Then, the shop chair essentially ended the meeting by dismissing people, saying, "Can we have more discussion about this as a key four group? Thank you very much everyone!"

One other plant was recommended by the senior manufacturing group as a possible site for the evaluation. This plant visit involved a senior manufacturing executive, three Quality Network leaders, one GMS employee, and several members of our research team. On our way to the plant, the senior manufacturing executive was confident that this plant would allow us to conduct the evaluation, as this passage from the field notes makes clear: "He talked about how he anticipated no problems in terms of conducting an implementation and evaluation at [the plant]. He said that he had a great relationship with the plant manager and that she was very smart—as were her staff and the union leaders. He felt that things would go very smoothly." His introductory remarks at the meeting also exuded his confidence: "[One of our greenfield plants] has launched their plant with these tools. Now we need a [brownfield] plant to take these tools on. You are really the demonstration plant—I won't say guinea pigs [laughing]. Hopefully we can roll this out to every assembly and stamping plant [in the United States]. There is a lot riding on your shoulders . . . I'd like to kick this off here and give it six months of work with intermediate updates."

As the meeting proceeded, plant leaders at this second potential demonstration plant expressed concerns that paralleled those of the first potential demonstration plant, as well as those articulated by the Quality Network. These concerns reflected some of the same cultural obstacles (i.e., ethnocentrism, resistance to change, cross-cultural conflict). They asked about who would fund the effort and learned that they would be largely responsible. They indicated that nothing in the collaboration tools seemed different from what was already being done at the plant: "We try to emphasize that collaborative environment here routinely. If we can't relate this [collaboration tool effort] to Quality Network and GMS, it will look like something different to employees. We have emphasized collaboration. We've been pretty successful. They [plant employees] can demonstrate some awareness of it." They pointed out that they had an ongoing "cultural training" program for employees. The plant manager also stated, "Then you got issues like he's [shop chair] got to get reelected." (In a follow-up conversation, she indicated, "When they [the UAW] are getting ready for elections, they just do not like to make a move [on any new initiatives] because it hurts them politically.") At the end of our visit, we toured the plant with the personnel director, captured in this excerpt from the field notes: "He said that the points that we were making about the importance of collaboration were really good, and that while this was a good plant, there were areas of the plant that could really benefit from the use of the tools. The collaboration in those areas was somewhat spotty."

Our efforts to conduct an evaluation of the collaboration tools were unsuccessful. We were unable to persuade the local plant leadership of two different plants to approve and support the evaluation despite endorsement from both senior manufacturing executives and Quality Network leaders. Not only did the GM plant management and local union leaders in each plant agree that they did not want to participate in the evaluation, they were successful in opposing the requests from their own (GM and International UAW) leaders. We suspect that issues in the broader environment associated with the GM-UAW relationship accounted for the refusal by both plants to work with us. Informal discussion about the then-upcoming 2007 national labor negotiations were already underway, with formal negotiations scheduled to begin within one to two months of our plant visits. The message was already circulating that GM would be seeking significant concessions from the UAW because GM's per-hour labor costs were uncompetitive compared with the Japanese transplants, and that GM's survival was at stake. Thus, while our research group had senior executive support for the evaluation, these same executives and their local plant management were reluctant to add any additional stress at the local level. Moreover, launching a new initiative (like the evaluation) that did not immediately and visibly relate to GM's bottom line was not a top priority.

Our experience suggests that environmental interference can have an important impact on organizational-culture-change efforts. Cultural transformation is difficult and complex even when there is significant leadership support for the change efforts. Sometimes change requires the "right" environment combined with the "right" timing; in the case of the proposed evaluation, it appears we had neither. Other factors may have been at play in preventing the evaluation, such as our lack of direct personal or professional contacts or advance buy-in at the two potential demonstration plants. Given the shifting cultural and environmental circumstances, it is probably worth a shot at reintroducing the initiative at a later time when there is more openness to innovative ideas and cultural change.

Conclusions

We contend that the collaboration tools could and should be potentially powerful devices for transforming parts of the old way at GM (as discussed in earlier chapters) so that the culture progresses toward the cultural ideal. First, the tools are the result of a research study in which collaboration surfaced strongly and repeatedly as the most important element to GM employees in their worldview of the future. Second, they reflect the inputs of both study participants and researchers; both groups built on each other's knowledge, ideas, and experiences in crafting the tools. Third, they have the potential to let members of the culture learn, explore, maintain, or change the existing culture so that they can move closer to the ideal. Fourth, the tools are designed for low-context organizational cultures where people can benefit from the written documentation and the opportunities to learn and practice what the tools teach. Fifth, the tools are flexible in that they can be applied in many different contexts (e.g., meeting starters, conversations between superiors and subordinates, problem-solving efforts). Finally, we know that the tools are successful in engaging employees to cooperate and collaborate with each other toward plant goals. Both the pilot test and the ongoing use of the tools at the greenfield plant attest to their success.

The resistance of some manufacturing plants and GMS staff to implementation did not reflect rejection of the collaboration tools (as tools). Instead, the issues were the need for new training in using the tools (which had a dollar value associated with it that they would have to absorb); acceptance of a new, "collaborative" way of doing work and process; and acceptance of a set of tools that they had not developed, all at a time of severe organizational stress. Strong leadership commitment, patience, and persistence are critical elements for successful cultural transformation.

Tools or applications, such as the ones developed at GM, can be an essential component in the cultural-transformation process. For those organizations that consider collaboration an in-house weakness, the collaboration tools can be used more or less off the shelf with minor modifications. Typically, however, the tools serve a more general function as a model for reinforcing the cultural ideal or desired transformation. They represent the types of applications that organizations can develop to align with their own perspectives on the ideal. Indeed, organizations can use the tools to guide their own "fieldwork" with employees on their cultural ideals. In short, our tools can help organizations ask themselves the "right" questions, explore alternative options, and chart a path to the future that makes sense to them.

CHAPTER 8

LESSONS LEARNED, FUTURES PLANNED

In this book we have explored about one hundred years of cultural transformations within automotive manufacturing. We examined major shifts in the structure and dynamics of work in the United States, emphasizing especially the contrasts between mass production and flexible and lean production. We developed two models of cultural transformation—one focusing on the elements of cultural adaptiveness, cultural responsiveness, and cultural problem solving, and the other that uses the metaphor of a bridge to focus on organizational-culture-change processes. We described a consensus-based cultural ideal for GM's manufacturing culture that identifies one possible model for GM as it heads into its future. We also introduced a set of tools that GM and other U.S.-based organizations can use to facilitate the change process where change in collaboration, cooperation, and relationships are needed. Each of these aspects of manufacturing culture has the potential to yield benefits not only for GM and other U.S. manufacturing organizations but also for other U.S. organizations as well. Our focus in this chapter is to consider the lessons from this study of manufacturing culture and the ways in which those lessons are applicable to issues of cultural transformation in the American workplace.

LEARNING FROM PRODUCTION-WORK PARADIGMS

Production-work paradigms and the firms associated with them are situated within a particular historical and cultural context. These paradigms are affected by both conditions internal to the firm and conditions external to the firm. An interesting lesson that arises from their history is captured in the aphorism that "the more things change, the more they stay the same," or perhaps more accurately, change does not go in a straight line; it spirals back on itself with increasing refinement because of the need to "improve" existing processes. This historical information identifies many of the areas of tension and transformation that must be addressed in the development of any new production-work paradigm—including the extremes of hierarchy, individualism, and conflict orientation—as well as the elements that must carry forward to make that paradigm feasible.

Mass Production

Ford was a master at cultural transformation. Building on the processes and experiences of earlier industries, he developed an approach and a scale to the organization of work that was more efficient and profitable than ever seen before in the automotive industry. He created an organization that valued creativity, innovation, openness to technical changes, and experimentation, though only among "experts." As his success grew, he solved his human resources problem in a way—a five-dollar-per-day wage—that lives in legend. Eventually, he and his company lost much of their ability to adapt and misread both the market and his work force. But the production-work paradigm that Ford pioneered was not changed significantly by Ford's decline. General Motors had a similar mass-production approach for decades. The paradigm as it played out on the plant floor was not changed fundamentally by the influence of the UAW. The durability of mass production through prosperity, depression, strikes, and war attests to its adaptiveness and responsiveness. It was not until sixty years after Ford's innovative work that the flexible and lean production-work paradigm came to automotive manufacturing.

What Ford can teach us today is to think of the organization and its people as a system. Everything was constructed to be consistent with his vision of the ideal, from hiring, to product, to the organization of work. Through his holistic orientation to production, he tried to optimize the entire organization, keeping in mind his goal to produce vehicles that an increasingly greater proportion of America could purchase. As problems arose in his factories (e.g., absenteeism and turnover, rise in materials costs), he did not ignore them but sought workable solutions. Organizations can benefit from a systems-thinking approach. It is worth the effort to step back, identify the goals, obstacles, and enablers, and develop a balanced, multipronged approach to systematically improve the organization.

Flexible and Lean Production

TPS, the gold standard of flexible and lean systems, teaches additional lessons. Constrained by resources, focused on changeable customer demands, and shaped by an orientation to the group (rather than the individual), a flexible and lean production system developed at Toyota. Over time, the firm changed from hierarchically focused control over incremental innovation to team-focused control (or empowerment) *for* innovation. Production flow, standardized work as a platform for improvement, and the removal of all forms of waste were made possible by innovative ideas and problem-solving skills from groups across the organization. The ability to gather, learn, borrow, adapt, implement, improve, and integrate has become a Toyota hallmark, setting it apart from its competitors. Decades of training in developing quality and reliable products through incremental improvement helped to create and sustain a favorable public perception. Toyota, too, sought compliance from employees, along with loyalty and hard work, though it was more successful in creating a positive image of its production culture to those outside its organization than was Ford.

One of the lessons from Toyota is its ability to build connections both within and beyond its manufacturing system and learn from those connections. It activates its networks in the search for new knowledge and information created outside its organizational boundaries. It then uses its high-context culture to its advantage, facilitating information sharing and learning within the organization for the benefit of the whole. Low-context organizations could consider ways of adapting key elements of the Toyota approach to learning—connecting, sharing, and diffusing. Simple questions can be used to probe a low-context organization's current learning processes:

- Describe the connections your organization has with its external customers—their number, quality, frequency, timeliness, and value. How could those connections be more useful to your organization?
- What kinds of knowledge and information are exchanged between your organization and its external customers? How balanced is the flow of knowledge and information between your organization and its external customers?
- Under what circumstances are the inputs from external-customer discussions disseminated (or not disseminated) within your organization? How could the channels for diffusing those inputs be improved?

By asking and answering these questions, organizations can examine their own learning process, determine what adjustments, if any, are necessary, and improve their own adaptiveness and responsiveness.

The Hybrid of Mass Production with Flexible and Lean

At the start of its second century of operations, GM is a mix of mass-production principles and flexible-and-lean-production methods (referred to as GMS). Its production culture is a hybrid. Stories and examples from the plant floor portray a cultural shift away from individualized work to shared work, from individually generated work-task solutions to group problem solving, and from production quotas as the primary metric to a "balanced scorecard" in which multiple measures are evaluated (e.g., quotas, quality, health and safety, throughput). This hybrid system came to be associated with significant improvements in vehicle quality and productivity. Conterminously, the firm found selected ways to partner (more often) with union leaders and launch innovative manufacturing initiatives—one of which, GMS, seems to hold the most promise. Employees continue to struggle with GM's silo-ed and autonomous cultural tradition and its parochial, not-invented-here orientation. With its public image still tarnished, the bankruptcy crisis has been reshaping GM's goals and priorities, including the potential for a transformed culture.

An important lesson from GM is that production-work paradigms and organizational cultures can, and do, change. Shortly after GM was established, it adapted mass production for a diverse product offering; since then, its production paradigm has evolved to be more similar to TPS. GM's culture has changed in other ways, including in its emphasis on teams and teamwork, its growing interest in partnering with the UAW, and its improved competitive record. The evidence is clear that GM has been aware of changes in environmental conditions and has been following an incremental strategy for transformation at least since the mid-1980s.

Its adaptiveness may be at an all-time high given the bankruptcy proceedings and the continuing pressure from external stakeholders (e.g., media, GM's board) to "fix the culture." At the same time, there are warnings for other organizations based on the GM experience. Organizations need to pay close attention to the conditions in the broader environment that can impact their operations. They also need to focus on their own internal cultural conditions to ensure that any changes they make are appropriate, consistent with their assessment of the external environment, speedy, fully implemented, and continually reinforced to mitigate any cultural drift.

Learning from Cultural Transformation

This book describes two models for cultural change within a manufacturing environment. Each of the models draws from multiple theories of cultural change (including national-culture and organizational-culture change theories), as well as the research conducted for the Ideal Plant Culture project. The models represent descriptions of the lessons we learned about cultural transformation. The two models provide a framework for understanding evolutionary, transformational change. Other organizations can adapt the key elements of these models for their own transformations.

Cultural Transformation Model

The cultural transformation model focuses on the cognitive (ideological) and processual conditions that impact cultural transformation. One key element of this model is cultural adaptiveness, or the ability to modify existing elements of an organizational culture to fit changing needs within the broader external culture by understanding the need to change, identifying cultural elements that should be changed, and understanding the cultural environment that will facilitate or hinder change. Another important element is cultural responsiveness, or the ability of the organization to change in a timely and focused manner that accommodates existing cultural processes by transforming them into newly configured processes. The intersection of adaptiveness and responsiveness is the transformative process that we have called cultural problem solving. This cultural transformation model is particularly important for understanding perspectives on the cultural ideal and the need for a "new way."

Several lessons emerged from developing the transformation model that other organizations should find useful. First, we learned that identifiable goals or end points that focus and target the transformation process are necessary. Second, creating an incremental process of change (based on increasing stability in the system), rather than an abrupt change (which members of the culture may see as threatening or destabilizing), is preferable. Third, we discovered the need for a clear feedback loop that both measures progress toward change and provides information on the environmental conditions that impact, redirect, or modify the change in negative directions; these environmental conditions can be both macro (e.g., economic downturn, bankruptcy) or micro (e.g., a local plant conflict between the union and management) in scope. Essentially the culture must show more willingness to change that unwillingness, must be aware that change is needed, and must be willing to accept, adapt, and incorporate appropriate change that moves it toward a consensual end point or goal.

The Bridge Model of Transformation

The Bridge Model focuses on the cultural-change processes at the individual, small-group, and organizational level. It contains the primary ideas and conditions that must be incorporated in any successful cultural problem-solving process for complex organizations. It includes the identification of general obstacles to cultural transformations, enablers for successful transformations, and cultural-change tools that move the culture toward and reinforce the consensus ideal. This model is important in helping us understand the broad environmental conditions that have a strong impact on cultural transformations. The Bridge Model produced a number of desired cultural problem-solving results, because it allowed us to (1) identify the cultural conditions that are in play (e.g., a relationship, a cultural value, a way of doing something) that are either hindering or assisting desired change, (2) identify the response to the problem that best resolves the problem in a positive direction, and (3) provide an integrated approach for implementing a solution.

Elements that hinder or prevent change were often the first dimension of the cultural-transformation process that we noticed. Any form of cultural change, from sweeping cultural revolutions to small changes in material culture, always meets some level of resistance. In our analysis of GM manufacturing culture, we were able to identify, confirm, and elaborate on seven barriers to change that must be addressed if the transformation is to be successful. These obstacles to change apply within and beyond manufacturing organizations and therefore will be useful to U.S. organizations generally:

- Having to learn a new culture
- Ethnocentrism
- Cross-cultural conflict
- Resistance to change
- Cultural dilemmas
- Cultural contradictions
- Cultural drift

Most of the obstacles are associated with positive aspects of the existing culture, which we call enablers—the second core element of the Bridge Model. Unlike the obstacles, the enablers are culture specific rather than generic. For GM, they reflect dimensions of manufacturing culture that are captured in views of the cultural ideal and that relate to plant-floor relationships, work practices and processes, work force characteristics, and the physical plant. We recommend that organizations going through some form of planned transformation take the time to search out the enablers that are active in their organizational culture. That way, when the enablers are applied to foster cultural transformation, they will be most effective. Successful enablers for change should include the following guidelines to yield effective change rather than "lip service" change:

- The enabler should have a clear and consensus-driven goal that supports the appropriate direction of desired change.
- The enabler should support incremental rather than abrupt change unless fully disruptive change is the only alternative.
- The enabler should take advantage of local environmental conditions rather than impose a completely new environment.
- The enabler should be viewed as pragmatic or achievable rather than "pie in the sky."
- The enabler should produce minimum interference in routine, daily life while also supporting timely change.
- The enabler must solve known problems.

Following these guidelines will allow organizations to engage in non-disruptive or minimally disruptive cultural transformations.

LEARNING FROM THE CULTURAL IDEAL

We described the cultural-transformation process at GM based on the stories, statements, and behaviors of study participants in the Ideal Plant Culture project. A consensus view of a cultural ideal emerged from across GM's manufacturing organization. This consensus view specified the importance of building and maintaining a culture of collaboration as the avenue for improving organizational effectiveness. Collaboration, or working together toward organizational goals, was also desirable because it reduced the level of tension and conflict, created a sense of community within the work environment, and helped people feel that they were contributing to the organization in important ways. There are lessons from the GM case for other U.S. organizations that want to learn about their own ideal culture and work to attain it.

Developing a Common Understanding of the Ideal

The convergence of viewpoints about the ideal makes some sense given that culture is a collective experience. There are cultural rules operating within the organization, norms for behavior, and shared beliefs, assumptions, and expectations that make the cultural context distinctive. These dimensions of culture are transmitted to newcomers during the acculturation process with the intent of "bringing them up to speed" with the knowledge to be able to function in the culture. Organizations can examine their employees' perspectives for convergence. Some organizations may discover that a consensus viewpoint emerges—as in the GM case. A virtue of a consensus view of the ideal is that organizational "buy-in" is immediate; employee views of the ideal match, enabling the organization to move on to the next steps in the cultural-transformation process. Other organizations may find multiple views of the ideal within their employee population. In that case, the kinds of stories and examples employees tell will furnish some clues to explain the divergence and suggest a way forward.

Understanding employee views of the ideal can help organizations frame their future and identify a set of strategies to help secure that future. The ideal reflects a cultural theme that can be described in a single phrase (e.g., culture of collaboration) and that helps to focus the organization's activity. The ideal represents a state that has not yet been achieved and, indeed, may never be attained completely. The ideal typically compares favorably with past or current experiences, making the contrast poignant and easily understandable. The strategies derived from employees' cultural ideal have an empirical basis as well. Their comments about the ideal typically reflect those aspects of the current culture that require expansion, preservation, modification, or termination. We found that by exploring a range of employee views, many of the potential strategies of the future were embedded in actions that were working well in the current state.

The ideal must be consistent with the overall organizational goals and objectives. Organizations exist for particular reasons (e.g., to offer services, manufacture products, deliver value to customers, increase revenue). Both process (or cultural ideal) and outcome (or end goals) matter. Therefore, a dual focus is most effective. Organizations can develop ways of interfacing and satisfying their external customers while doing so in the spirit of their cultural ideal. That way they achieve their product or service goals and succeed in realizing their ideal. If organizations only focus on the process (as happened at Spring Hill with consensus decision making), then the goals will not be met. By contrast, if organizations only focus on the end goals (as happened in the GM truck plant in the mid-1980s), then the culture suffers with long-term, devastating results.

Focusing on the Ideal

Raising awareness of the ideal in a low-context organizational setting is a first and necessary step. It is important to formalize the ideal and cultural direction as a way to reinforce the change process. The ideal must be made explicit so that it is recognizable in various ways (e.g., focus of company task force, work-group or department slogan) using various means (e.g., conversations, speeches, newsletters, requirement on annual employee evaluations) throughout the organization. The ideal also must be measurable so that its impact on organizational operations, products, and services can be teased out. Metrics related to the ideal can be developed, tested, and then implemented to drive home the point that the ideal matters; such metrics must be viewed within the context of the overall organizational goals. In low-context cultures without these kinds of "cultural" metrics, it is easy to ignore the message or intent of the ideal and decide against trying to achieve it. Formalization through metrics makes the ideal stand out.

Operationalizing Collaboration as the Cultural Ideal

The cultural ideal of collaboration at GM has the potential to become a cultural ideal within U.S. organizations generally, in part because of rising global competition. Indeed, one persistent theme in our findings was that cooperation and group relationships play an important role in successful manufacturing cultures. An emphasis on collaboration is likely to be an area of opportunity for low-context American workplaces, since so much of the work currently done there is done by individuals in isolation from others. The American orientation to work is often contrasted with the orientation to work in high-context cultures. The cultural focus in high-context cultures is on relationships that structure how everything gets done—including information sharing, learning, and work. High-context cultures assume the importance of collaborative relationships in the workplace because the welfare of the group matters.

There are some models for collaboration in the American workplace. As discussed in this book, teams of manufacturing employees have become a critical part of the coordination and problem solving in assembly work. Partnerships often exemplify a collaborative approach.

Examples of collaborative arrangements include university researchers working in conjunction with corporate employees (as in our anthropological research group), small organizations that pool their skills and talents to offer their services to a larger organization or community, or universities that work with firms, nonprofit organizations, or other universities toward some end goal.[1] Informal partnering also occurs within many U.S. organizations when groups have to work together across organizational boundaries.

A collaborative approach has a number of benefits with respect to the internal dynamics of American work organizations. If tasks are assigned to a group, the end result has the potential to be more robust due to the input of multiple people. If that group works together to complete the tasks, the potential for developing strong collaborative relationships is possible; these relationships are not necessarily friendships but rather cooperative, work-related interactions based on mutual respect and trust. If strong collaborative relationships develop in the workplace, there is likely to be a greater familiarity with competencies, increased sharing of work-related knowledge and insights, an improved understanding of how the work of the group aligns with organizational goals, and less internal conflict. The combination of these benefits has the potential to lead to improved organizational effectiveness and organizational performance.

Putting this culture of collaboration into practice requires changing some of the expectations surrounding how work is typically done. One set of solutions is driven by the jobs and their requirements. Entire jobs could be shared if employees are cross-trained and have the necessary competencies and skills. Parts of a job also could be shared—say, under particular conditions (e.g., when there is a deadline, when the office gets busy). Another set of solutions could involve information exchanges designed to highlight collaborative behavior. Meetings could start with a "collaboration message" in which an attendee describes how collaboration was a factor in the success of a project. Supervisors could praise the efforts of particular "teams" in face-to-face discussions. A third set of solutions is driven by employee-evaluation systems (both informal and formal). Work group members could assess each other in terms of the roles they play in the group and the impact of those roles in the final outcome. Compensation, or at least some portion of it, Could be based upon employees' "teamwork" skills, especially their willingness and efforts in contributing to the shared work.

Learning from the Ethnographic Process

The process of gathering and validating ethnographic data as it pertains to cultural transformation and views of the ideal offers several lessons. First, our experience was that employees have perspectives to share. Seasoned employees have knowledge of and experience with past conditions and circumstances; they are positioned to offer a historical viewpoint. Recently hired employees notice cultural elements that the more seasoned employees take for granted (because the latter have come to accept those elements as "normal" and usual). Employees are, in fact, the cultural experts. They are culturally competent in their own organizational culture because they have a direct, personal association with it. They have the stories, the examples, and the cases at the ready. Their cultural experiences can be put to good use in shaping the ideal.

Second, we found, by and large, that employees were eager to share their thoughts on what the ideal should be. They liked being asked for their opinion and they liked articulating their perspective. They found our questions about the ideal culture and how it might help improve their work culture and working conditions interesting to explore. Far from threatening, our questions stimulated employees to imagine a different world—a better world. Thinking about and responding to the questions was largely a positive and enjoyable experience.

Third, we sought a mix of employees in each of the four manufacturing plants associated with our project to ensure that we were capturing a range of work experiences and job types. As we validated our findings, we discovered that the collaborative ideal held throughout GM's U.S. manufacturing operations. It is important to have a mix of organizational roles.[2] For example, in a small business like a medical practice, it would be important to gather the perspectives of those in key roles (e.g., physician, medical assistant, office manager). It also might be possible to gather insights from other similar medical practices—whether through discussion, observation, or existing research literature. Indeed, partnering with similar organizations might be a useful way to compare and contrast insights and to discuss potential strategies and recommendations for change.

Another question concerns who should solicit views of the ideal. Our project involved a mix of full-time GM employees, contracted university researchers, and business consultants/contract employees. Having the project sponsored by GM and having GM researchers involved made access to manufacturing facilities and senior leaders easier. It also signaled that the project was important and relevant

and therefore worth employees' time. Having "outside" researchers involved brought additional skill sets to the project and may have
increased the perception of objectivity. Adopting a similar strategy
with both insiders and outsiders might be helpful to organizations that
do not have the necessary (or sufficient) in-house talent to engage in
this kind of project. In addition, this strategy may mitigate employee
concerns about confidentiality. An alternative to the mixed strategy is
to find an outside group (e.g., university researchers, consultants) to
gather and analyze the feedback.

LEARNING FROM CULTURAL TOOLS

Developing tools or applications to target the cultural ideal is an
important way of facilitating organizational-culture change. In GM,
the structure, content, and goals of the ten collaboration tools were
designed to accommodate the problem-solving elements of the Bridge
Model while helping to foster a culture of collaboration. The tools
target an improved understanding of collaboration, address some of
the specific obstacles to a more collaborative culture, utilize culturally
embedded enablers to reinforce the positive aspects of the existing
culture, and provide a way of measuring progress toward the cultural
ideal. Most of what we learned came from the tools' content and the
design considerations for deployment in GM. We describe here what
might be helpful to organizations as they begin the journey of cultural
transformation.

Pragmatic Enablers for Cultural Transformation

Part of our project mission was to leave GM's manufacturing culture with useful applications that could foster continuous movement
toward the ideal. We have found that the collaboration tools serve
that purpose. Because the tools target a variety of cultural issues—
from learning how to ask objective questions to figuring out the best
approaches for reducing workplace conflict—they can address a range
of problems on the plant floor. The tools also fall into broad categories by their primary function. Some are designed to help employees
understand what collaboration is, others to help employees practice
their collaborative skills, and still others to measure the extent of collaboration in the work culture. These different functions take into
account the variation in levels of ability, skill, and experience with
respect to GM's cultural ideal.

Some organizations may want to use the collaboration tools we developed as an off-the-shelf set of applications, particularly if they decide to focus on collaboration as their cultural ideal. American workplaces stand to benefit from an emphasis on collaboration because of their long-standing tradition of individualized work and their targeted focus on work tasks. The collaboration tools are sufficiently generic that they will work in many organizational settings beyond manufacturing. In the event that specific details of the tools do not apply or do not translate easily, discussion around those details can reveal insights that become springboards for future organizational activity.

Alternately, organizations may want to use our tools as examples of the kinds of applications that could be developed given their culture, their challenges, and their cultural ideals. Thus, the targeted focus or content of their tools would reflect their own cultural environments. In addition, organizations may want to prepare for the likely variation in familiarity, interest, or competency with the cultural ideal that becomes their target for cultural change. Organizations are likely to find, as we did, that people exhibit different levels of competency with respect to the cultural ideal. For example, organizations could develop tools for those with limited skills or experience related to the ideal (in our case, someone who does not routinely act in ways perceived as collaborative), as well as for those with significant abilities and experience. In general, the tools should function to help close the gap between the current state and the ideal and then help sustain or reinforce that ideal in the long term.

Organizational cultures also have to focus attention on the dynamics of the current state. In our study, we identified a set of cultural tensions between necessary but competing elements of manufacturing culture. One example is the tension between hierarchy and teamwork—the need to have clear direction and the need to have flexible and creative work teams. Another example is the tension between standardization and constant improvement. Standardization is crucial in producing a predictable level of productivity, while creativity is critical for achieving a new and better level of standardization and remaining competitive in the face of other people's creativity. The continuing resolution of these types of "cultural contradictions" or Cultural Hot Spots (as we labeled one of our collaboration tools), is an important goal or direction for any version of a cultural ideal that might be adopted in the United States. They are directly related to or embedded in the need to evaluate, change, and improve relationships within the workplace.

Tools are only effective if they are endorsed and used consistently by people throughout the organization. We found that cultural transformation is easier to achieve and sustain if the tools are supported and endorsed by key organizational members with a people-centered orientation and a long-term vision for change. It is best if this group includes "informal" leaders as well as individuals in formally designated leadership roles. In the GM case, it mattered to have the support of both types of leaders—one reflecting the informal cultural system and the other the formal organizational hierarchy. With endorsement coming from different parts of the cultural system, the likelihood of a successful transformation is increased.

Stories as Powerful Motivators for Change

People tell stories whether it be by the water cooler or on the plant floor. Stories are a social currency shared among organizational members. Like culture, stories belong to everyone and are told to pass on information and lessons about cultural matters. One virtue of stories is that individuals can generally "see" themselves in the roles of the characters, understand and appreciate the story's message, and relate the story to their own life experiences. In our study, stories were one of the key ways in which we were able to learn about manufacturing culture. Later, we were able to use the stories to describe and explain that culture, documenting those same stories as part of the collaboration tools. Even for a group of researchers like us, the storytelling activity became a collaborative, participatory, and reciprocal effort involving us in the cultural transformation process. Organizations can build on the personal associations, memories, and cultural experiences depicted in stories and through storytelling. Planned efforts for organizational-culture change would do well to incorporate stories into their design to guide and drive the change process.

We discovered significant interest across GM manufacturing in the stories we collected. One reason for the interest was that formal efforts to document stories to illustrate some collective cultural experience were rare. A second reason was that stories make particular cultural "points." The stories we were told often contrasted the current state and desired ideal or future state of the organization. The Hoist Story, for example, emphasizes the frustrations in dealing with both a production manager and a supplier who were not eager to work with the engineer and his team. The cultural "point" of this story was that the engineer and team worked together with the supplier in ways that exemplified the ideal of collaboration and fixed the hoist problem.

The stories we collected were so compelling that, even in our retelling of a story "slightly incorrectly" (say, at a meeting), employees typically gave us the benefit of the doubt. They would "correct" the inaccuracy, often with a smile, and then put their full attention into discussing the story's overall message.

Diversity in Tool Design

As we began developing the collaboration tools, we tried to accommodate the low-context cultural environments of GM manufacturing. Members of low-context cultures work better when information is provided that is "spelled out in detail." Indeed, the change process itself is more likely to be successful if employees have access to the written documentation and then can use it as a basis for organizational conversations and discussions. Consequently, we created collaboration tools in both hard copy and electronic forms so that they could be reproduced and shared. U.S. organizations interested in creating their own applications should consider the importance of the written word.

We also spent considerable time working with a diverse group of union and management leaders when developing the tools. They were able to provide us with specific kinds of content guidance on some of the prototype tools, as well as ideas for new tools that could be created. As part of this multiyear exchange with the leadership team, our awareness of existing GM applications (through Quality Network and GMS) grew. The final version of the collaboration tools is compatible with and complementary to these earlier union and corporate efforts. Applications that "fit in" to the current culture in terms of format and process are likely to be perceived as more user friendly and helpful than those that do not.

A related issue when developing cultural applications for use in organizational settings concerns how and when people learn. Accommodating different learning styles can be overlooked when planning for organizational change. Some people are visual learners, while others are auditory, and still others use a combination of methods to acquire new knowledge and skills. We talked with employees about when and where the tools might be used and learned that there were many possibilities for their use (e.g., during group meetings, as decision-making support for a single individual, in one-on-one conversations). Because some people were more likely to use the tools as members of a group and others were more likely to use them on their own, we designed the tools to accommodate both situations.

Organizations developing their own applications should recognize differences in learning styles by building in a diversity of format into the tool design.

Perhaps the most frequent way in which the tools have been used is when groups assemble for a particular purpose (e.g., at a staff meeting, in a work-group discussion). The exercises associated with the tools encourage group learning. A particular exercise from one of the tools could be selected for discussion on a given day. Creative brainstorming typically occurs as the ideas are discussed and debated with the goal of finding the appropriate solution. This form of group learning, through the use of the exercises, is culturally consistent with the usual practices of groups getting together to resolve technical issues in GM.

A different learning format is associated with the Individual Relationship Effectiveness Metrics Tool. This application promotes learning through introspection. It helps the individual understand the current state of his or her collaborative abilities, thereby creating a baseline. As that individual revisits the tool on subsequent occasions, it is possible to see the extent to which the baseline changes over time. Exercises completed on one's own reaffirm the notion that each person is part of the process for change. Working with tools as an individual, rather than as a member of a larger group, provides useful insight for that individual who then may be able to apply those insights within the organizational culture.

A third format incorporated into the collaboration tools is the use of video and the visual aspects of computer simulation. This format offers a visual focus for the learner that can reinforce the cultural ideal and may be entertaining as well. Indeed, when we were developing the *ExplorePlantCulture* computer game, we found that it would be considered within the genre of "serious games" because of its learning emphasis. Reactions to verbal and nonverbal actions shown visually provide additional depth and detail about plant life. Seeing these details seems to help viewers stay focused on learning. The visual format also encourages those watching the video or playing the game to place themselves in the "shoes" of the characters, a parallel with the ways stories appear to affect employees. Computer simulation, thus, presents employees with an interactive learning experience. The game helps players see the impact of the decisions they make on plant culture—both through immediate visual reinforcement of the gauges that are linked with their decision choices and through a summary explanation of how collaboratively the players worked to solve plant problems. The feedback we received from players was positive, and the game turned out to be a platform for learning lessons about the ways that tools can be developed and deployed. At the same time, the development costs (e.g., time, effort, dollars) were significantly higher than the other collaboration tools. Other organizations may want to use the game we developed (as one option for focusing on aspects of organizational-culture change) or investigate simulations on the open market as alternatives to developing their own simulation in-house.

REMEMBERING BACK AND LOOKING FORWARD

As we were finalizing the book's manuscript, we asked each other what we had found remarkable about working on the Ideal Plant Culture project. Tracy Meerwarth emphasized the "soup-to-nuts" process from data gathering, to analysis and validation, to applications development. What was valuable about the project was the opportunity to learn directly from people on the plant floor, take what was learned, and make those lessons available to the broader manufacturing culture. Part of the satisfaction was in "nailing" the cultural analysis, and the rest was in seeing the collaboration tools used to reinforce the kinds of changes that people on the plant floor said they wanted most.

In thinking about this same question, Elizabeth Briody referenced a quote that we had heard many times and in many ways: "It's all about relationships." This quote has a particular interpretation. It refers to relationships that are based on cooperation, trust, and respect—the cultural ideal of collaboration. Employees want to be able to interact effectively with each other, work with others to find solutions to plant problems, and contribute their skills and talents to plant goals. The meaning behind the quote is simple, yet profound. American work culture, traditionally, has not paid attention to collaboration because what has mattered was getting the job done. What we have learned from working on this book is that ordinary (and extraordinary) working people are telling us loudly and clearly that the culture must change. Collaboration does matter and should be cultivated and celebrated; without it, having an impact becomes much more elusive.

One of the things that Bob Trotter found remarkable about the Ideal Plant Culture project was the way in which our existing theories provided a powerful framework for identifying the obstacles and enablers captured in the project and in the Ideal Cultural Model. He also found that our methods provided excellent processes for creating and affirming the cultural models, for understanding the successes and failures of the transformation process, and for providing a roadmap of how other organizations could follow out these same theories and processes to their own benefit.

This book provides a window into the many different ways that the cultural transformation process plays out within American manufacturing culture. It is grounded in historical and ethnographic data gathered over a long period of time, based on careful analysis, and validated by tough critics throughout an organization desperately trying to change and resisting change simultaneously. It expands the literature on organizational-culture change by introducing the cultural ideal (a consensus view from employees) as a way to direct and guide the change process. Through the Bridge Model, it illustrates the known cultural obstacles with the culture-specific enablers and collaboration tools to achieve and sustain that ideal, making the transformation process useful for change-management practitioners. The book also argues strongly for a new work paradigm for the American workplace. With collaboration as a foundation, working relationships become stronger, information sharing and learning occur more readily, and work cultures become more effective in achieving their goals.

Notes

Foreword

1. Jordan 2013.

Chapter 1

1. Briody and Trotter 2008, 4.
2. Briody, Cavusgil, and Miller 2004.
3. In-depth ethnographies (i.e., descriptive accounts of a particular culture) can be thought of as case studies. Their power and strength lie in features such as the multiple methods used in data gathering, the length of the field period, the composition of the sample, and the cycle of exploration, confirmation, and validation of the cultural patterns. Ethnographies yield cultural complexities that can be compared and contrasted with other complex systems (Schensul and LeCompte 1999; Harris 2001).
4. Womack, Jones, and Roos 1990.
5. Keller 1989, 21.
6. UAW stands for the International Union, United Automobile, Aerospace and Agricultural Implement Workers of America. It is the body that represents almost all GM hourly employees in the United States.
7. Alland 1973.
8. Steward 1955; Driver 1973; Schneider 1977.
9. Sahlins and Service 1960; Barth 1967, 1972.
10. Barth 2000; Sahlins 2000; Denison and Mishra 1995.
11. The seminal work on context was done by E. T. and M. R. Hall (Hall and Hall 1987, 1989). Researchers in cross-cultural communication and cross-cultural training specialists have used their work extensively, particularly in relation to Internet learning, art, managerial practices, negotiation, and conflict (Twu 2009; Ito 2005; Salleh 2005; Ting-Toomey 1999; Brislin 1993).
12. Since GM's culture is strongly embedded in the American culture, and GM has been struggling to change and adapt for so long, it becomes an ideal empirical example.
13. There are varying models and metaphors for this interaction. A simple one is a Hegelian dialectic that has a dominant culture viewpoint (thesis)

countered by an alternative viewpoint (counter-thesis or antithesis) that results in a cultural transformation synthesizing the two—in our case, a manufacturing culture adapting to a changing global environment.

14. We use the term "employee" or "plant personnel" to mean any individual working in that manufacturing culture regardless of job classification or status. When role or status is relevant to the particular example, we use a more specific identifier (e.g., engineer, salaried employee, plant leader).

15. Holland and Quinn 1987; Kleinman 1980.

16. While this approach has been used predominantly in medical anthropology and health care studies, it is currently being used successfully in industrial ethnographies that are directed at cultural change (Paolisso 2007), conflict and conflict resolution (Hirsch 2000), and the development of changes in belief systems (Shepherd, McMullen, and Jennings 2007).

17. Trotter and Schensul 1998; Strauss and Quinn 1997.

18. In our work, we also link a cultural-models approach to the current trend in "design anthropology," or client-centered (participatory) design within manufacturing systems or organizational development (Jordan 2003; Lengwiler 2008; Wasson 2002; Salvador, Bell, and Anderson 1999; Trigg and Anderson 1996). These studies show the increasing productivity payoff for paying attention to multiple stakeholder groups when designing products or processes targeted at meeting both industrial and cultural goals in business organizations.

19. Varenne 1977.

20. Tocqueville 1990b; Bellah et al. 1985.

Chapter 2

1. Staudenmayer, Tyre, and Perlow 2002; Britan and Denich 1976; Chance 1960.

2. A typical way to illustrate these conditions is to portray groupings of subcultures, organizational cultures, and regional, national, and international cultures as nested or interfacing entities (Jordan 1994).

3. Hall and Hall 1989, 147.

4. Gannon and Associates 1994, 312.

5. Briody, Cavusgil, and Miller 2004.

6. Hall and Hall 1987, 42.

7. Fujimoto 1995; Wada 1995.

8. Kuhn 1986.

9. Hounshell 1995.

10. Wada 1995.

11. Williams, Haslam, and Williams 1992; Ling 1990.

12. Sloan 1963.

13. Kuhn 1986.

14. Gerth and Mills 1946, 59. Other writers have used this concept as well (Hirst and Zeitlin 1991; Teague 1990), though Williams, Haslam, and Williams (1992) argue that there is no value in using the ideal-type heuristic if the key elements contributing to it can be disproven, as they claim to have done with the mass production "stereotype" at Ford's Highland Park plant. We believe that the empirical findings of Williams, Haslam, and Williams may reveal some features of mass production in its earlier forms, reflecting what was going on at that particular plant at a particular point in time.

15. Harris 2001.

16. Piore and Sabel 1984.

17. Hounshell 1983, 1.

18. Hirst and Zeitlin 1991, 2.

19. Hounshell 1983, 10–11.

20. Ling 1990; Lewchuk 1987.

21. Shimada 2007.

22. Coy 1989.

23. Hounshell 1983, 3.

24. Ling 1990, 103.

25. Hounshell 1983, 218; emphasis in original. The Model T is generally considered as the first affordable car ever produced. It was made between 1908 and 1927 by Ford Motor Company and has been referred to colloquially as the "Tin Lizzie" or "Flivver."

26. Lewchuk 1987.

27. Williams, Haslam, and Williams 1992.

28. Hounshell 1983.

29. Ling 1990.

30. Hounshell 1983, 247.

31. Applebaum 1984a.

32. Braverman 1974.

33. Hounshell 1983.

34. Wollering, quoted in Hounshell 1983, 221.

35. Ford 1926, 822.

36. For example, in the 1830s, it took about two hundred hours of labor to make a buggy by hand; by 1865, it took only about forty hours due to increased mechanization (Ling 1990, 108).

37. Hounshell 1995.

38. Ling 1990.

39. Williams, Haslam, and Williams 1992, 527.

40. Hirst and Zeitlin 1991, 3.

41. Nash 1984.

42. Coy 1989, 3.

43. Kuhn 1986, 4.

44. Williams, Haslam, and Williams 1992, 542.

45. Ford 1922, 22.

46. Lewchuk 1987.
47. Ling 1990, 142.
48. Hounshell 1983. Taylor (1911) emphasized the subdivision of work tasks based on time and motion studies as a way to improve efficiency and productivity.
49. Lewchuk 1987.
50. Ling 1990.
51. Lewchuk 1987, 35.
52. Ling 1990, 114.
53. Lewchuk 1987.
54. Hounshell 1983, 11.
55. Nevins and Hill 1954, 270–71.
56. Ling 1990; Lewchuk 1987.
57. Ling 1990, 129.
58. Applebaum 1984a.
59. Ford 1922, 103.
60. Ling 1990, 129.
61. Ling 1990, 129.
62. Hounshell 1983.
63. Hounshell 1983, 290.
64. Hounshell 1983, 290.
65. Goody 1989, 238–42.
66. Berden 1989.
67. Applebaum 1984b, 42.
68. Ling 1990, 132.
69. Lewchuk 1987, 59.
70. Ling 1990, 147.
71. Ling 1990, 155.
72. Ford 1922, 92.
73. Coy 1989.
74. Applebaum 1984.
75. Ford 1922, 60.
76. Hounshell 1983, 327.
77. Ford 1922, 86.
78. Ford 1922, 98, 100.
79. Deafenbaugh 1989.
80. See Detroit Institute of Arts.
81. Hounshell 1983, 323, 327.
82. Hounshell 1983, 259.
83. Shiomi and Wada 1995.
84. Piore and Sabel 1984, 17.
85. Hirst and Zeitlin 1991, 7.
86. Whyte 1991, 124.
87. Dertouzos et al. 1989.
88. Womack, Jones, and Roos 1990.
89. Womack et al. 1990, 13–14.

90. Liker 2004.
91. Camuffo and Volpato 1995; Piore and Sabel 1984.
92. The word *toyoda* means "abundant rice fields." Kiichiro Toyoda and other members of the automobile department of Toyoda Automatic Loom chose the name "Toyota" for the new company because of its "clarity in sound and potential advertising appeal" (Cusumano 1985, 59).
93. Becker 2001.
94. Nonaka 1995,
95. The word *andon* in Japanese means "lantern."
96. Holweg 2007, 421.
97. Cusumano 1985, 66.
98. Wada 1995.
99. Cusumano 1985.
100. Wada 1995, 14.
101. Cusumano 1985, 60–66, 70.
102. Cusumano 1985, 265.
103. Ohno in Wada 1995, 22.
104. Whyte 1991, 130.
105. Holweg 2007.
106. Ohno interview quoted in Wada 1995, 21.
107. Wada 1995.
108. Cole 1995, 374.
109. Imai 1986, 26–27.
110. Ford 1922, 100.
111. Cusumano 1985.
112. Deming 1982, 23–24.
113. Deming 1982, 88.
114. Nonaka 1995; Dertouzos et al. 1989; Imai 1986.
115. Whyte 1991, 106.
116. Cusumano 1985, 117.
117. Cusumano 1985.
118. Hamada 1991.
119. Hall and Hall 1987, 76–77.
120. Cusumano 1985.
121. Cusumano 1985, 123.
122. Fujimoto 1995, 211.
123. Shiomi 1995, 43.
124. Tomlinson 2005, 288.
125. Shiomi 1995.
126. Hirst and Zeitlin 1991.
127. Cusumano 1985, 180–81.
128. Cusumano 1985, 183.
129. Hall and Hall 1987, 8.
130. Cusumano 1985, 180–81; Ling 1990, 129.
131. Stewart and Raman 2007, 80.
132. Holweg 2007, 422.

133. Wada 1995.
134. Ishikawa 1985.
135. Cleveland 2006; Sobek, Ward, and Liker 1999.
136. Nemoto 1987, 207.
137. Stewart and Raman 2007; Nemoto 1987.
138. Liker 2004, 251–56.
139. Whyte 1991, 127.
140. Goody 1989.
141. Compare to Liker 2004.
142. Mehri 2005, xiv.
143. Kamata 1982, 25.
144. Kamata 1982, 42.
145. Kamata 1982, 37.
146. Mehri 2006, 25.
147. Mehri 2006, 36.
148. Mehri 2006, 34.
149. Mehri 2006, 32.
150. Mehri 2006, 28.
151. Mehri 2006, 28.
152. Mehri 2006, 28.
153. A number of writers have commented on this theme of incremental improvement in Toyota's culture (Stewart and Raman 2007; Mehri 2006; Wada 1995; Suzaki 1993), though it is less clear at what point incremental improvement became a prominent feature. Certainly, some of Toyota's early practices appeared more like breakthroughs linked with measured risk than incremental improvements associated with risk aversion.
154. Holstein 2009, 5.
155. Sloan 1963, 69.
156. General Motors Corporation 1924, 8.
157. Kuhn 1986.
158. Hounshell 1983, 267.
159. Sloan 1963, 54.
160. Sloan 1963, 49–50.
161. Kuhn 1986, 25. Interestingly, Kuhn (1986, 8) dismissed Sloan's "decentralization thesis as a myth," arguing that Sloan started the trend to centralization by imposing strict financial controls over the divisions.
162. Kuhn 1986.
163. Levin 1990, 143.
164. Levin 1990, 142.
165. Kuhn 1986, 27.
166. Ford was aware of the "continuous selling" strategy in which new models were manufactured on a regular basis; the "old bicycle trade" engaged in this practice (Ford 1922, 56). Ford made a conscious decision to improve

upon his existing model rather than offer a variety of new models. His philosophy was to manufacture his product "so strong and so well made that no one ought ever to have to buy a second one" (Ford 1922, 57).

167. Ford 1922, 72.
168. Briody, Cavusgil, and Miller 2004.
169. Cray 1980.
170. Levin 1990, 144.
171. Lichtenstein 1995, 292.
172. Lichtenstein 1995, 221.
173. Cray 1980, 402.
174. Wysner 1994, 61.
175. Briody 1995.
176. Levin 1990; Keller 1989.
177. Keller 1989, 21–26.
178. Cray 1980, 468–69.
179. Wysner 1994, 192.
180. Nader 1965.
181. Wright 1979.
182. Cray 1980, 467.
183. Wysner 1994; Levin 1990.
184. We cite some of our own interview data to supplement what is publicly available on these innovative partnerships.
185. Keller 1989, 92.
186. Womack, Jones, and Roos 1990, 82–84.
187. Holweg 2007.
188. Keller 1989, 133, 136.
189. Whyte 1991, 133.
190. Stewart and Bennett 1991.
191. Holstein 2009.
192. Keller 1989, 37.
193. Maynard 1995, 50–51.
194. Wysner 1994, 197.
195. Briody, Cavusgil, and Miller 2004, 7.
196. Once we engaged these senior leaders in discussion, we found that they were generally receptive to the Ideal Cultural Model of collaboration.
197. Deming 1982.
198. Juran 1988.
199. Crosby 1979.
200. Weekley and Wilbur 1996.
201. Keller 1989, 246.
202. Holstein 2009, 75.
203. Holstein 2009, 77.

CHAPTER 3

1. At the time the book prospectus was reviewed, we were asked to address issues of research objectivity and independence, since one of the authors and three members of our six-person research group were GM employees (the others being university-contract and outside consultants). The study design is probably the best defense of the independence of the research. The purpose of the ethnographic method is to provide a culturally valid view of a system that combines the insider perspective (i.e., culturally significant, culturally relevant, and culturally relative—an "emic" view) with the addition of an outsider (i.e., "etic" or objective) view (Bernard 2000; Hymes 1964). Other factors pertained to our research group culture. To work together over a several-year period requires honesty, accuracy, and completeness with respect to the data collection, analysis, and generation of results. Moreover, as researchers, we must abide by the ethics of our professional associations (e.g., the National Association for the Practice of Anthropology, the Society for Applied Anthropology) regarding the collection, analysis, and publication of ethnographic data.
2. Briody 1992.
3. Deming 1982.
4. Katz 1985.
5. Briody 1992.
6. Womack, Jones, and Roos 1990.
7. Crosby 1979, 1.
8. Dertouzos et al. 1989, 19, 177.
9. Harbour and Associates conduct productivity studies of virtually all automotive manufacturing operations in the United States. This calculation is based on linking together two similar productivity variables—workers per daily production unit and worker hours per vehicle. In 1979, 5.12 workers in the United States, Canada, and Mexico were required to produce one production unit compared to 4.88 workers per unit by 1989 (Harbour and Associates 1990, 127). The approximate number of workers per unit in 1986 was 4.95, while the 1999 figure was 3.09 (Harbour and Associates 2000, 50); productivity between 1986 and 1999 improved by 38 percent. Harbour switched to an hours-per-vehicle calculation (HPV) as part of an overall change in methodology in 1999. GM's HPV measure improved by a further 25 percent in the United States, Canada, and Mexico between 1999 (29.64; Harbour and Associates 2000, 50) and 2007 (22.19; Oliver Wyman 2008, 40). Thus, total productivity over the entire period from 1986 to 2007 was 54 percent.
10. Hours per vehicle statistics in 2007 were as follows: Nissan (23.44), Ford (22.65), Toyota (22.35), GM (22.10), Chrysler (21.31), and Honda (20.9). Honda and Toyota data are estimates (Oliver Wyman 2008, 14).

11. In 1989, J. D. Power reported 167 PP 100 (both cars and trucks) compared with 97 PP 100 in 1997. J. D. Power launched the second generation of the Initial Quality Study in 1998; the series between 1989 and 1997 and 1997 and 2008 were spliced. Using the new series, PP 100 dropped from 220 in 1997 to 119 in 2008 (J. D. Power and Associates 1989–2008). Another study redesign known as the third generation Initial Quality Study was launched in 2006, though it did not create the sharp fluctuations that appeared in 1998.

12. Using 1993 data as the baseline, this policy set a target of a 50 percent reduction in occupational injuries and illness rates within three years (i.e., by the end of 1996; General Motors Corporation 1995, 20). GM achieved a 52.5 percent reduction in lost work day case rates and a 44 percent reduction in "recordable" occupational injuries and illnesses over this three-year period (General Motors Corporation 1998, 14).

13. General Motors Corporation 1998, 14; 2005, and personal communication with GM Health Care Initiatives staff.

14. The term "recordables" refers to workplace injuries and illnesses requiring medical treatment more than simple first aid per OSHA (Occupational Safety and Health Administration, U.S. Department of Labor) regulations. Recordables must be documented and reported.

15. General Motors Corporation 1998, 14; 2005; and personal communication with GM Health Care Initiatives staff. Specific rates for individual firms cannot be compared because they are not publicly available (General Motors Corporation 1998, 14).

16. All of the named individuals in the stories were given pseudonyms to protect their confidentiality.

17. Don's job involved representing hourly employee concerns to plant management. His job was a full-time, elected UAW position.

18. Ling 1990.

CHAPTER 4

1. Bernard 2000; Schensul and LeCompte 1999.
2. Bernard 2006.
3. Swanson and Holton 2005.
4. Kedia 2008; Smith, Pyrch, and Ornelas Lizardo 1993; Cernea 1992a; Cernea 1992b; Cernea 1992c; Minkler et al. 2003; Shalowitz et al. 2009.
5. Tax 1964; Ablon 1977; Wulff and Fiske 1987; Fiske 2006.
6. While gathering field data during either the research phase or validation phase, we followed two practices. If we were engaged in casual conversations or in observation of work-related activities, we tried to remember as much as possible so that we could tape record our recollections soon after leaving the field. If we were involved in a formal interview or participating in a meeting (or validation session), we typically took

notes and tried to get as close-to-verbatim statements as possible. Only after leaving the interview or meeting would we tape record our notes. Tape recording in the field was not appropriate for three reasons. First, it was not a practice with which most GM employees were comfortable. Second, study participants in some locations told us tape recording was not allowed. Third, the ambient noise in the manufacturing plants made tape recording impractical. We later transcribed, edited (as necessary), and made available all of our field data to all members of our research group.

7. Chick 2000; Kirk and Miller 1986.
8. Jordan 2003.
9. Bernard 1998; Bernard 2000; Schensul and LeCompte 1999; Trotter and Schensul 1998.
10. Hounshell 1983, 327.
11. The Prototype Bridge Model is the simplest form of the bridge/ transformation model. As we explored the old way–new way dichotomy throughout the project, the bridge became more elaborate, as did the environment surrounding the bridge, the territory the bridge spanned, and the end point of the transformation process. This visual metaphor is elaborated in succeeding chapters of the book.
12. Meerwarth, Briody, and Kulkarni 2005.
13. Compare to Turner, Katz, and Hurd 2001; Wheeler 1985.
14. Team coordinators are hourly employees who know all the jobs in their area. In team-concept plants, TCs are referred to as group leaders. They are there to assist when an hourly employee asks for help with a work task. They also fill in for hourly employees who need a quick break or who are absent. They are typically paid at a higher hourly rate than an assembler.
15. Schensul and LeCompte 1999; Harris 2001.
16. It is worth noting that GMS and Star Point developed outside the United States and then filtered back to GM's U.S. operations. We know from the culture-change literature that change often begins on the periphery and works its way to the core.
17. Weekley and Wilbur 1996, 122.
18. Weekley and Wilber 1996, 122–23.
19. Weekley and Wilber 1996, 79.
20. Trist 1981; Trist et al. 1963.
21. Lewin 1958; Tuckman and Jensen 1977.
22. Many of these same features appeared in the interviews that formed the foundation for the Quality Network's beliefs and values.
23. Standardization involves documenting, following, and completing work tasks according to particular standards and methods. The performance level achieved becomes the platform for future improvements.

CHAPTER 5

1. Goodenough 1999; White 1959; Barnett 1953.
2. Goodenough 1963; Wallace 1956.
3. Barnett 1983; Goodenough 1999; White 1959.
4. Fiske 1991; Goodenough 1999.
5. Connell, Klein, and Meyer 2003, 159.
6. Jordan 1996, 28.
7. Manufacturing coordinators had supervisory responsibility over several foremen as well as the hourly employees supervised by those foremen.
8. Stamping plants have large presses that "stamp," or shape, the sheet metal into the various parts of the vehicle body (e.g., hoods, doors, quarter panels).
9. A millwright is a member of the skilled trades who maintains and cares for mechanical equipment. We often saw millwrights moving equipment.
10. A stud gun is a piece of equipment used to attach studs to sheet metal. Studs flow through hoses, or "pipes," to stud guns, which are robot controlled and located on the end of the robot arm.
11. Our research team was fortunate to have been on site when this particular stud gun malfunctioned. Tracy Meerwarth was able to observe the interaction among plant personnel as the equipment was being repaired. Later, Elizabeth Briody and Bob Trotter interviewed the electrician involved in the repair to gather further information on the technical and cultural issues associated with the breakdown.
12. Before anyone can enter the robot cell, a lock-out procedure has to be performed. Safety protocol requires that each person entering the robot cell put a lock on the entry panel box, which disables all control power in the cell. Other locks are put on any piece of equipment that will be worked on. The locks signal that employees are in the robot cell.
13. The banks refer to the number of completed jobs that are waiting to move to the next area of the line.
14. Frequently, there are changes that get captured in these stories that are unique to the time and place but many more that are part of on-going cultural processes that provide important lessons for plants in very different situations.
15. Briody 1992.
16. It is possible to make the case that GM's complexity (e.g., hierarchical and compartmentalized organizational complexity, geographic complexity, cultural complexity) is more analogous to a national-level governmental bureaucracy than a business organization. To the extent that that analogy holds, it is then possible that the forms of evolutionary organizational-culture change that we are advocating might be seen as too slow, too spotty, and too strongly resisted to allow GM to transform into the needed model for twenty-first-century manufacturing success. Some individuals might propose the need for revolution, not evolution,

since revolution (or at least rebellion) is the common form of paradigm change for governments. They might state that perhaps GM has grown so large and complex that it has outgrown the opportunity for implementing the kind of incremental and evolutionary change that we are proposing in this book. Yet it is also the case that gradual cultural evolution is possible for governments, and the most common forms of transformation we have found in our study are evolutionary, not revolutionary.

Chapter 6

1. Barnett 1953; Parsons and Shills 1962; Barth 1967; Wallace 1972.
2. Wax 1993; Batteau 2000; Leung et al. 2005.
3. Barger 1977; Hollan 2000.
4. Serageldin et al. 1995.
5. Denison and Mishra 1995.
6. Labianca, Gray, and Brass 2000.
7. Cernea 1992a; Cernea 1992b.
8. Serageldin et al. 1995.
9. Funnell and Smith 1981; Spindler and Spindler 1982; Schwartz 1981.
10. Wolcott 1991; Durrenberger 2002.
11. Romer 1960.
12. Kottak 1990, 722.
13. Kottak 1990, 723.
14. We use the term "recipe" to refer to a summary statement or general guideline. This concept is explained more fully in Chapter 7.
15. A recordable is incident which requires an investigation per U.S. Occupational Safety and Health Administration regulations.

Chapter 7

1. Compare to Kedia 2008; Minkler et al. 2003.
2. Wulff and Fiske 1987; Tax 1964.
3. Briody, Meerwarth, and Trotter, forthcoming.
4. The collaboration tools have been copyrighted and are available for public use (Briody et al. 2007).
5. This example was a clear signal to our research group of the distinction between the UAW as an institution and UAW members who agreed to serve as study participants, advisory committee members, and pilot participants. Rarely had we encountered any unwillingness on the part of hourly employees to contribute to the Ideal Plant Culture project. The UAW institutional resistance emerged as our project became more visible and required senior GM manufacturing-leader intervention.
6. Briody et al. 2008.
7. A score of one represents a low, or poor, demonstration of the cultural theme. A score of five reflects a mixed demonstration of the theme

(e.g., some behaviors are rated high and others rated low; all behaviors hover around the average). A score of ten indicates a high, or strong, demonstration of the cultural theme. Relationships and work process were the two key cultural themes that emerged in a content analysis of the actual stud gun observation. The relationship theme consisted of the elements of relationship health, recognizing effort, and job empathy. The work process theme included role effectiveness, support, and task responsiveness.

8. The phrase "key four" refers to the plant manager and plant personnel director along with the president of the union local and the head of the bargaining committee.

9. SPQRC is an acronym for a set of measures used in manufacturing. The "S" stands for safety, "P" is for people, "Q" is for quality, "R" is for responsiveness, and "C" is for cost.

CHAPTER 8

1. Briody and Trotter 2008.
2. Johnson 1990.

REFERENCES

Ablon, J. 1977. Field methods in working with middle class Americans: New issues of values, personality and reciprocity. *Human Organization* 36 (1): 69–72.

Alland, A., Jr. 1973. *Evolution and human behavior: An introduction to Darwinian anthropology.* Garden City, NY: Anchor Books.

Applebaum, H. 1984a. Theoretical introduction. In *Work in non-market and transitional societies*, ed. H. Applebaum, 1–38. Albany, NY: State University of New York Press.

———. 1984b. Introduction: Theory and the anthropology of work. In *Work in non-market and transitional societies*, ed. H. Applebaum, 39–44. Albany, NY: State University of New York Press.

Barger, W. K. 1977. Culture change and psychosocial adjustment. *American Ethnologist* 4 (3): 471–95.

Barnett, H. G. 1953. *Innovation: The basis of cultural change.* New York: McGraw-Hill.

———. 1983. *Qualitative science.* New York: Vantage.

Barth, F. 1967. On the study of social change. *American Anthropologist* 69:661–69.

———. 1972. Analytical dimensions in the comparison of social organizations. *American Anthropologist* 74 (1): 207–20.

———. 2000. Reflections on theory and practice in cultural anthropology: Excerpts from three articles. In *The unity of theory and practice in anthropology: Rebuilding a fractured synthesis*, ed. C. E. Hill and M. L. Baba. *National Association for the Practice of Anthropology Bulletin* 18:147–63.

Batteau, A. W. 2000. Negations and ambiguities in the cultures of organization. *American Anthropologist*, n.s., 102 (4): 726–40.

Becker, R. M. 2001. Lean manufacturing and the Toyota Production System. *Automotive Manufacturing and Production* 113 (6): 64–65.

Bellah, R. N., R. Madsen, W. M. Sullivan, A. Swidler, and S. M. Tipton. 1985. *Habits of the heart: Individualism and commitment in American Life.* New York: Harper & Row.

Berden, F. 1989. Trade and markets in precapitalist states. In *Economic Anthropology*, ed. S. Plattner, 78–107. Stanford, CA: Stanford University Press.

Bernard, H. R., ed. 1998. *Handbook of methods in cultural anthropology.* Walnut Creek, CA: Altamira.

————. 2000. *Social research methods: Qualitative and quantitative approaches.* Thousand Oaks, CA: Sage.

————. 2006. *Research methods in anthropology: Qualitative and quantitative approaches.* Lanham, MD: Altamira.

Braverman, H. 1974. *Labor and monopoly capital: The degradation of work in the twentieth century.* New York: Monthly Review.

Briody, E. K. 1992. Quality vs. quantity: How an assembly plant work force adapts. GM Research Publication No. 7784, Warren, MI.

————. 1995. Culture's effects on GM's corporate restructurings. GM Research Publication No. 8289, Warren, MI.

Briody, E. K., T. L. Meerwarth, and R. T. Trotter, II. Forthcoming. A story's impact on organizational culture change. *Journal of Organizational Change Management.*

Briody, E. K., S. T. Cavusgil, and S. R. Miller. 2004. Turning three sides into a delta at General Motors: Enhancing partnership integration on corporate ventures. *Long Range Planning* 37:421–34.

Briody, Elizabeth K., Tracy L. Meerwarth, Robert T. Trotter II, and Randombyte Software. 2008. *ExplorePlantCulture* PC Game. http://www.randombyte.com.

Briody, E. K., and R. T. Trotter II. 2008. *Partnering for organizational performance: Collaboration and culture in the global workplace.* Lanham, MD: Rowman & Littlefield.

Briody, E. K., R. T. Trotter II, T. L. Meerwarth, and G. H. Sengir. 2007. *Collaboration tools for designing and implementing an ideal manufacturing culture in the U.S.* U.S. Copyright Registration, TX 6-680-935, March 31.

Brislin, R. 1993. *Understanding culture's influence on behavior.* Fort Worth, TX: Harcourt Brace College.

Britan, G., and B. S. Denich. 1976. Environment and choice in rapid social change. *American Ethnologist* 3 (1): 55–72.

Camuffo, A., and G. Volpato. 1995. The labour relations heritage and lean manufacturing at Fiat. *International Journal of Human Resource Management* 6 (4): 795–824.

Cernea, M. M. 1992a. The building blocks of participation: Testing a social methodology. In *Participatory development and the World Bank: Potential directions for change*, ed. B. Bhatnagar and A. C. Williams, 96–108. World Bank Discussion Papers No. 183. Washington, DC: World Bank.

————. 1992b. *The building blocks of participation: Testing bottom-up planning.* World Bank Discussion Papers No. 166. Washington, DC: World Bank.

————. 1992c. Re-tooling in applied social investigation for development planning: Some methodological Issues. In *Rapid assessment procedures— Qualitative methodologies for planning and evaluation of health related programmes*, ed. N. S. Scrimshaw and G. R. Gleason, 11–23. Boston, MA: International Foundation for Developing Countries (INFDC).

http://www.unu.edu/unupress/food2/UIN08E/uin08e00.htm (accessed November 12, 2007).

Chance, N. A. 1960. Culture change and integration: An Eskimo example. *American Anthropologist*, n.s., 62 (6): 1028–44.

Chaplin, C. 1936. *Modern times*. Directed and produced by Charles Chaplin. United Artists. Accessed from Google Films, http://video.google.com/videoplay?docid=893627879073510155.

Chick, G. 2000. Writing culture reliably: The analysis of high-concordance codes. *Ethnology* 39 (4): 365–93.

Cleveland, J. 2006. The Toyota product development system's implementation challenges. *Automotive Design and Production* 118 (5): 16–20.

Cole, R. E. 1995. Reflections on organizational learning in U.S. and Japanese industry. In *Engineering in Japan: Japanese technology-management practices*, ed. J. K. Liker, J. E. Ettlie, and J. C. Campbell, 365–79. New York: Oxford University Press.

Connell, N. A. D., J. H. Klein, and E. Meyer. 2003. "Are you sitting comfortably? Then I'll begin (to transfer some knowledge?)": Narrative approaches to the transfer and interpretation of organisational knowledge. Proceedings of the Knowledge Management Aston Conference 2003. Aston Business School, Birmingham, UK, 152–63.

Coy, M. W. 1989. From theory. In *Apprenticeship: From theory to method and back again*, ed. M. W. Coy, 1–11. Albany, NY: State University of New York Press.

Cray, E. 1980. *Chrome Colossus: General Motors and its times*. New York: McGraw-Hill.

Crosby, P. B. 1979. *Quality is free: The art of making quality certain*. New York: McGraw-Hill.

Cusumano, M. A. 1985. *The Japanese automobile industry: Technology and management at Nissan and Toyota*. Cambridge, MA: Harvard University Press.

Deafenbaugh, L. 1989. "Hausa weaving: Surviving amid the paradoxes. In *Apprenticeship: From theory to method and back again*, ed. M. W. Coy, 163–79. Albany, NY: State University of New York Press.

Deming, W. E. 1982. *Out of the crisis: Quality, productivity and competitive position*. Cambridge, MA: MIT Press.

Denison, D. R., and A. K. Mishra. 1995. Toward a theory of organizational culture and effectiveness. *Organization Science* 6 (2): 204–23.

Dertouzos, M. L., R. K. Lester, R. M. Solow, and the MIT Commission on Industrial Productivity. 1989. *Made in America: Regaining the productive edge*. Cambridge, MA: MIT Press.

Detroit Institute of Arts. http://www.dia.org/education/rivera/ubfil2.htm.

Driver, H. E. 1973. Cultural diffusion. In *Main Currents in Cultural Anthropology*, ed. R. Naroll and F. Naroll, 157–83. New York: Appleton-Century-Crofts.

Durrenberger, E. P. 2002. Structure, thought, and action: Stewards in Chicago union locals. *American Anthropologist*, n.s., 104 (1): 93–105.

Fiske, A. P. 1991. *Structures of social life: The four elementary forms of human relations.* New York: Free Press.

———. 2006. Anthropology in pursuit of public policy and practical knowledge. *National Association for the Practice of Anthropology Bulletin* 26 (1): 82–107. Arlington, VA: American Anthropological Association.

Ford, H. 1922. *My life and work.* In collaboration with Samuel Crowther. London: William Heinemann.

———. 1926. "Mass Production." In *Encyclopedia Britannica*, ed. J. L. Garvin, 13th ed., vol. 30. 821–23.

Fujimoto, T. 1995. A note on the origin of the "Black Box Parts" practice in the Japanese motor vehicle industry. In *Fordism transformed: The development of production methods in the automobile industry*, ed. H. Shiomi and K. Wada, 184–216. Oxford, UK: Oxford University Press.

Funnell, R., and R. Smith. 1981. Search for a theory of cultural transmission in an anthropology of education: Notes on Spindler and Gearing. *Anthropology and Education Quarterly* 12 (4): 275–300.

Gannon, M. J., and Associates. 1994. *Understanding global cultures: Metaphorical journeys through 17 countries.* Thousand Oaks, CA: Sage.

General Motors Corporation. 1924. *Sixteenth annual report of the General Motors Corporation (year ended December 31, 1924).* Detroit, MI: General Motors.

———. 1995. *Environmental report.* Detroit, MI: General Motors.

———. 1998. *1997 General Motors environmental, health and safety report.* Detroit, MI: General Motors.

———. 2005. *Corporate responsibility report.* Detroit, MI: General Motors.

Gerth, H. H., and C. W. Mills, ed. 1946. *From Max Weber: Essays in sociology.* New York: Oxford University Press.

Goodenough, W. H. 1963. *Cooperation in change: An anthropological approach to community development.* New York: Russell Sage Foundation.

———. 1999. Outline of a Framework for a Theory of Cultural Evolution. *Cross-cultural Research* 33 (1): 84–107.

Goody, E. N. 1989. Learning, apprenticeship, and the division of labor. In *Apprenticeship: From theory to method and back again*, ed. M. W. Coy, 233–56. Albany, NY: State University of New York Press.

Hall, E. T., and M. R. Hall. 1987. *Hidden differences: Doing business with the Japanese.* Garden City, NY: Anchor/Doubleday.

———. 1989. *Understanding cultural differences: Germans, French and Americans.* Yarmouth, ME: Intercultural.

Hamada, T. 1991. *American enterprise in Japan.* Albany, NY: State University of New York Press.

Harbour and Associates. 1990. *The Harbour report a decade later: Competitive assessment of the North American automotive industry 1979–1989.* Rochester, MI: Harbour and Associates.

————. 2000. *The Harbour Report 2000: Manufacturing analysis, company by company, plant by plant.* Rochester, MI: Harbour and Associates.

Harris, M. 2001. *The rise of anthropological theory: A history of theories of culture.* Walnut Creek, CA: Altamira.

Hirsch, J. L. 2000. Culture, gender, and work in Japan: A case study of a woman in management. *Ethos* 28 (2): 248–69.

Hirst, P., and J. Zeitlin. 1991. Flexible specialization versus post-Fordism: Theory, evidence, and policy implications. *Economy and Society* 20 (1): 1–56.

Hollan, D. 2000. Constructivist models of mind, contemporary psychoanalysis, and the development of culture theory. *American Anthropologist*, n.s., 102 (3): 538–50.

Holland, D., and N. Quinn. 1987. *Cultural models in language and thought.* Cambridge, UK: Cambridge University Press.

Holstein, W. J. 2009. *Why GM matters: Inside the race to transform an American icon.* New York: Walker.

Holweg, M. 2007. The genealogy of lean production. *Journal of Operations Management* 25:420–37.

Hounshell, D. A. 1983. *From the American system to mass production 1800–1932: The development of manufacturing technology in the United States.* Baltimore, MD: Johns Hopkins University Press.

————. 1995. Planning and executing "Automation" at Ford Motor Company, 1945–65: The Cleveland engine plant and its consequences. In *Fordism transformed: The development of production methods in the automobile industry,* ed. H. Shiomi and K. Wada, 49–86. Oxford, UK: Oxford University Press.

Hymes, D. 1964. Toward ethnographies of communication: The analysis of communicative events. In *Language and Social Context,* ed. P. Giglioli, 21–44. Harmondsworth, England: Penguin Books.

Imai, M. 1986. *Kaizen: The key to Japan's competitive success.* New York: Random House Business Division.

Ishikawa, K. 1985. *What is total quality control? The Japanese way.* Englewood Cliffs, NJ: Prentice Hall.

Ito, K. 2005. A history of manga in the context of Japanese culture and society. *Journal of Popular Culture* 38 (3): 456–75.

J. D. Power and Associates. 1989–2008. *Initial quality study.* Westlake Village, CA: McGraw-Hill.

Johnson, J. C. 1990. *Selecting ethnographic informants.* Qualitative Research Methods Series No. 22. Newbury Park, CA: Sage.

Jordan, A. T. 1994. Organizational culture: The anthropological approach. In *Practicing anthropology in corporate America: Consulting on organizational culture,* ed. A. T. Jordan. National Association for the Practice of Anthropology Bulletin 14, Arlington, VA: American Anthropological Association.

————. 2013. Transforming culture: creating and sustaining a better manufacturing organization. *Anthropology of Work Review* 34(1): 55–57.

————. 1996. Critical incident story creation and culture formation in a self-directed work team. *Journal of Organizational Change Management* 9 (5): 27–35.

————. 2003. *Business anthropology*. Prospect Heights, IL: Waveland.

Juran, J. M. 1988. *Juran on planning for quality*. New York: Free Press.

Kamata, S. 1982. *Japan in the passing lane: An insider's account of life in a Japanese auto factory*. New York: Pantheon Books.

Katz, H. C. 1985. *Shifting gears: Changing labor relations in the U.S. automobile industry*. Cambridge, MA: MIT Press.

Kedia, S. 2008. Recent changes and trends in the practice of applied anthropology. *National Association for the Practice of Anthropology Bulletin* 29 (1): 14–28.

Keller, M. 1989. *Rude awakening: The rise, fall, and struggle for recovery of General Motors*. New York: William Morrow.

Kirk, J., and M. L. Miller. 1986. *Reliability and validity in qualitative research*. Beverly Hills, CA: Sage.

Kleinman, A. 1980. *Patients and healers in the context of culture: An exploration of the borderland between anthropology, medicine, and psychiatry*. Comparative Studies of Health Systems and Medical Care No. 5. Berkeley, CA: University of California Press.

Kottak, C. P. 1990. Culture and economic development. *American Anthropologist*, n.s., 92 (3): 723–31.

Kuhn, A.J. 1986. *GM passes Ford, 1918–1938: Designing the General Motors Performance-Control System*. University Park, PA: Pennsylvania State University Press.

Labianca, G., B. Gray, and D. J. Brass. 2000. A grounded model of organizational schema change during empowerment. *Organization Science* 11 (2): 235–57.

Lengwiler, M. 2008. Participatory approaches in science and technology: Historical origins and current practices in critical perspective. *Science, Technology and Human Values* 33 (2): 186–200.

Leung, K., R. S. Bhagat, N. R. Buchan, M. Erez, and C. B. Gibson. 2005. Culture and international business: Recent advances and their implications for future research. *Journal of International Business Studies* 36 (4): 357–78.

Levin, D. 1990. *Irreconcilable differences: Ross Perot versus General Motors*. New York: Penguin Books.

Lewchuk, W. 1987. *American technology and the British vehicle industry*. Cambridge, UK: Cambridge University Press.

Lewin, K. 1958. Group decision and social change. In *Readings in Social Psychology*, 3rd ed., ed. E. E. Maccoby, T. M. Newcomb, and E. L. Hartley, 197–211. New York: Henry Holt.

Lichtenstein, N. 1995. *The most dangerous man in Detroit: Walter Reuther and the fate of American labor*. New York: Basic Books.

Liker, J. K. 2004. *The Toyota way: 14 management principles from the world's greatest manufacturer.* New York: McGraw-Hill.

Ling, P. J. 1990. *America and the automobile: Technology, reform, and social change.* Manchester, UK: Manchester University Press.

Maynard, M. 1995. *Collision course: Inside the battle for General Motors.* New York: Birch Lane.

Meerwarth, T. L., E. K. Briody, and D. M. Kulkarni. 2005. Discovering the rules: Folk knowledge for improving GM partnerships. *Human Organization* 64 (3): 286–301.

Mehri, D. 2005. *Notes from Toyota-Land: An American engineer in Japan.* Ithaca, NY: IRL Press, an imprint of Cornell University Press.

———. 2006. The darker side of lean: An insider's perspective on the realities of the Toyota Production System. *Academy of Management Perspectives* 20 (2): 21–42.

Minkler, M., A. G. Blackwell, M. Thompson, and H. Tamir. 2003. Community based participatory research: Implications for public health funding. *American Journal of Public Health* 93:1210–13.

Nader, R. 1965. *Unsafe at any speed.* New York: Grossman.

Nash, J. 1984. The anthropology of work. In *Work in non-market and transitional societies*, ed. H. Applebaum, 45–55. Albany, NY: State University of New York Press.

Nemoto, M. 1987. *Total quality control for management: Strategies and techniques from Toyota and Toyoda Gosei.* Englewood Cliffs, NJ: Prentice Hall.

Nevins, A., and F. E. Hill. 1954. *Ford: The times, the man, the company.* New York: Charles Scribner's Sons.

Nonaka, I. 1995. The development of company-wide quality control and quality circles at Toyota Motor Corporation and Nissan Motor Co. Ltd. In *Fordism transformed: The development of production methods in the automobile industry*, ed. Haruhito Shiomi and Kazuo Wada, 139–59. Oxford, UK: Oxford University Press.

Oliver Wyman. 2008. *The Harbour Report 2008: North America manufacturing, company by company, plant by plant.* New York: Oliver Wyman, MMC.

Paolisso, M. 2007. Cultural models and cultural consensus of Chesapeake Bay blue crab and oyster fisheries. In *Anthropology and fisheries management in the United States: Methodology for research*, ed. P. Ingles and J. Sepez, 123–35. National Association for the Practice of Anthropology Bulletin No. 28. Berkeley, CA: University of California Press.

Parsons, T., and E. Shills, ed. 1962. *Toward a general theory of action.* New York: Harper & Row.

Piore, M. J., and C. F. Sabel. 1984. *The second industrial divide: Possibilities for prosperity.* New York: Basic Books.

Romer, A. S. 1960. *Man and the vertebrates.* Vol. 1. Harmondsworth, England: Penguin Books. (Orig. pub. 1954).

Sahlins, M. D. 2000. *Culture in practice: Selected essays.* New York: Zone Books.

Sahlins, M. D., and E. R. Service. 1960. *Evolution and culture.* Ann Arbor, MI: University of Michigan Press.

Salleh, L. M. 2005. High/low context communication: The Malaysian Malay style. Proceedings of the 2005 Association for Business Communication Annual Convention, Irvine, CA.

Salvador, T., G. Bell, and K. Anderson. 1999. Design Ethnography. *Design Management Journal* 10 (4): 35–41.

Schensul, J. J., and M. D. LeCompte. 1999. *The ethnographer's tool kit.* 7 vols. London, UK: Altamira.

Schneider, H. K. 1977. Prehistoric transpacific contact and the theory of culture change. *American Anthropologist* 79 (1): 9–25.

Schwartz, T. 1981. The acquisition of culture. *Ethos* 9 (1): 4–17.

Serageldin, I., A. Steer, M. M. Cernea, J. A. Dixon, E. Lutz, S. Margulis, M. Munasinghe, and C. Rees. 1995. Making development sustainable: From concepts to action. Environmentally Sustainable Development Occasional Paper Series No. 2. Washington, D.C: World Bank.

Shalowitz, M. U., A. Isacco, N. Barquin, E. Clark-Kauffman, R. D. Delger, D. Nelson, A. Quinn, and K. A. Wagenaar. 2009. Community-based participatory research: A review of the literature with strategies for community engagement. *Journal of Developmental and Behavioral Pediatrics* 30 (4): 350–61.

Shepherd, D. A., J. S. McMullen, and P. D. Jennings. 2007. The formation of opportunity beliefs: Overcoming ignorance and reducing doubt. *Strategic Entrepreneurship Journal* 1 (1–2): 75–95.

Shimada, I. 2007. *Craft production in complex societies: Multicraft and producer perspectives.* Salt Lake City, UT: University of Utah.

Shiomi, H. 1995. The formation of assembler networks in the automobile industry: The case of Toyota Motor Company (1955–80). In *Fordism transformed: The development of production methods in the automobile industry,* ed. H. Shiomi and K. Wada, 28–48. Oxford, UK: Oxford University Press.

Shiomi, H., and K. Wada, eds. 1995. *Fordism transformed: The development of production methods in the automobile industry.* Oxford, UK: Oxford University Press.

Sloan, A. P. 1963. *My years with General Motors,* ed. J. McDonald and C. Stevens. Garden City, NY: Doubleday.

Smith, S., T. Pyrch, and A. Ornelas Lizardo. 1993. Participatory action-research for health. *World Health Forum* 14 (3): 319–24. http://whqlibdoc .who.int/whf/1993/vol14-no3/WHF_1993_14(3)_p319-324.pdf (accessed December 4, 2007).

Sobek, D. K., II, A. C. Ward, and J. K. Liker. 1999. Toyota's principles of set-based concurrent engineering. *Sloan Management Review* 40 (2): 67–83.

Spindler, G., and L. Spindler. 1982. Do anthropologists need learning theory? *Anthropology and Education Quarterly* 13 (2): 109–24.

Staudenmayer, N., M. Tyre, and L. Perlow. 2002. Time to change: Temporal shifts as enablers of organizational change. *Organization Science* 13 (5): 583–97.

Steward, J. H. 1955. *Theory of culture change: The methodology of multilinear evolution.* Urbana, IL: University of Illinois Press.

Stewart, E. C., and M. J. Bennett. 1991. *American cultural patterns: A cross-cultural perspective.* Rev. ed. Yarmouth, ME: Intercultural.

Stewart, T. A., and A. P. Raman. 2007. Lessons from Toyota's long drive. *Harvard Business Review* 85 (7–8): 74–83.

Strauss, C., and N. Quinn. 1997. *A cognitive theory of cultural meaning.* Cambridge, UK: Cambridge University Press.

Suzaki, K. 1993. *The new shop floor management: Empowering People for Continuous Improvement.* New York: Free Press.

Swanson, R. A., and E. F. Holton III, eds. 2005. *Research in organizations: Foundations and methods of inquiry.* San Francisco: Berrett-Koehler.

Tax, S. 1964. The uses of anthropology. In *Horizons of Anthropology*, ed. S. Tax, 248–58. Chicago, IL: Aldine.

Taylor, F. W. 1911. *The principles of scientific management.* New York: Harper and Brothers.

Teague, P. 1990. The political economy of the regulation school and the flexible specialization scenario. *Journal of Economic Studies* 17 (5): 32–54.

Ting-Toomey, S. 1999. *Communicating across cultures.* New York: Guilford.

Tocqueville, A. de. 1990. *Democracy in America.* Vol. 2. New York: Vintage Books. (Orig. pub. 1845).

Tomlinson, P. R. 2005. The overseas entry patterns of Japanese automobile assemblers, 1960–2000: Globalisation of manufacturing capacity and the role of strategic contingency. *International Journal of Automotive Technology and Management* 5 (3): 284–304.

Trigg, R. H., and S. I. Anderson. 1996. Introduction to this special issue on current perspectives on participatory design. *Human-Computer Interaction* 11 (3): 181–84.

Trist, E. L. 1981. The evolution of socio-technical systems: A conceptual framework and an action research program. Occasional Paper No. 2. Toronto, ON: Ontario Quality of Working Life Center.

Trist, E. L., G. W. Higgin, H. Murray, and A. B. Pollock. 1963. *Organizational choice: Capabilities of groups at the coal face under changing technologies: The loss, rediscovery and transformation of a work tradition.* London: Tavistock.

Trotter, R. T., II, and J. J. Schensul. 1998. Methods in applied anthropology. In *Handbook of methods in cultural anthropology*, ed. H. R. Bernard, 691–736. Walnut Creek, CA: Altamira.

Tuckman, B. W., and M. A. C. Jensen. 1977. Stages of small group development revisited. *Group and Organization Management* 2 (4): 419–27.

Turner, L., H. C. Katz, and R. W. Hurd. 2001. *Rekindling the movement: Labor's quest for relevance in the 21st century.* Ithaca, NY: Cornell University Press.

Twu, H-L. 2009. Effective wiki strategies to support high-context culture learners. *TechTrends* 53 (5): 16–21.

Varenne, H. 1977. *Americans together: Structured diversity in a Midwestern town.* New York: Teachers' College Press.

Wada, K. 1995. The emergence of the "flow production" method in Japan. In *Fordism transformed: The development of production methods in the automobile industry,* ed. H. Shiomi and K. Wada, 11–27. Oxford, UK: Oxford University Press.

Wallace, A. F. C. 1956. Revitalization movements. *American Anthropologist* 58:264–81.

———. 1972. Paradigmatic processes in culture change. *American Anthropologist,* n.s., 74 (3): 467–78.

Wasson, C. 2002. Collaborative work: Integrating the roles of ethnographers and designers. In *Creating breakthrough ideas: The collaboration of anthropologists and designers in the product development industry,* ed. S. Squires and B. Byrne, 71–90. Westport, CT: Bergin and Garvey.

Wax, M. L. 1993. How culture misdirects multiculturalism. *Anthropology & Education Quarterly* 24 (2): 99–115.

Weekley, T. L., and J. C. Wilbur. 1996. *United we stand: The unprecedented story of the GM-UAW quality partnership.* Ed. B. R. Creedon. New York: McGraw-Hill.

Wheeler, H. N. 1985. *Industrial conflict: An integrative theory.* Columbia, SC: University of South Carolina Press.

White, L. A. 1959. *The evolution of culture: The development of civilization to the fall of Rome.* New York: McGraw-Hill.

Whyte, W. F. 1991. *Social theory for action: How individuals and organizations learn to change.* Newbury Park, CA: Sage.

Williams, K., C. Haslam, and J. Williams. 1992. Ford versus "Fordism": Beginning of mass production? *Work, Employment and Society* 6 (4): 517–55.

Wolcott, H. F. 1991. Propriospect and the acquisition of culture. *Anthropology and Education Quarterly* 22 (3): 251–73.

Womack, J. P., D. T. Jones, and D. Roos. 1990. *The machine that changed the world: The story of lean production.* New York: Harper Perennial.

Wright, J. P. 1979. *On a clear day you can see General Motors: John Z. De Lorean's look inside the automotive giant.* Grosse Pointe, MI: Wright Enterprises.

Wulff, R., and S. Fiske. 1987. *Anthropological praxis: Translating knowledge into action.* Boulder, CO: Westview.

Wysner, J. 1994. *Every purse and purpose: General Motors and the automotive business.* Davisburg, MI: Wilderness Books.

Index

CPSIA information can be obtained at www.ICGtesting.com
Printed in the USA
BVOW03s2227190214

345447BV00006B/91/P